MUSIC AND NEW TECHNOLOGY

– the MIDI connection

Gabriel Jacobs and

Panicos Georghiades

SIGMA PRESS
Wilmslow, England

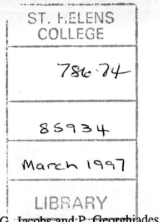
© 1991, G. Jacobs and P. Georghiades

Many of the designations used by manufacturers and sellers to distinguish their products are claimed as trademarks. The publisher has made every attempt to supply trademark information about manufacturers and their products mentioned in this book and due acknowledgment is hereby made of all legal protection.

Typeset and Designed by Sigma Hi-Tech Services Ltd, Wilmslow, UK

First published in 1991
Sigma Press, 1 South Oak Lane, Wilmslow, Cheshire SK9 6AR, UK

First printed 1991
Reprinted 1992

Printed in Malta by
Interprint Ltd.

ISBN: 1-85058-231-9

British Library Cataloguing in Publication Data
A CIP catalogue record for this book is available from the British Library

Acknowledgments
Within this book, various proprietary trade names and names protected by copyright are mentioned for descriptive purposes. Due acknowledgment is hereby made of all legal protection and registration.

Foreword

Many times in the past I have been asked the same question: What do I think about keyboards, synthesisers, and the modern technology?

I always find it extremely difficult to give a simple answer, one which can cover the full implications of the question. The reason for this is obvious. I don't know what it is that I am dealing with. Are we defining keyboards as things which have keys, an instrument ready to be played by humans, or are they things which appear to have keys but are far from being an instrument?

You see, it was inevitable that from the moment Man invented the first drum, flute, bow, string, and the like, he created something out of a specific need to produce sound in his own time and in his own way. Unlike the invention of the wheel, when an inevitable pattern was started that would lead us ultimately to conquer space, it is apparent to me that with instruments today we have not, so far, gone on to conquer creation. The reason for this is simple. Through our investment, and therefore our belief that technology will lead us to the mastery of creation, we might commit the error of underestimating, more and more, the Human factor, which is a far better machine in this area.

In other words, instead of using the technology to our own advantage, we are the ones who have become progressively more used, and for me, who have been a believer in technology since my childhood, the way of development has turned into a nightmare, due mainly to the monopoly of the approach taken by designers and manufacturers, who are responsible for the lack of playability and the lack of instant access. Instead of shortening the distance between the moment of creation and execution, the reverse has applied, and this distance now grows bigger by the day.

We understand however that, after all, there is nothing wrong with technology; it is simply the design which is at fault. It is known throughout the history of Humanity that many great and important discoveries end up being used in the wrong way and for the wrong reasons. In this area, therefore, I hope and I wish that we begin to pay a far greater attention to the problem, because music, and of course creation, are serious matters, far more so than sheer entertainment or easy commercial gains. Music, and creation in general, are the safety valve for the human race – not forgetting, of course, humour.

I appeal to you all, therefore (the reader as well as the various manufacturers) to take this matter very seriously, and to create a paradise of technology – one not made in order to look at, but to inhabit – achieving thereby, at last, contact with the Universal Law.

Vangelis

P.S. It is not by chance that various early Greek philosophers talked constantly about the music of the spheres!

Preface

In the last few decades, new technology has made it possible for a composer to be creator, instrumentalist, conductor and recording technician combined. The laughable one-man band has been replaced by the perfectly serious one-man orchestra.

With a little equipment, a modicum of musical knowledge, and a minimum of instrumental playing skill (even none at all) complete performances of original compositions can be created from scratch. And herein lies a bone of contention. More people than ever - especially young people - have been attracted into composition by the fact that comparatively little training is now needed in order to make a start, a source of disdain and irritation for certain traditionalists whose domain has been invaded by what they consider to be mere dabblers.

We would be the first to agree that outlandish claims for what modern technology can do for the proverbial man in the street have to be greeted with a raised eyebrow. It may now be very easy to produce impressive sounds in a narrow range of musical styles, but high levels of accomplishment in any field, whether technical, interpretative or creative, are never easily achieved. The music of Vangelis and other similar futuro-classical composers cannot be reduced to a few facile technological formulae. In other words, the fact that composition has been freed of certain obstacles does not mean that the ultimate goal of greatness is any more attainable than in the past, nor that study and practice have lost all significance. Technology, musical knowledge and playing skills go hand in hand, and any one of them, or any combination of the three, can lead to musical creativity. If technology alone can lead to it, so much the better. Greatness is another matter.

Just as it was essential for most of yesterday's composers to be able to play a keyboard for the purposes of orchestration - Berlioz is the best-known exception -

it is necessary for today's composers who wish to take advantage of the new technology to be able to use a music *studio*, that is to say the range of equipment required for electronic music (not necessarily a special room). Producers such as Alan Parsons, Quincy Jones, and the Stock, Aitken & Waterman trio have used a studio just as Stokowski has used the orchestra, that is to say to create their own distinct sound.

Using a studio means acquiring skills which until recently would have been considered peripheral to composition, if not irrelevant, including some knowledge of the physics of sound and of the way in which computers work. Trained musicians who have little understanding of electronic technology will have to come to terms with some unfamiliar concepts. Computers do not function like the human mind: they have no inherent sense of pitch, rhythm or expression, nor do they talk the same language as human beings. But once some basics have been understood, it soon becomes clear that their ability to process information very rapidly turns them into excellent labour-saving musical devices, and even aids to creativity. A crash course on computers, which assumes no previous understanding of them, can be found in Chapter 2.

Those with little or no musical training but who know about computers will find, too, that music and electronics can be married quite happily, and part of the aim of this book is to explain the basis of that union. Nevertheless, it is not possible to create music without at least a bare minimum of musical understanding. This minimum is set out as a course in the basic concepts of music in Chapter 13. Those with no musical knowledge are advised to take the course as one of the first steps.

Those who know nothing about either music or electronics will be able to learn something about the tools available for rapidly expressing musical ideas which in former times, without years of painstaking study, would almost certainly have lain dormant. Technology cannot reduce those years to an instant, nor can it fuel great music if talent is missing, but it can grease the parts of the musical engine so that it will run on low power.

About the Authors

The authors of this book have published extensively, both separately and as a team, on MIDI and other music-related topics in specialist magazines and in the UK national press.

Gabriel Jacobs at one time played the clarinet and saxophone professionally, but now lectures and researches in French and Business Computing in the University of Wales, Swansea. He is co-editor of *Interactive Multimedia*, an international journal devoted to developments in the integration of text, graphics and sound on computers.

He comes from a wholly musical background. His grandfather (Sam Sanderson) was a well-known bandleader of the twenties and thirties, and his mother (Esther Sanderson) was a professional soprano who, before the Second World War, made many BBC broadcasts and cut a number of records.

Panicos Georghiades is a part-time professional composer, with works accepted by the BBC. He researched for a while in computer-related subjects at the University of Wales, Swansea, and at present runs his own software and systems-analysis computer company.

He too comes from a musical background, having been trained as an instrumental player. He desperately wanted to be a professional composer, but his amateur playing skills and his parents said No. He went to college instead, but as soon as computers had developed to the point of being able to make music, his problems were over.

Acknowledgements

The authors gratefully acknowledge the contributions made by the following professionals who read the manuscript of this book and made invaluable suggestions:

Steve Evans (composer)
Paul Fletcher (multimedia consultant)
Penny Jacobs (musician)
Anton Mullan (composer)
Laurie Scott-Baker (composer)
Ian Wright (computer programmer)

CONTENTS

1. The MIDI Studio. 1
  1.1 Structure of the MIDI Studio. 3
  1.2 Parts of the MIDI Studio. 4
    1.2.1 The Computer 4
    1.2.2 The MIDI Interface. 5
    1.2.3 MIDI Instruments 6
    1.2.4 Sequencers. 6
  1.3 Buying the Basics. 8
  1.4 Beyond the Basics 9
    1.4.1 Sound Modules. 9
    1.4.2 Sound Mixers. 11
    1.4.3 Extra Software 11
  1.5 The Human Voice and Natural Instruments. 15
  1.6 Polishing Off. 16
  1.7 Mastering 17
  1.8 Listening. 17

2. Computers for Music. 18
  2.1 A Crash Course in Computing. 19
    2.1.1 Processors 19
    2.1.2 Internal Memory. 19
    2.1.3 Storage 20
    2.1.4 Monitors 21
    2.1.5 Computer Input Devices 22
    2.1.6 Operating Systems 23
    2.1.7 Printers 24
    2.1.8 Modems. 25
    2.1.9 Multi-tasking 26
    2.1.10 Networking 27
  2.2 Makes of Computer 27
    2.2.1 The IBM PC, its Compatibles, and the PS/2. 28
    2.2.2 Apple and the Macintosh. 30
    2.2.3 The Atari ST 31

2.2.4 Commodore 32
2.2.5 Acorn 33
2.2.6 The Yamaha CX5 35
2.2.7 The NeXT Computer 35
2.2.8 The Amstrad PCW 35
2.3 Making the choice 36
2.3.1 Choice Checklist for Computers 36

3. MIDI - the Theory 38
3.1 The MIDI Software Standard 39
3.1.1 MIDI Channels 39
3.1.2 Kilobaud 39
3.1.3 Serial Communication 43
3.1.4 Synchronous and Asynchronous Communication 43
3.1.5 A Word on Hexadecimal Notation 45
3.2 The MIDI Hardware Standard 45
3.2.1 Sockets 45
3.2.2 Cables 46
3.2.3 Connecting Instruments in Series 46
3.2.4 Connecting in a Star Shape 47
3.3 MIDI Messages 47
3.3.1 Program Change Messages 51
3.3.2 Controller Messages 51
3.3.3 Finer Increments 52
3.3.4 Aftertouch 55
3.3.5 System-exclusive Messages 56
3.3.6 Classification of MIDI messages 57

4. MIDI Interfaces and MIDI Accessories 61
4.1 Interfaces, Specifications and Standards 61
4.1.1 MIDI Interfaces and Synchronisation 63
4.1.2 Beyond the 16-Channel Barrier 66
4.2 MIDI Interfaces for the IBM PC andCompatibles 67
4.2.1 The Roland MPU-401 67
4.2.2 MPU for MCA 68
4.2.3 Standard MPU-compatible Interfaces 68
4.2.4 Non-MPU-compatible Interfaces 70
4.2.5 Interfaces Incorporating Sound 70
4.3 MIDI Interfaces for Apple Computers 71
4.4 The Atari ST 72
4.5 The Commodore Amiga 73
4.6 MIDI Interfaces for Acorn computers 74
4.7 Other MIDI Interfaces 74
4.7.1 Amstrad PCW and other computers 74
4.7.2 Generic Interfaces 74

4.8 Choice Checklist for MIDI Interfaces 75
4.9 MIDI Accessories 76
    4.9.1 MIDI Through Units 76
    4.9.2 MIDI Merge Units 76
    4.9.3 MIDI Patch Bays and MIDI Switches 76
    4.9.4 MIDI-to-CV Converters 77
4.10 Products 78

5. Sequencers 80
5.1 Tracks 84
    5.1.1 Other Track Considerations 85
5.2 Recording 86
    5.2.1 Time Signature and Tempo 87
    5.2.2 Count-in 87
    5.2.3 Punch In/Out 87
    5.2.4 Other Recording Features 87
5.3 Play Features 88
    5.3.1 Mute and Solo 88
    5.3.2 Play Range and Loop Play 88
    5.3.3 Change Parameters while in Play Mode 88
    5.3.4 Jukebox 89
5.4 Edit Features 89
    5.4.1 Displaying Events as Musical Notation 89
    5.4.2 Displaying Events on a Grid 90
    5.4.3 Displaying Events on a List 91
    5.4.4 Displaying other MIDI data 92
    5.4.5 Editing Individual Notes 92
    5.4.6 Editing Individual MIDI Events 93
    5.4.7 Editing by Blocks 93
5.5 Transforming MIDI Events 94
    5.5.1 Pitch Transformations 94
    5.5.2 Other Transformations 95
5.6 Graphs 97
5.7 Tempo and Synchronisation 97
    5.7.1 Tempo track 97
    5.7.2 External Synchronisation 98
5.8 File Handling 98
    5.8.1 Save Individual Tracks or Patterns 98
    5.8.2 Standard MIDI Files 99
    5.8.3 System-exclusive Information 99
5.9 Other Sequencer Functions 100
    5.9.1 Reverse in Time 100
    5.9.2 Arpeggios from Chords and Glissandos from Note Sequences 100
    5.9.3 Automatic Creation of Tremolos and Trills 100
    5.9.4 Notepads 101

        5.9.5 Undo. 101
    5.10 Choice Checklist for Sequencers. 101
    5.11 Products 102

6. MIDI Instruments and other Input Devices 106
    6.1 Computer Keyboard 107
    6.2 MIDI Keyboards 108
        6.2.1 Facilities on MIDI Keyboards 109
        6.2.2 Other Characteristics of MIDI Keyboards 113
        6.2.3 Choice Checklist for Keyboards 113
    6.3 MIDI Guitars. 114
        6.3.1 Choice Checklist for MIDI Guitars 115
    6.4 Wind Controllers 115
    6.5 MIDI Drums 117
    6.6 Alternative Instruments. 118
    6.7 Pitch-to-MIDI Converters 119
    6.8 Data Entry Pads. 120
    6.9 Digital Faders 120
    6.10 MIDI Implementation Chart for Input Devices. 120
    6.11 Products 122

7. MIDI Output. 123
    7.1 Sound Synthesis. 123
        7.1.2 Envelopes 124
        7.1.3 Waves. 126
    7.2 Synthesising Devices 129
        7.2.1 Types of Instruments. 129
    7.3 Types of Sound Creation. 132
        7.3.1 Synthesised Sound 132
        7.3.2 Natural Sound by Sampling. 134
        7.3.3 Chipboard Sounds. 138
        7.3.4 A New Generation of Synthesisers? 139
        7.3.5 Acoustic Sound 139
    7.4 Polyphony and Multi-timbrality 140
        7.4.1 Polyphony and Multi-timbral Sound Modules. 142
    7.5 Choice Checklist for Output Devices 142
        7.5.1 MIDI Implementation Chart for Output Devices. 143
    7.6 MIDI Lighting. 143
    7.7 Products 145

8. Creative Sound 153
    8.1 Sound Editors 154
        8.1.1 Sound Editors at Work 155
    8.2 Finding the Right Combination 157
        8.2.1 Assignment of the Sound-producing Oscillators 158

8.2.2 Other Parameters Affecting the Sound. 160
8.3 Editing Samples. 160
8.4 Editing Multi-timbral Settings 161
8.4 Librarians 163
8.5 Editors for Non-instrumental MIDI Equipment 163
8.6 Alternative Tuning 163
8.7 Products 166

9. Practical Sound. 168
9.1 Sound Mixers. 168
  9.1.1 Individual Channel Controls. 170
  9.1.2 Overall Signal Controls 175
  9.1.3 The Range of Available Mixers 176
  9.1.4 General Advice on Choosing Mixers. 176
  9.1.5 Choice Checklist for Mixers. 177
9.2 Effects - the Spices of Sound. 178
  9.2.1 Analogue and Digital Effects Units. 178
  9.2.2 Available Effects 180
  9.2.3 Choice Checklist for Effects Units 185
9.3 Products 185

10. Adding Acoustic Sounds. 188
10.1 Microphones 189
  10.1.1 Types of Microphones. 189
  10.1.2 Microphone Characteristics 190
  10.1.3 Recommendations. 192
10.2 Multi-track Tape Recorders 193
  10.2.1 Types of Multi-track Tape Recorders. 193
  10.2.2 Sound Signals and Noise Reduction 194
10.3 Synchronising with an Acoustic Performance. 195
  10.3.1 General Considerations 196
  10.3.2 A Sync Session using FSK Tape-Sync. 196
  10.3.3 A Sync Session using Time Code 197
  10.3.4 Synchronisation Hints 198
10.4 Analogue and Digital Recorders. 198
  10.4.1 Analogue Recording 198
  10.4.2 Digital Recording 199
10.5 Monitoring and Mastering 201
  10.5.1 Monitoring. 201
  10.5.2 Mastering. 206
10.6 Products 209

11. Aids to Composition. 215
11.1 Algorithmic Composers. 216
11.2 Arrangers. 219

11.3 A Plea for Artificial Intelligence. 221
11.4 Products 221

12. Music Notation Software **223**
12.1 Methods of Input 224
   12.1.1 Input from the Computer Keyboard. 224
   12.1.2 Mouse Input. 225
   12.1.3 Input with a MIDI Instrument in Step Time 225
   12.1.4 Input with a MIDI Instrument in Real Time. 226
   12.1.5 Input from Disk 226
12.2 Output of the Score. 226
   12.2.1 Printing 226
   12.2.2 Output to Standard MIDI Files 229
   12.2.3 Output to MIDI Instruments. 229
   12.2.4 Monitoring Output 229
12.3 Editing 230
   12.3.1 Editing Screens. 230
   12.3.2 Editing Facilities. 230
12.3.3 Musical Symbols 231
12.4 Computer Hardware Requirements 232
12.5 Score Editor Checklist. 233
12.6 Products 234

13. Musical Education **236**
13.1 The Theory of Music - A Crash Course for the Absolute Beginner. 236
13.2 What is Music? 237
   13.2.1 Rhythm 237
   13.2.2 Pitch 238
13.3 Musical Notation 240
   13.3.2 Qualifiers and Other Signs. 243
13.4 Putting it into Practice. 244
13.5 Glossary of Musical Terms 244
13.6 Educational Software 247
   13.6.1 Examples. 248
   13.6.2 Choice Checklist for Educational Software. 251
   13.6.3 Products. 251

14. Selling Music **252**
14.1 Practical Advice in Specific Areas. 253
14.1.1 Popular-Song Writing 254
14.1.2 Library Music (Production Music). 256
14.1.3 Film 257
14.2 Locating Companies and Using Organisations 259
14.3 Royalties and Copyright 259
14.4 The PR Factor. 260

Postface: A Last Word 261

Appendix A: MIDI Messages. 262
  MIDI Message Specification. 262
  A.1 Channel Messages. 263
    A.1.1 Channel Voice Messages 263
    A.1.2 Channel Mode Messages. 264
  A.2 System Messages. 265
    A.2.1 System-exclusive Messages. 265
    A.2.2 System-common Messages 266
    A.2.3 System Real-time Messages 267

Appendix B: Addresses and Publications 268
  B.1 Assocations and Official Bodies. 268
  B.2 Companies. 269

Glossary 278
Index 288

Preliminaries

Product selection

In many product categories there are hundreds of available options, and space has not allowed us to give a comprehensive coverage. Products mentioned in the various lists in this book represent a selection, based for the most part on how well they typify the category to which they belong, how popular they are, and their quality and value for money in our judgement.

Product prices

For the most part, we do not give exact retail prices for individual products. It is a fact of life in the electronic music industry that if a product, particularly a hardware product, does not sell well in its first year, it is heavily discounted in the next (it is therefore often worthwhile buying equipment which was released more than a year ago). In addition, new equipment models appear at frequent intervals, and old models (whether or not they have sold well) are often deleted from a producer's catalogue, though they may still be readily available from distributors and dealers, and the same is true to a certain extent of software packages. On top of that, prices vary from time to time and from dealer to dealer.

For these reasons, broad price categories are given in preference to the prices themselves (except when it comes to very expensive equipment). These categories should be taken to be very rough guides only, intended as they are merely to give an idea of cost. The categories are as follows:

A: less than £50

B: £50 to £150

C: £150 to £250

D: £250 to £400

E: £400 to £600

F: £600 to £1,000

G: £1,000 to £2,000

H: £2,000 to £3,000

Products priced higher than category H are indicated with an approximate amount.

Product location

The USA is better served than the UK when it comes to electronic musical equipment of all kinds because its total market is so much larger. There is of course nothing to stop anyone in the UK ordering directly from the USA, though this can obviously pose problems if the equipment fails. Our advice to UK readers is to buy from a UK distributor unless a specific piece of equipment fits the bill so well, from the points of view of features and price, that no substitute will do. In many cases, the same applies to software.

It is also worth mentioning that there is a flourishing second-hand market in electronic musical equipment, and that there are therefore bargains to be had by scouring the classified advertising sections of specialist magazines.

The word *synthesiser*

Modern musical technology is intimately bound up with sound synthesis - that is to say the creation of sound from scratch by electronic means, as opposed to banging, blowing, scraping or using the voice. Any device which can synthesise sound is technically a synthesiser. *However, the term (or its abbreviation* synth*) is now firmly embedded in everyday musical vocabulary as denoting a piano-like keyboard. In this book we use the word in both its everyday sense of a keyboard, and that of a synthesising device of any kind, allowing the context to make it plain which sense is intended, or specifying the distinction if there can be any doubt.*

The word *composer*

The word composer *is used in this book in its widest sense, that is to say not necessarily merely that of a professional 'serious' composer. It includes amateur and professional songwriters, jingle writers, writers of backing-tracks, in fact anyone who creates music.*

1

The MIDI Studio

MIDI and Digital Information

MIDI – The Concept

MIDI – *Musical Instrument Digital Interface* – began in 1981, when three men working with companies producing electronic musical instruments met at the exhibition of the US National Association of Music Merchants (NAMM) and discussed ways in which synthesiser keyboards of different makes could be made to communicate with each other.

This facility was becoming increasingly necessary as musicians using synthesisers tried to link them together – each make of keyboard produced a slightly different sound, and the result was a thicker overall sound texture. This solved Rick Wakeman's concert problem of trying to play seven or so synthesisers with only two hands. But it was well-nigh impossible to achieve this without re-wiring the insides of the synthesisers because each make used different control methods.

As a consequence of the meeting, one of the men involved (Dave Smith) wrote a proposal for a universal standard, and he presented it at a conference of audio engineers a few months later. He called it the Universal Synthesiser Interface, which turned out to be the direct precursor of MIDI.

When the major manufacturers of electronic instruments met at the 1982 NAMM exhibition, an outline of what we now know as MIDI was drafted, and by early 1983 electronic keyboards with integral MIDI sockets were beginning to appear. The full specification was released in August 1983, shortly after which the International MIDI Association was formed in the USA, and in Japan the Japanese MIDI Standards Committee. Once the two major countries involved in manufacturing electronic instruments had agreed the standard, it was assumed that it would be immediately accepted world-wide. In fact, it was not until 1984 that the American MIDI Manufacturers' Association published a definitive standard.

At that time, personal computers were just beginning to be widely used, and the temptation to link them with electronic instruments was very strong, since their processing power could be put to good musical use. This trend has never ceased, so that today MIDI has in many circles come to mean connecting musical instruments to computers. And MIDI has established itself so firmly as a standard that nobody seriously interested in producing music using a computer can consider being without it.

MIDI allows a musical score to be entered into a computer by playing each part on an instrument conforming to the MIDI standard and connected to the computer via a special cable. The computer can then be used to play back many instruments simultaneously, thus allowing a single composer or arranger to create an orchestral sound. The computer can also store the performance on disk, synchronise musical compositions with tape recorders, make lights flash for stage performances, and even send a complete score through the telephone line from one part of the world to another, to be played back and heard exactly as it was recorded.

These wonders are made possible by the fact of the *D* in MIDI – Digital. And one of the most important concepts to understand in the context of computers, MIDI and modern electronic devices of all kinds, is the difference between digital and analogue information.

In a nutshell, digital information is composed of distinguishable steps, while analogue information is continuous. Take an everyday example: a clock with hands for hours, minutes and seconds is analogue, while a digital clock displays numbers (digits). An analogue clock presents information (the time) in a continuous band as the tips of its hands move in a circle. A digital watch presents the same information but in increments. It may be that those increments are very small, down to a hundredth of a second or less, but they are nevertheless steps which can be distinguished, whereas the hand of an analogue clock moves smoothly and continuously.

It is possible to convert information from an analogue to a digital form and vice versa, and the same example of a clock can be used to illustrate one of the processes. When we look at an analogue clock face and tell the time, whether we say it is five past nine or 9.05, the angles of the hand have been converted from analogue to digital information. We might need greater accuracy and say that it is 9.05 and 25 seconds. All that has happened is that the increments have become smaller. Indeed, we have no practical way of describing the time except by performing an Analogue to Digital conversion.

Analogue to Digital (A/D) and Digital to Analogue (D/A) conversion are, in certain circumstances, an essential part of modern electronics sound devices. Sound reaches our ears as an analogue signal – varying loudness, for example, does not arrive in distinguishable steps – whereas modern computers and MIDI devices process sound digitally. If a computer or other electronic device is to understand an analogue signal, such as a musical sound, its pitch and loudness must first be converted to digital form. Equally, for a MIDI digital signal representing that sound to be played back via an instrument and amplified through a loudspeaker, its pitch and volume must be converted back to analogue form. A/D converters are also used to map the texture of sounds.

Details of the way in which MIDI handles its digital data are given in Chapter 3.

1.1 Structure of the MIDI Studio

A modern music studio – housed in a room to itself or in some corner of one – is made up of a number of parts. They usually come as separate pieces of equipment linked together by cables.

Many pieces of equipment are manufactured in a standard size, in which case they are said to be *19-inch rack-mountable* or simply *rack-mounted*, that is to say that they are of a standard width and have holes on their front panels so that they can be screwed into a rack (a trolley or firm-standing frame) which is actually 18 15/16 inches (480 mm) wide. The height of a rack-mounted piece of equipment is given in *Units*, one Unit being 1.75 inches (45.2 mm). A rack-mounted device which is specified as *1U* is one Unit high. The advantages of a rack are that it saves space and keep things tidy, and a trolley is useful for stage work.

Among the equipment, whether rack-mounted or not, will probably be found a computer, a sound mixer, a synthesiser keyboard, sound modules, and other pieces of hardware designed for producing specific sound effects. In later chapters we shall delve into the mysteries of these units, describing them in detail, exploring their possibilities and limitations, and recommending particular products to suit particular needs. Here, however, we shall merely take a bird's eye view of them, and of what puts them all together: MIDI.

MIDI is sometimes referred to as a communication protocol or standard. This is because apart from direct MIDI commands (instructions), there are also definitions of how musical information is to be transmitted between the various parts of a studio, as well as specifications for the hardware connections: the types of cables and plugs that should be used, and so forth.

The basic MIDI concept is best described using an analogy. The human body has many systems working within it, the blood and the nervous system being examples. The blood system transfers substances to the various parts of the body, while the nervous system for the most part carries commands between the brain and the muscles and organs. These systems interact with the breathing system, the digestive system, the lymphatic system and so on.

Similarly, the modern music studio has many systems working in conjunction with each other. The picture may be one of a jumbled spaghetti of wires, but within it there are actually well-defined separate systems. The most obvious of these is the one carrying the mains electrical power. Another one, like the human blood system, is a collection of wires carrying the sound signals and other information between the various pieces of equipment.

A modern studio also has a nervous system. This is a network of cables carrying MIDI commands and data between a computer and various sound-producing and sound-processing devices. Although, in terms of complexity, there is no comparison between the human nervous system and a MIDI network, there are nevertheless many similarities between the brain (the computer) and its outer organs (the peripheral equipment), and it can be useful to think of a MIDI studio in these terms.

This book covers the separate parts of the MIDI studio in detail. Figure 1.1 indicates where the parts are specifically dealt with.

1.2 Parts of the MIDI Studio

These, then, are the tools of the trade, and to get the best out of MIDI means having access to certain important ones.

1.2.1 The Computer

MIDI does not in itself require a computer, but computers are becoming increasingly essential in a MIDI studio. For problem-free results, a computer of reasonable power is required, though the power of the machine does not necessarily make any difference to the final result – the music. This is an important point and it has been vital to the success of MIDI. However, the computer must be capable either of handling MIDI directly via one of its *ports* (outlets), or of linking up with an added MIDI interface (see Section 1.2.2 below).

Most modern personal computers can handle MIDI in one way or another – the Atari ST, the IBM PC and its compatibles (PCs), the Apple Macintosh, and the Commodore Amiga are the most widely known and used.

More about computers, including a crash course for novices and descriptions of the capabilities of different makes, can be found in Chapter 2.

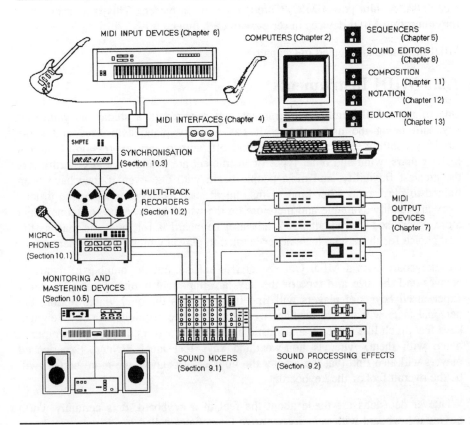

Figure 1.1: The parts of a modern MIDI studio

1.2.2 The MIDI Interface

An interface is a connection between two separate pieces of equipment. It may itself be a piece of equipment, or it may be a standard set of rules. The term *MIDI interface* is therefore not as logically misleading as it at first may seem. The acronym MIDI already contains the *I* of *Interface*, but this refers to the standard. By (in effect) repeating the word *interface*, a distinction is made between the MIDI standard and that standard as used in a piece of hardware.

A MIDI interface is, then, a piece of hardware which sits somewhere between the computer and a MIDI device such as a MIDI musical instrument (or it may be incorporated into the computer or into the MIDI device). It has at least two sockets (ports) on it: MIDI In and MIDI Out. These are more or less self-explanatory: a MIDI cable links the In port on the computer to the Out port on an instrument, and vice versa. A third port – MIDI Through – is often present. This is a special port for connecting MIDI devices in series with each other.

MIDI interfaces are treated in Chapter 4.

1.2.3 MIDI Instruments

One or more MIDI musical instruments are required in a studio, a synthesiser keyboard being the usual choice. It has ordinary piano-style keys and some auxiliary controls to turn features on and off, and to vary expression. Although MIDI guitars, wind and other types of instrument are available, a keyboard offers the greatest flexibility, and most people begin with one even if they have been trained to play some other kind of instrument such as the trumpet or the drums. They are readily available and therefore on the whole better value for money than more specialised instruments. A synthesiser keyboard is for the same reasons the best choice for those who have never learned to play any musical instrument at all.

Any keyboard with a MIDI Out socket will suffice, but the number of available octaves and the size and type of the keys are important points to consider. Most experienced keyboard players will find full-size keys the only viable option, but personal taste will dictate whether *weighted* keys are required or not. Weighted keys feel much like those of an acoustic piano (piano players therefore feel more at home with them) whereas non-weighted keys feel much lighter. Experienced players will also find that the greater the number of octaves, the more natural will be the overall feel of the keyboard.

Whatever decisions are made about the feel of a keyboard, it is certainly worth buying a keyboard with *velocity-sensitive* (sometimes called *touch-sensitive*) keys. Velocity-sensitive keyboards work like those of an ordinary piano (although to a more limited degree), in that the harder they are hit, the louder the sound. This facility is important not only for experienced piano players, who can find it difficult to play the organ, for example, because their fingers do not control the volume as they touch the keys, but also for people with no keyboard experience, since it comes fairly naturally to expect a light touch to produce a soft sound and thump to produce an uproar. Without a velocity-sensitive keyboard, it is impossible to control the volume and the *timbre* (colour, texture – sometimes pronounced *tamber*) of a given note relative to its neighbours. There are many velocity-sensitive keyboards on the market, some of them reasonably priced.

MIDI instruments are covered in Chapters 6 and 7.

1.2.4 Sequencers

A sequencer is essential in order to maximise the use of MIDI. It may come as a piece of hardware, though more usually these days as a software package running on a computer (this is therefore the type we shall describe here), and it requires a little more initial explanation than the other parts of a MIDI studio.

A sequencer records note information coming from a MIDI source such as a MIDI musical instrument, and plays it back. Musical phrases can be recorded, then edited, transposed to different key signatures, assigned to different instruments, and saved on computer disk for later use, either in the sequencer's own format, or in some cases as *standard MIDI files*. These are collections of data stored on disk in a standardised format, which means that they can understood by different sequencers and other pieces of musical software, provided that the software in question has been written with them in mind.

A number of different tracks are available on a sequencer so that a complete orchestral score can be laid down. With the sequencer in Play mode, the data from each track is distributed back to MIDI instruments, or to other MIDI devices for further processing.

Essentially, then, sequencing software turns a computer into a tapeless multi-track tape recorder. But the difference between a multi-track tape recorder and a sequencer is that an ordinary (analogue) tape recorder records the actual sound of a performance, whereas a sequencer records *information about* a performance.

In practice, one of the principal effects of this is that the information can be entered into the computer either in real time (played at normal speed on a MIDI musical instrument), or at a slower tempo, or even discontinuously note by note, a process known as *step-time input*. In other words, a composer is no longer limited by an inability to play an instrument properly. Furthermore the quality of a recording is not diminished through the tape medium during the recording and playback processes – transferring sound from one tape recorder to another, and simply recording to tape, inevitably result in a loss of sonic quality. This does not apply to digital multi-track tape recorders, but their price generally puts them out of reach of all but professionals or the most dedicated amateurs.

Generally speaking, the basic screen of a sequencer displays the tracks, together with graphic representations of information about them such as the bars of music which have been recorded. It also displays information such as the title of the composition and the tempo at which it is to be played. An Edit screen then allows the MIDI data to be viewed in more detail for any individual track. This is mainly information about the music – notes, pitch, duration, attack – but other information about the sound may also be shown, like vibrato, pitch bends (bending the pitch up or down, as is achieved by pulling the string on a guitar after it has been made to sound), position in the stereo spectrum, or other niceties of musical expression.

Any of this information can be changed on-screen – individual notes or groups of notes, bars, whole tracks or groups of tracks – using tools similar to those of word processing and desktop publishing: Delete, Insert, Cut, Paste, and so on.

The history of the sequencer is a fascinating one. Details of its origins can be found in Chapter 5 (where sequencers are treated), but it is worth briefly noting here the way in which the sequencer has changed over the last decade, since the change has been central to the development of MIDI in the context of computers.

In the early 1980s, the only word processors available were so-called dedicated machines. As their name suggests (at least to the computer-literate) they were capable of doing one thing only, that is processing words. Then came the personal computer which could be made to do all kinds of things by inserting different program disks into the disk drive. This proved to be a revolution, because now the same machine could be used for word processing, databases, spreadsheets, accounts, and myriad other applications. Furthermore, such computers made a better job than their dedicated predecessors even of word processing because they had more disk storage and more internal memory.

This is much the case with the history of sequencers. Less than a decade ago, they were dedicated boxes with some buttons, a one-line display, and a few recording tracks. With the advent of the personal computer, sequencers started to appear on disk as pieces of software. And just as word processors based on personal computers offer more storage and greater flexibility than did their dedicated counterparts, so do disk-based sequencers.

It should be said, however, that dedicated sequencers have not been displaced to the same extent as dedicated word processors. Not only that, but new and better models, sometimes challenging the sophistication of software sequencers, still appear from time to time. The main reason for this is that there is still a demand for portable dedicated sequencers intended for stage performances. But their future is doubtful now that laptop computers which can run sequencing software are becoming widely available.

1.3 Buying the Basics

The above equipment and software represent the basic MIDI studio, and one way of setting it up is to buy a starter pack. There are several available, some of them offering a MIDI interface and sequencer for less than the price of certain interfaces alone. The choice depends partly on cost, partly on the facilities provided, and partly on the range and extent of upgrade paths, all of which will be dealt with later in this book.

It is worth emphasising at this point, however, that there is a complex inter-relationship between cost, features, and requirements.

For a start, not all MIDI information can be handled by all pieces of MIDI hardware – MIDI equipment comes in a range from MIDI-dumb to MIDI-genius, with price being only a rough indication of its usefulness in particular circumstances. For example, there are cheap synthesiser keyboards which do not have velocity-sensitive keys. At perhaps three times the price there are keyboards which give not only velocity sensitivity but also *aftertouch* sensitivity. This means that the depth to which a key is pressed will affect the timbre of the sound, usually making it brighter. Yet the cheaper synthesiser might produce four different sounds at the same time, while the more expensive model may produce only two.

Buying MIDI equipment, then, requires some knowledge and some thought. It is a minefield through which this book is intended as a guide.

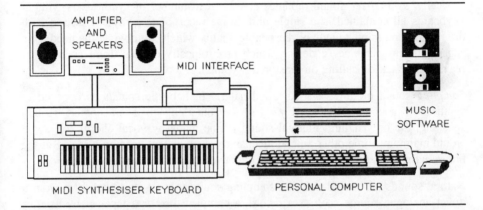

Figure 1.2: A basic MIDI set-up

1.4 Beyond the Basics

Vade retro Satanas!

It goes almost without saying that beginners should not normally invest in expensive extras. But MIDI is dangerously addictive. A basic set-up may soon seem far too basic, and there are many optional MIDI studio devices to tempt enthusiasts.

The essential factors which make devices *MIDI devices* are that they have in them a microchip which can understand MIDI information, and one or more MIDI sockets. Beyond those common factors the range they cover is very wide.

1.4.1 Sound Modules

A sound module is a musical instrument in a box – it cannot be played on its own, only via MIDI. A *multi-timbral* sound module is an electronic instrument ensemble – it can produce a number of different sounds (timbres) simultaneously, that is to say *polyhonically* (*polyphonic* means multi-part). A relatively simple keyboard synthesiser can produce one by one the sounds of a flute, a pipe organ, a bird, a ringing telephone ... whatever. A multi-timbral sound module can produce all these at the same time – typically up to eight, chosen from a stored library of perhaps hundreds of them.

Sound modules are fully covered in Chapters 7 and 8, but our bird's eye view distinguishes two varieties: *synthesiser modules* and *sampling modules*. Prices in both cases depend on the available amount of polyphony, the sound quality, the number of audio outputs, and the editing features.

Basically, *synthesiser* sound modules consist of a number of synthesisers without keyboards all contained in a single unit. Some incorporate a rhythm section with drum and percussion sounds of reasonable quality which can obviate the need for a separate drum machine (a device which electronically creates drum sounds and plays them back by calling on its stored rhythms).

Sampling sound modules use so-called natural or acoustic sounds as opposed to synthesised sounds. The word *natural* is something of a misnomer: strictly speaking, the only natural musical sound is one made by vocal chords (or, some would maintain, some other animal mechanism such as that used by birds). But the phrase *natural instrument* is these days synonymous with *acoustic instrument*.

Natural sounds are recorded in the sampling sound module in digital form from a direct analogue source such as a record, a compact disc or a tape, or by using a microphone, and the results can be impressive. In general, however, although there are models available within the price range of the average amateur, very high-quality sampling sound modules are bought by teams of professionals rather than by home enthusiasts.

A synthesiser sound module, on the other hand, would normally be the next piece of MIDI equipment to buy after having set up a basic studio composed of computer (and interface if the computer requires one), synthesiser keyboard and sequencing software, and especially so if orchestral sounds or special effects are required.

As far as choosing a sound module is concerned, it is worth remembering that no matter how good the music or how sophisticated the recording and processing equipment, the final result depends as much as anything on the equipment used to produce the sound. The output should be clear and free of hiss or other electronic noise, and the timbre of each instrument should be as close as possible to what is in the mind of the musician. Getting the sounds right for a recording from the beginning saves time and trouble. Trying to change them at later stages with the use of sound-processing effects units is costly and messy.

One sound module is adequate for reproducing a small ensemble. However, if the objective is the sound of the luscious strings of Stokowski-like orchestrations, the closely harmonised textures of a 1940s big band, or the wall of sound created by the Pet Shop Boys, a single sound module is not enough.

The number of sound modules in a system therefore depends on musical tastes and ambitions, but when it comes to the cost of a studio this number has also to be offset against the quality and features of individual modules.

An important factor in creating a 'thick' texture is an adequate polyphonic capability, and it is worth paying a little more for a little more polyphony, since the more polyphony a system can handle, the closer it will get to a realistic symphonic sound. Consider that when the strings in a symphony orchestra are playing a five-note chord, the sound may be produced by over 60 instruments playing at the same time, each being very slightly out of tune with the others. It is this out-of-tuneness which creates the pleasing sound of strings and choirs, and which is so difficult to reproduce on electronic instruments. It is a curious fact that in music we get more pleasure out of nearness to perfection than perfection itself.

It is therefore wise to buy at least one sound module which is advanced and flexible in its MIDI implementation. This can be used for instruments which play solo parts, while cheaper sound modules can be used for playing chords, though we should stress that advanced modules for solo parts are comparatively expensive.

Many sound modules have a Stereo Out socket, which means that if three modules are used, six sound signals have to be mixed into a stereo signal. But to do this, yet another piece of equipment is required: a sound mixer.

1.4.2 Sound Mixers

The final sound of a performance comes out of a pair of speakers. Sound mixers are devices which combine many individual sound sources into a stereo signal, and which also have facilities for sending sounds off to effects units (see Section 1.6 below) for further processing before the final mix is made.

More details about sound mixers and effects can be found in Chapter 9.

1.4.3 Extra Software

MIDI studio extras are available not only as pieces of hardware. The peripheral aspects of the Muse have not escaped the two-finger players – the computer programmers – and a very wide range of software is available to suit every musical need. Indeed, confusion about music software is common precisely because there are so many different types of program available. A simple way of understanding the position as far as MIDI is concerned is always to bear in mind that there are six basic software categories:

❏ Sequencing programs for recording and editing performances, as described above in Section 1.2.4

❏ Score editors, which are desktop music-publishing packages

❏ Sound editors (sometimes called *synthesiser voice editors*) and Librarians, both being software add-ons for, among other devices, synthesiser keyboards and sound modules

❏ Integrated packages which combine some or all of the above

❏ Educational programs

❏ Experimental composition programs for generating musical ideas.

Score Editors

For good-quality musical scores to be produced on a regular basis in *hard copy* (printed on paper) a score editor – sometimes called a notation program – is necessary. This is essentially a desktop-publishing program, and for some people it may be as much a part of a MIDI studio as their synthesiser keyboard, while for others it may be quite unnecessary.

In the early 1980s when word processing first took the world by storm, those of us interested in music were unable clearly to see how the same treatment could in practice be applied to musical notation, despite the optimistic prognostications of early computer-music gurus. After all, a word processor merely has to deal with the letters of the alphabet, word and line spacing, page breaks, and so forth. The equivalent music processor would have to deal with myriad extra complexities such as beamed notes, double staves with notes running into each other, and a host of diacritical marks with complex rules governing where and how to use them.

In fact it took a few years for true notation processors to become available, and when they first appeared they were expensive and cumbersome. We remember using an early one and finding that writing all but the simplest score by hand was easier and quicker, offered infinitely more flexibility, and with the steady hand of one of us actually gave better results.

That situation has changed for three main reasons. First, advances in printer technology have put high-quality output within the grasp of ordinary people. Secondly, the market for music programs running on computers, at first seen by software houses as too specialised to warrant development costs, has blossomed. Thirdly, the graphical techniques used in desktop-publishing packages have quite naturally spilled over into the area of notation processing. There are now a number of more or less *WYSIWYG* (What You See Is What You Get) score editors which give publishing-quality results. It should be stressed, however, that score editing is recorded separately while listening to the rest. This is similar to recording different MIDI instruments on the tracks of a sequencer, but in this case only acoustic sounds are recorded. This method was extensively used in the 1970s, when tape recorders of 24 or 48 tracks allowed musicians like Tomita, Vangelis, Jarre and Wakeman to create symphonic sounds all by themselves. However, with computers and MIDI, the number of tracks needed on tape has been reduced to the number of acoustic sounds used. So, a 4-track recorder which ten years ago would have been considered adequate for only very amateur use, today can offer semi-professional standards. One track can contain a tape-sync code which will run the computer and all the MIDI instruments, leaving three free tracks for vocals, a guitar, a saxophone or some other acoustic instrument.

Multi-track tape recorders exist in both cassette and reel-to-reel form. Cassette recorders tend to be cheaper. They are adequate, and many composers are happy with them. Most good models will run at double the normal speed of 4.5 cms per second, and feature noise reduction for improved performance.

For natural sounds, a microphone is of course a must, and whereas it is possible elsewhere in the studio to economise on a piece of equipment in order to finance some other material, with microphones this is more often than not a mistake. Microphones represent the one area in the entire range of studio equipment where price really does equal quality, and where bargains are few and far between.

The use of natural sounds within MIDI is treated in various parts of this book, but see especially Chapter 10, and for types of microphones Section 10.1.

1.6 Polishing Off

There are many sound effects which can be added to a recording to make it more interesting. Sound effects produced within a MIDI studio do not mean recordings of bird song, gunshots or other sounds available on a BBC Sound Effects record used for adding a sound track to a home movie. MIDI sound effects are ways of processing the raw sounds of synthesisers and sound modules, as well as the sounds of natural instruments and the human voice.

Reverberation (usually called simply *reverb*) enriches dry sounds. Delay and echo can add mystery to vocals. Special effects such as flanging, pitch shifting and phasing – difficult if not impossible to describe in words, but which should be heard at some time during the MIDI learning process – can create an outer-space atmosphere. Chorus, which can multiply a single sound creating what is called *pseudo many*, is often used to improve synthesised strings. Enhancers are used to transform bathroom-quality voices and make them caress, instead of scratch, the listener's eardrums.

not an easy process, and the panacea it may appear to offer in the hyperbole of advertisements has to be viewed with a good dollop of circumspection.

Notes can be input either directly from a computer, from a compatible sequencer, or from a MIDI musical keyboard via a MIDI interface, either in real or step time. And some of the available score editors are very intelligent. They come with facilities like user-defined sensitivity levels for the real-time input of chords (since a player may not press all the keys at exactly the same moment), transposition from one key to another, automatic beaming (joining) of groups of notes with the correct slope, and so on. And they of course all have the normal editing functions found on word processors, such as saving, deleting and copying marked blocks.

Score editing is fully described in Chapter 12.

Sound editors and Librarians

Sound editors are computer versions of the functions found in synthesiser keyboards used for editing *voices* (instrument or other sounds). Many synthesisers are programmable, and can be made to produce a great variety of voices, from trumpets and bells to strings and thunderstorms. But even professional keyboards are often limited to a single-line Liquid Crystal Display (LCD) and allow programming of only one setting at a time. This makes programming an unattractive proposition if it is something which will be done frequently.

Sound editors, on the other hand, allow full-screen editing on a computer, as well as allowing sounds to be manipulated in other ways. They are often available as separate modules, each for a different model of instrument. They are sometimes called *synthesiser voice editors* (or just *voice editors*), or *patch* editors (for reasons which are given in Chapter 8 Section 8.4). Sounds are sent to the computer from the keyboard or sound module, are edited with the software, then sent back to the keyboard or sound module for storage.

Librarians add to the power of sound editors. A synthesiser keyboard may be capable of storing, say, 32 sounds in its internal memory. Using a librarian, *banks* of sounds can be created with a sound editor (or they can be bought ready-made). Individual sounds can then be taken from any one of the banks in order to make up a new bank, which can then be stored on disk ready for sending to the synthesiser whenever it is required. Librarians are therefore sound-information management tools.

Some sound editors, and even some sequencers, have built-in librarians, but librarians can also be bought as stand-alone pieces of software. They represent an inexpensive way of storing sounds, because most synthesisers store them on rather expensive RAM (Random Access Memory) or ROM (Read Only Memory) cards and cartridges, whereas computer-disk storage is cheap. For the price of a typical cartridge holding perhaps 64 sounds, it is possible to buy a librarian which will allow a thousand sounds or more to be stored on a single floppy disk. This is something they often forget to say in music shops. Note, however, that synthesisers with their own floppy-disk storage are beginning to appear.

Sound editors and librarians are treated in Chapter 8.

Integrated packages

Many of the features of sequencers, score editors and the like can be found in so-called integrated packages. The simplest of these are essentially just a sequencer and score editor in one, though some incorporate facilities found in sound editors.

Integrated packages in the area of MIDI are no different from those in other areas of computing. Many integrated business packages incorporating a word processor, a database, a spreadsheet and a communications program, allow data to be exchanged between the modules, something which overcomes the annoying incompatibility of separate programs from different software houses. You can be fairly certain, however, that each module will not be equal in quality with its neighbour. You can also be certain, unless you are buying a top-quality and therefore expensive package, that at least some of the modules will be of a quality or range which are inferior to equivalent stand-alone packages.

Educational software

Almost as soon as computers had become items affordable by schools and parents, educational software packages on every subject began to appear, and there has been a growth market in the area ever since. A computer is well suited to musical education because most personal computers have at least some internal sound-producing capability, and MIDI can enhance this.

Musical education software can be found in many varieties, from keyboard training to music theory. Some packages are more interactive than others, and some are meant for absolute beginners while others are aimed at tutoring people who already have a basic musical knowledge.

As a general rule, care has to be exercised in evaluating computer-assisted learning software, and especially so in music where taste and personal judgement can play such a major part. It should always be remembered that a program may appear to show intelligence, but it knows only what its programmers have written into it, and poorly designed software can do as much educational damage as educational good, especially in advanced applications.

Educational software is treated in more detail Chapter 13 Section 13.5.

Experimental hardware and software

A computer can do an enormous amount of the work which used to be obligatory for composers. Whatever may be said to the contrary, however, they cannot as yet be real substitutes for the creative process. Computers and MIDI are merely tools, and the human brain is still the only device which can create art. We are aware how contentious such a statement will be in certain circles – after all, computers have created so-called poetry, so-called paintings and so-called music. We stand firm.

Nevertheless, the work of composition can be eased not merely by having the computer perform repetitive or boring tasks: computers can also be programmed to add something of their own. There are pieces of hardware and software which will take care of the basics of arranging pieces of music. They give instant results, which is what today's three-minute culture demands. It may all taste like instant coffee, but that is good enough for most people, who are no more prepared to go to the trouble of a real capuccino than they are to slave over harmonic theory and counterpoint.

In our view, such efforts at automation should not be disparaged, partly because they represent experiment, and partly because the results they give can actually be useful if they are thought of as prototypes rather than finished products. They are dealt with in Chapter 11.

1.5 The Human Voice and Natural Instruments

However interesting and subtle the music produced by the MIDI studio we have so far described, synthesised sounds tend to sound synthesised, and the quality of a performance can be considerably enhanced by using a mixture of synthesised and acoustic sounds.

The easiest way of interfacing with human voices or conventional instruments is to create the computerised accompaniment first, and sing or play along with it afterwards. However, it is better from a musical standpoint to work the other way round by adding a synthesised accompaniment to an acoustically-produced main melody. This involves recording the main voice or instrument on a tape recorder, then synchronising the computer accompaniment with it.

Some MIDI interfaces are capable of producing *tape-sync* (tape synchronisation) code for synchronising MIDI note information with a tape recorder holding the acoustic performance. The theory behind sync code is described in Chapter 4 Section 4.1.1, and the practice in Chapter 10 Section 10.3.

Multi-track tape recorders are essential if natural sounds are regularly to be incorporated into MIDI performances, since they allow each instrument to be

Although until two years ago each of these effects would have required a considerable financial outlay, most of them can today be found in one box called a Multi-Effect Digital Sound Processing Unit – a mouthful, but a very useful piece of hardware usually offering some pre-set and some programmable effects. More details of such equipment appear in Chapter 9 Section 9.2.

1.7 Mastering

Mastering means creating a master recording in stereo.

For those interested in MIDI music merely for the pleasure of hearing their own compositions, an ordinary hi-fi system will suffice. But those who wish to make copies of recordings perhaps in order to market them, should consider some semi-professional equipment. In the old days – a little over five years ago – this would have been a reel-to-reel analogue tape recorder. Today, the magic word is again *digital*. More on mastering can be found in Chapter 10 Section 10.5.

1.8 Listening

There are many other add-ons available for the MIDI studio. Indeed, it is possible to go on adding ever-more sophisticated pieces of machinery, from specialised music entry pads to digital faders. The only limiting factors are finance, the physical space available for the equipment ... and ears.

Subsequent chapters in this book contain advice and recommendations about particular brands of MIDI equipment, but it cannot be over-stressed that music is about hearing. Before buying anything, it is imperative to hear MIDI studios actually work. If as yet you do not have any equipment of your own nor access to any, visit a music or computer shop where it is on sale, and listen. No book can be a complete substitute for listening when it comes to choosing MIDI material.

2

Computers for Music

A MIDI studio does not have to include a computer. All that is needed is to connect two synthesisers together via their MIDI sockets and technically this is a MIDI studio. But the processing power of computers is the natural concomitant of MIDI, and they have come to be inextricably linked with it. The additional functional benefits they supply are many, and certainly outweigh their cost.

There is vast choice of computers, and the computer-ignorant buyer is probably more of a potential victim than in any other area of consumer electronics. When buying any piece of equipment, from a refrigerator to a camcorder, by definition the more you know about the facilities it offers, the more informed will be your choice. With computers such knowledge is vital, and the beginner is therefore at a considerable disadvantage. The average salesperson in a High-Street store knows enough about digital watches and even video cassette recorders to be able to advise in general terms. When it comes to computers, few such sales people can offer anything but the most basic advice.

However, armed with a little understanding of the components of a computer, the wretched first-time buyer is at least in a position to ask the right questions, either of a High-Street salesperson or a specialist dealer. The following section is therefore intended for those who wish to buy a computer for musical purposes, but who know little or nothing about the subject.

2.1 A Crash Course in Computing

2.1.1 Processors

The heart of a computer is a microprocessor called the CPU (Central Processing Unit), often referred to simply as the *processor*. This controls the basic functions of the computer such as arithmetic and logic.

The difference between the processors of various computers is an essential part of the differences in the way they perform, and one of the most significant among these differences is the speed at which they can handle operations. One way of thinking about a microprocessor is as a pathway with a number of tracks along it, and the wider the path, the greater the number of tracks. Early microcomputers were based on processors with eight tracks or *bits* (see Chapter 3, Section 3.1.2 for a more accurate explanation of bits) and were therefore known as 8-bit computers. They are still produced, but 1981 saw the appearance of 16-bit processors in personal computers, which were faster because the wider pathway allowed them to handle more information, and to address (use) larger areas of memory. They are now the norm, but 32-bit processors (which are that much more powerful) are also found on higher-end machines.

The speed at which the processor and its associated chipset runs (affecting the number of operations it can perform in a given time, and other factors) is called its *clock speed*, which is measured in MegaHertz (MHz). By today's standards, less than 3 MHz is slow, and over 20 MHz is fast. Clock speed is not everything by any means, but it is a fair indicator of performance (in machines other than those which use a RISC system – Reduced Instruction Set Computer – such as the Acorn Archimedes).

Most serious machines offer add-ons to make the processor more efficient, the two most important of which are a maths co-processor and a Digital Signal Processor (DSP). A maths co-processor takes care of many of the arithmetical operations, thus leaving the CPU to get on with other things. A DSP can specifically handle the arithmetic involved in processing digital audio signals, and is therefore a step up for the musician from a maths co-processor.

2.1.2 Internal Memory

The internal memory of a computer is divided between ROM and RAM. ROM stands for Read-Only Memory, and it contains certain basic instructions about how the computer is to perform. The fact that it is read-only means that it cannot be changed by the user. RAM stands for Random Access Memory, and is used for two purposes: as a temporary store for instructions required to run a program, and as a temporary store for a user's data.

When a computer is switched off, normally everything in RAM is lost, so data has to be transferred to a disk for more permanent storage in the form of *files*, each with its own filename. For example, a piece of music which has been produced on a sequencer will be stored in a file on disk. The sequencer program itself is not re-stored since it has not been changed.

RAM is measured in *Kilobytes*, usually written as *K*. A byte is the equivalent of a single character typed at a computer keyboard, and a kilobyte is roughly 1,000 bytes, so 512K means about 512,000 characters, say 85,000 words. MIDI information is stored not as textual characters or words but in a special way, though the basic processes taking place in RAM are identical.

Most modern computers come with a minimum of 512K of RAM as standard, and some high-end machines come with *megabytes* (Mb) of RAM, that is to say thousands of kilobytes. The amount of RAM in a computer can be a critical factor for MIDI purposes. With many MIDI applications (particularly sequencers), the bigger the internal memory of the computer, the greater the potential file size. A small amount of RAM will in some cases limit the duration of a piece of music and/or the number of instruments used in orchestration. RAM can normally be upgraded to a larger amount, but many pieces of software are written to run with only the standard amount in order not to limit the market to upgraded machines.

2.1.3 Storage

Storage refers to files stored on a medium such as a cassette tape or a disk. Cassette tapes are hardly used these days, and the disk is the basic computer storage medium. Floppy disks are so called because they are round and made of very thin material which bends easily. But they are encased in a thicker material, of a square shape, for protection. They are inserted into a floppy-disk drive in (or connected to) the computer, which is then able to *read* files they contain into its RAM, and to *write* files on them for permanent storage. Floppy disks, like audio and video tapes, can be re-written over many times.

Floppy disks come in various sizes and are capable of storing different amounts of data, though the amount they can store is not related in a linear way to their physical size. The most common sizes are 3.5 inch (inside a fairly rigid plastic case) and 5.25 inch (inside a thin cardboard case). The former are more robust, since 5.25 inch disks can easily be bent even inside their cardboard covering.

The amount of data a disk can hold is often referred to as its *format*, measured in kilobytes (K), as with RAM. Modern sequencers are capable of generating large MIDI files, and it is important that the disk format of a computer is large enough to contain the largest file envisaged. MIDI software written for specific computers will of course take their particular disk formats into account, but floppy storage affects the design specifications of many pieces of software, and can be a limitation.

not an easy process, and the panacea it may appear to offer in the hyperbole of advertisements has to be viewed with a good dollop of circumspection.

Notes can be input either directly from a computer, from a compatible sequencer, or from a MIDI musical keyboard via a MIDI interface, either in real or step time. And some of the available score editors are very intelligent. They come with facilities like user-defined sensitivity levels for the real-time input of chords (since a player may not press all the keys at exactly the same moment), transposition from one key to another, automatic beaming (joining) of groups of notes with the correct slope, and so on. And they of course all have the normal editing functions found on word processors, such as saving, deleting and copying marked blocks.

Score editing is fully described in Chapter 12.

Sound editors and Librarians

Sound editors are computer versions of the functions found in synthesiser keyboards used for editing *voices* (instrument or other sounds). Many synthesisers are programmable, and can be made to produce a great variety of voices, from trumpets and bells to strings and thunderstorms. But even professional keyboards are often limited to a single-line Liquid Crystal Display (LCD) and allow programming of only one setting at a time. This makes programming an unattractive proposition if it is something which will be done frequently.

Sound editors, on the other hand, allow full-screen editing on a computer, as well as allowing sounds to be manipulated in other ways. They are often available as separate modules, each for a different model of instrument. They are sometimes called *synthesiser voice editors* (or just *voice editors*), or *patch* editors (for reasons which are given in Chapter 8 Section 8.4). Sounds are sent to the computer from the keyboard or sound module, are edited with the software, then sent back to the keyboard or sound module for storage.

Librarians add to the power of sound editors. A synthesiser keyboard may be capable of storing, say, 32 sounds in its internal memory. Using a librarian, *banks* of sounds can be created with a sound editor (or they can be bought ready-made). Individual sounds can then be taken from any one of the banks in order to make up a new bank, which can then be stored on disk ready for sending to the synthesiser whenever it is required. Librarians are therefore sound-information management tools.

Some sound editors, and even some sequencers, have built-in librarians, but librarians can also be bought as stand-alone pieces of software. They represent an inexpensive way of storing sounds, because most synthesisers store them on rather expensive RAM (Random Access Memory) or ROM (Read Only Memory) cards and cartridges, whereas computer-disk storage is cheap. For the price of a typical cartridge holding perhaps 64 sounds, it is possible to buy a librarian which will allow a thousand sounds or more to be stored on a single floppy disk. This is something they often forget to say in music shops. Note, however, that synthesisers with their own floppy-disk storage are beginning to appear.

Sound editors and librarians are treated in Chapter 8.

Integrated packages

Many of the features of sequencers, score editors and the like can be found in so-called integrated packages. The simplest of these are essentially just a sequencer and score editor in one, though some incorporate facilities found in sound editors.

Integrated packages in the area of MIDI are no different from those in other areas of computing. Many integrated business packages incorporating a word processor, a database, a spreadsheet and a communications program, allow data to be exchanged between the modules, something which overcomes the annoying incompatibility of separate programs from different software houses. You can be fairly certain, however, that each module will not be equal in quality with its neighbour. You can also be certain, unless you are buying a top-quality and therefore expensive package, that at least some of the modules will be of a quality or range which are inferior to equivalent stand-alone packages.

Educational software

Almost as soon as computers had become items affordable by schools and parents, educational software packages on every subject began to appear, and there has been a growth market in the area ever since. A computer is well suited to musical education because most personal computers have at least some internal sound-producing capability, and MIDI can enhance this.

Musical education software can be found in many varieties, from keyboard training to music theory. Some packages are more interactive than others, and some are meant for absolute beginners while others are aimed at tutoring people who already have a basic musical knowledge.

As a general rule, care has to be exercised in evaluating computer-assisted learning software, and especially so in music where taste and personal judgement can play such a major part. It should always be remembered that a program may appear to show intelligence, but it knows only what its programmers have written into it, and poorly designed software can do as much educational damage as educational good, especially in advanced applications.

Educational software is treated in more detail Chapter 13 Section 13.5.

Experimental hardware and software

A computer can do an enormous amount of the work which used to be obligatory for composers. Whatever may be said to the contrary, however, they cannot as yet be real substitutes for the creative process. Computers and MIDI are merely tools, and the human brain is still the only device which can create art. We are aware how contentious such a statement will be in certain circles – after all, computers have created so-called poetry, so-called paintings and so-called music. We stand firm.

Nevertheless, the work of composition can be eased not merely by having the computer perform repetitive or boring tasks: computers can also be programmed to add something of their own. There are pieces of hardware and software which will take care of the basics of arranging pieces of music. They give instant results, which is what today's three-minute culture demands. It may all taste like instant coffee, but that is good enough for most people, who are no more prepared to go to the trouble of a real capuccino than they are to slave over harmonic theory and counterpoint.

In our view, such efforts at automation should not be disparaged, partly because they represent experiment, and partly because the results they give can actually be useful if they are thought of as prototypes rather than finished products. They are dealt with in Chapter 11.

1.5 The Human Voice and Natural Instruments

However interesting and subtle the music produced by the MIDI studio we have so far described, synthesised sounds tend to sound synthesised, and the quality of a performance can be considerably enhanced by using a mixture of synthesised and acoustic sounds.

The easiest way of interfacing with human voices or conventional instruments is to create the computerised accompaniment first, and sing or play along with it afterwards. However, it is better from a musical standpoint to work the other way round by adding a synthesised accompaniment to an acoustically-produced main melody. This involves recording the main voice or instrument on a tape recorder, then synchronising the computer accompaniment with it.

Some MIDI interfaces are capable of producing *tape-sync* (tape synchronisation) code for synchronising MIDI note information with a tape recorder holding the acoustic performance. The theory behind sync code is described in Chapter 4 Section 4.1.1, and the practice in Chapter 10 Section 10.3.

Multi-track tape recorders are essential if natural sounds are regularly to be incorporated into MIDI performances, since they allow each instrument to be recorded separately while listening to the rest. This is similar to recording different MIDI instruments on the tracks of a sequencer, but in this case only acoustic sounds are recorded. This method was extensively used in the 1970s, when tape recorders of 24 or 48 tracks allowed musicians like Tomita, Vangelis, Jarre and Wakeman to create symphonic sounds all by themselves. However, with computers and MIDI, the number of tracks needed on tape has been reduced to the number of acoustic sounds used. So, a 4-track recorder which ten years ago would have been considered adequate for only very amateur use, today can offer semi-professional standards. One track can contain a tape-sync code which will run the computer and all the MIDI instruments, leaving three free tracks for vocals, a guitar, a saxophone or some other acoustic instrument.

Multi-track tape recorders exist in both cassette and reel-to-reel form. Cassette recorders tend to be cheaper. They are adequate, and many composers are happy with them. Most good models will run at double the normal speed of 4.5 cms per second, and feature noise reduction for improved performance.

For natural sounds, a microphone is of course a must, and whereas it is possible elsewhere in the studio to economise on a piece of equipment in order to finance some other material, with microphones this is more often than not a mistake. Microphones represent the one area in the entire range of studio equipment where price really does equal quality, and where bargains are few and far between.

The use of natural sounds within MIDI is treated in various parts of this book, but see especially Chapter 10, and for types of microphones Section 10.1.

1.6 Polishing Off

There are many sound effects which can be added to a recording to make it more interesting. Sound effects produced within a MIDI studio do not mean recordings of bird song, gunshots or other sounds available on a BBC Sound Effects record used for adding a sound track to a home movie. MIDI sound effects are ways of processing the raw sounds of synthesisers and sound modules, as well as the sounds of natural instruments and the human voice.

Reverberation (usually called simply *reverb*) enriches dry sounds. Delay and echo can add mystery to vocals. Special effects such as flanging, pitch shifting and phasing – difficult if not impossible to describe in words, but which should be heard at some time during the MIDI learning process – can create an outer-space atmosphere. Chorus, which can multiply a single sound creating what is called *pseudo many*, is often used to improve synthesised strings. Enhancers are used to transform bathroom-quality voices and make them caress, instead of scratch, the listener's eardrums.

Although until two years ago each of these effects would have required a considerable financial outlay, most of them can today be found in one box called a Multi-Effect Digital Sound Processing Unit – a mouthful, but a very useful piece of hardware usually offering some pre-set and some programmable effects. More details of such equipment appear in Chapter 9 Section 9.2.

1.7 Mastering

Mastering means creating a master recording in stereo.

For those interested in MIDI music merely for the pleasure of hearing their own compositions, an ordinary hi-fi system will suffice. But those who wish to make copies of recordings perhaps in order to market them, should consider some semi-professional equipment. In the old days – a little over five years ago – this would have been a reel-to-reel analogue tape recorder. Today, the magic word is again *digital*. More on mastering can be found in Chapter 10 Section 10.5.

1.8 Listening

There are many other add-ons available for the MIDI studio. Indeed, it is possible to go on adding ever-more sophisticated pieces of machinery, from specialised music entry pads to digital faders. The only limiting factors are finance, the physical space available for the equipment ... and ears.

Subsequent chapters in this book contain advice and recommendations about particular brands of MIDI equipment, but it cannot be over-stressed that music is about hearing. Before buying anything, it is imperative to hear MIDI studios actually work. If as yet you do not have any equipment of your own nor access to any, visit a music or computer shop where it is on sale, and listen. No book can be a complete substitute for listening when it comes to choosing MIDI material.

2

Computers for Music

A MIDI studio does not have to include a computer. All that is needed is to connect two synthesisers together via their MIDI sockets and technically this is a MIDI studio. But the processing power of computers is the natural concomitant of MIDI, and they have come to be inextricably linked with it. The additional functional benefits they supply are many, and certainly outweigh their cost.

There is vast choice of computers, and the computer-ignorant buyer is probably more of a potential victim than in any other area of consumer electronics. When buying any piece of equipment, from a refrigerator to a camcorder, by definition the more you know about the facilities it offers, the more informed will be your choice. With computers such knowledge is vital, and the beginner is therefore at a considerable disadvantage. The average salesperson in a High-Street store knows enough about digital watches and even video cassette recorders to be able to advise in general terms. When it comes to computers, few such sales people can offer anything but the most basic advice.

However, armed with a little understanding of the components of a computer, the wretched first-time buyer is at least in a position to ask the right questions, either of a High-Street salesperson or a specialist dealer. The following section is therefore intended for those who wish to buy a computer for musical purposes, but who know little or nothing about the subject.

2.1 A Crash Course in Computing

2.1.1 Processors

The heart of a computer is a microprocessor called the CPU (Central Processing Unit), often referred to simply as the *processor*. This controls the basic functions of the computer such as arithmetic and logic.

The difference between the processors of various computers is an essential part of the differences in the way they perform, and one of the most significant among these differences is the speed at which they can handle operations. One way of thinking about a microprocessor is as a pathway with a number of tracks along it, and the wider the path, the greater the number of tracks. Early microcomputers were based on processors with eight tracks or *bits* (see Chapter 3, Section 3.1.2 for a more accurate explanation of bits) and were therefore known as 8-bit computers. They are still produced, but 1981 saw the appearance of 16-bit processors in personal computers, which were faster because the wider pathway allowed them to handle more information, and to address (use) larger areas of memory. They are now the norm, but 32-bit processors (which are that much more powerful) are also found on higher-end machines.

The speed at which the processor and its associated chipset runs (affecting the number of operations it can perform in a given time, and other factors) is called its *clock speed*, which is measured in MegaHertz (MHz). By today's standards, less than 3 MHz is slow, and over 20 MHz is fast. Clock speed is not everything by any means, but it is a fair indicator of performance (in machines other than those which use a RISC system – Reduced Instruction Set Computer – such as the Acorn Archimedes).

Most serious machines offer add-ons to make the processor more efficient, the two most important of which are a maths co-processor and a Digital Signal Processor (DSP). A maths co-processor takes care of many of the arithmetical operations, thus leaving the CPU to get on with other things. A DSP can specifically handle the arithmetic involved in processing digital audio signals, and is therefore a step up for the musician from a maths co-processor.

2.1.2 Internal Memory

The internal memory of a computer is divided between ROM and RAM. ROM stands for Read-Only Memory, and it contains certain basic instructions about how the computer is to perform. The fact that it is read-only means that it cannot be changed by the user. RAM stands for Random Access Memory, and is used for two purposes: as a temporary store for instructions required to run a program, and as a temporary store for a user's data.

When a computer is switched off, normally everything in RAM is lost, so data has to be transferred to a disk for more permanent storage in the form of *files*, each with its own filename. For example, a piece of music which has been produced on a sequencer will be stored in a file on disk. The sequencer program itself is not re-stored since it has not been changed.

RAM is measured in *Kilobytes*, usually written as *K*. A byte is the equivalent of a single character typed at a computer keyboard, and a kilobyte is roughly 1,000 bytes, so 512K means about 512,000 characters, say 85,000 words. MIDI information is stored not as textual characters or words but in a special way, though the basic processes taking place in RAM are identical.

Most modern computers come with a minimum of 512K of RAM as standard, and some high-end machines come with *megabytes* (Mb) of RAM, that is to say thousands of kilobytes. The amount of RAM in a computer can be a critical factor for MIDI purposes. With many MIDI applications (particularly sequencers), the bigger the internal memory of the computer, the greater the potential file size. A small amount of RAM will in some cases limit the duration of a piece of music and/or the number of instruments used in orchestration. RAM can normally be upgraded to a larger amount, but many pieces of software are written to run with only the standard amount in order not to limit the market to upgraded machines.

2.1.3 Storage

Storage refers to files stored on a medium such as a cassette tape or a disk. Cassette tapes are hardly used these days, and the disk is the basic computer storage medium. Floppy disks are so called because they are round and made of very thin material which bends easily. But they are encased in a thicker material, of a square shape, for protection. They are inserted into a floppy-disk drive in (or connected to) the computer, which is then able to *read* files they contain into its RAM, and to *write* files on them for permanent storage. Floppy disks, like audio and video tapes, can be re-written over many times.

Floppy disks come in various sizes and are capable of storing different amounts of data, though the amount they can store is not related in a linear way to their physical size. The most common sizes are 3.5 inch (inside a fairly rigid plastic case) and 5.25 inch (inside a thin cardboard case). The former are more robust, since 5.25 inch disks can easily be bent even inside their cardboard covering.

The amount of data a disk can hold is often referred to as its *format*, measured in kilobytes (K), as with RAM. Modern sequencers are capable of generating large MIDI files, and it is important that the disk format of a computer is large enough to contain the largest file envisaged. MIDI software written for specific computers will of course take their particular disk formats into account, but floppy storage affects the design specifications of many pieces of software, and can be a limitation.

Formats for 3.5 inch and 5.25 inch disks normally range from 360K to 1,400K (1.4 Mb). But care is needed in dealing with these numbers because some manufacturers quote only the *unformatted* capacity of a disk. For instance, you may see a disk format quoted as 1 Mb, though when the disk is formatted ready for use, the maximum amount of data it can contain is only 720K.

Hard disks, as opposed to floppies, are usually permanent fixtures inside the computer (they are sometimes called fixed disks). They are sealed into the drive, can contain far more data than a floppy disk (typically between 20 and 100 Mb) and they have much faster access times, that is to say that the computer can read from and write to a hard disk far more rapidly than from or to a floppy disk. They are also said to be more reliable than floppy disks, though a great deal of work can be lost if they do fail. In particular, those which are not fully ruggedised (most are not) do not take kindly to being accidentally knocked. For these reasons, it is normal to make regular back-ups (safety copies) by copying files from a hard disk to floppy disks.

A hard disk with a comparatively fast access time (less than about 40/1000 of a second – 40 milliseconds) is necessary some for high-level MIDI programs, and normally, the larger the capacity of the disk, the faster the access time. A hard disk is also necessary for *dumping* sounds from a sampler (that is, storing the sounds of acoustic instruments or the human voice on disk), since this requires very large files, and for recording digitally direct to disk.

2.1.4 Monitors

Monitors (screens) come in various types. They can be monochrome or colour, and phosphorus-based or LCD (Liquid Crystal Display). LCD screens tend to be used in portable computers because they are lighter and consume less power. The most important measure of the display characteristics of monitors is the number of dots (called *pixels*) they can display, given in columns and lines, for example 640 x 350. This is their *resolution*, and it can be a critical factor in certain MIDI applications.

A high-resolution monitor is required for applications which include music-notation graphics, as in score editing, and for using Microsoft Windows or other software based on a graphical interface (see Section 2.1.5 below). Otherwise, it is perfectly possible to manage with medium resolution. As a rule of thumb, a resolution of 640 x 200 or less tends to be poor (even getting on for unusable) for notation graphics, while one of 640 x 350 and above is good.

A colour monitor is useful but not essential, and if price is the main consideration, on the whole it is better to opt for high-resolution monochrome than low-resolution colour. However, if colour is your choice, another factor is important for serious work: *dot pitch*. This is measured in fractions of a millimetre, and it is the distance between the three primary colours in any one dot. Colours are produced on a colour monitor by firing electrons at the screen from three separate guns: red, green and blue. The closer the targets are to each other, the less fuzzy the resulting coloured dot. So, the lower the dot pitch, the crisper the picture. A dot pitch of .31 and below is good for detailed work involving traditional notation.

The IBM PC and its clones have various standards for mono and colour monitors, and it is worth knowing about them because certain pieces of software will work satisfactorily only with some of them. For monochrome, the standards are Hercules, MDA (Monochrome Display Adapter) and VGA (Virtual Graphics Array). Colour monitors can also work in mono mode. The standards are CGA (Colour Graphics Adapter – 320 x 200 usually with four colours, or 640 x 200 mono), EGA (Enhanced Graphics Adapter – 640 x 200 or 320 x 350 with 16 colours), and VGA (640 x 480 with various colour modes). For traditional notation, EGA or VGA are often required.

A number of computers can work with an ordinary television, though the combination is not a good one for serious use (except in the newest multimedia machines such as the Commodore CDTV – see below Section 2.2.4). The quality of the display depends on the interface between the computer and the television set. This is a complex subject, but a general rule is that if the interface has a SCART connector, the results can be acceptable. A SCART connector is a 21-pin plug and socket, the plug being of a distinctive rectangular shape cut at an angle on one side. For most people, however, a dedicated high-resolution monitor is the best choice.

2.1.5 Computer Input Devices

Figure 2.1: A mouse

The kind of keyboard which comes with a computer is of little significance for MIDI applications. Far more important is the use of a mouse, which can replace the keyboard in many circumstances. A mouse gets its name from its shape, the cable linking it to the computer resembling a long tail.

A mouse is a pointing device: a tracker-ball underneath it registers its spatial coordinates as it is moved around, and these are translated into screen coordinates. The result is that a little picture (an arrow, a pointing finger or whatever) appears to move around the screen. A mouse is also equipped with one or more buttons. When these are pressed, the computer takes some action, for instance the same action which might be taken if the Enter (Return) key on the keyboard were pressed. When a button is pressed on a mouse, the term used to describe the action is a *click*. Thus, in some software documentation, you are asked to click on a certain part of the screen or on an option in a *menu* (list).

A mouse is an integral part of what is known as a WIMP environment, increasingly referred to these days as a GUI – Graphical User Interface. WIMP stands for Windows, Icons, Mouse, Pull-down menus (some people say the *P* stands for Pointer) which between them offer a graphical way of entering commands and data into a computer without having to type very much at the keyboard, and in some instances nothing at all. Such graphical interfaces are being used in MIDI software with increasing frequency even though they require large amounts of internal memory.

Windows are moveable and re-sizeable areas of the screen. Icons are representations of objects or ideas: an hour glass to indicate a *Please Wait* message, a double-sided arrow for dragging windows about by their borders, a dustbin representing deletion, and so on. Pull-down menus (sometimes called pop-up menus) are lists of available commands and options to be clicked on with the mouse.

A mouse is essential for some MIDI applications based on a GUI, while for others its use is optional, the alternative being to use the cursor (arrow) keys and the Enter key on the computer keyboard, though this is usually not as satisfactory as using a mouse. A mouse is particularly useful when it comes to editing MIDI data on the screen, either as graphs or musical notation, and as GUIs become ever more popular, so a mouse is becoming an increasingly important MIDI item.

2.1.6 Operating Systems

Imagine that you are a computer programmer in the 1950s. You know nothing about the internal workings of a computer, but are asked to write a program which adds together any two numbers entered by a user, prints the result on a printer, and stores it to magnetic tape. You cannot do it, because in order to write the program, you have to know how the machine has registered that a key has been pressed and which key, how it stores data in its internal memory, and how it sends it to a printer and to tape. In other words, to solve a trivial problem, you would be obliged to get deeply involved in the complexity of the machine's circuitry.

Today, operating systems take care of such matters. They decide where data will be stored in memory and where it will be held on a disk; they call in instructions as required; they detect input from a keyboard or other input device; they direct output as and when necessary to the correct destination (screen, printer, disk, communications port, whatever); and they tell you if something is wrong.

Each family of computers uses its own operating system, and though there are arguments about which is the best, software for particular computers is written to use the appropriate system. It may never be necessary to issue any commands at the operating-system level, though it is usually worth learning how to do so.

2.1.7 Printers

In musical applications, a printer is essential only for printing musical scores, though it can also be useful for producing hard copy of other information.

A *dot-matrix* printer is the cheapest variety. Dot-matrix printers have a print-head containing a matrix (rectangular printing mould) of needles. As the print-head moves along the printer carriage, appropriate needles are pushed forward, hit a ribbon, and patterns of dots are transferred to the paper. Dot-matrix printers normally have either 9 pins or 24 pins, the latter giving better resolution.

Ink-jet printers are dot-matrix printers which do not use a ribbon – the ink is sprayed directly on the paper. They can produce high-quality results, but are comparatively rare.

For publishing-quality print-outs of scores, a *laser* printer is required. Laser printers work something like a photocopier (and often look like one), and their flexibility and quality of output can be rivalled only by professional printing presses.

Daisy-wheel printers work by spinning a spoked wheel, with each spoke having a pre-formed character at the end of it. The appropriate character hits a ribbon and the shape is transferred to the paper. Daisy-wheel printers can therefore cope only with the characters on the spokes of the wheels available for them, and are of no use at all for most musical applications.

Unless you are using an Apple computer such as the Macintosh, which links perfectly with an Apple printer, with dot-matrix printers you should opt for one of the standard Epson range, or one which is Epson-compatible, because so much music software expects one of this kind. With laser printers (again with the exception of Apple), you should choose a Hewlett Packard (HP) Laserjet or compatible, for the same reason.

2.1.8 Modems

Figure 2.2: A modem

The word *modem* is derived from MOdulator/DEModulator. A modem allows computer data to be sent down an ordinary telephone line. It does this by translating the information coming out of the computer into audible tones (modulation) so that it can be handled by a telephone, which is equipped to deal with sound not numbers. A modem can also receive these tones and re-translate them into computer-readable form (demodulation). Two modems thus allow two-way communication between computers, however remote from each other, via the national or international telephone network.

Modems come in a box (external) or as cards which fit inside a computer (internal). In both cases, they are connected to the computer's communications port, and via a cable to a telephone wall-socket. They are controlled by a software communications package running on the computer, and the combined cost of such a communications set-up can be anywhere between under £100 and well over £500, depending on its sophistication. £250 buys a reliable set-up which is more than adequate for sending and receiving files.

You do not specifically require a modem for musical purposes except for transferring files urgently to another computer (that is to say without sending a disk in the post) or unless you wish to access an online system. Such systems are sometimes called Bulletin Boards, and there are many dotted around the UK, indeed around the world. They are accessed by dialling a data telephone number, after which the computer keyboard is used to send various commands via the modem, while incoming data is displayed on the computer screen.

Subscribing to such an online system can be useful for *downloading* software or data files (receiving them down the telephone line) and for obtaining advice from other subscribers, either by leaving a message on a public area of the system (such areas are sometimes called *conferences* or *notice boards*) or by sending it privately by electronic mail.

A number of online systems have a conference reserved for MIDI-related topics, where musicians can exchange ideas, read electronic versions of music magazines, access appropriate databases and so on. One system, however, is entirely devoted to music: The Music Network (TMN). This is split into many conferences ranging from those of a general musical nature to those intended for users of specific products, in some cases organised by the manufacturer and therefore working like a direct Help line. Various kinds of data and software can be downloaded, from synthesiser sounds in MIDI format to musical utilities and tools.

TMN is therefore an excellent forum for musicians. It represents a means of keeping up with the latest developments and, more importantly, of being in contact with people of the same ilk, not only in the UK but also world-wide. Composing can be a lonely business, and being able to discuss common interests with other musicians can be as much a boost to morale as a practical way of seeking help.

For most people in the UK, connection to TMN means either making a local telephone call to a *node* on a public data network (there are nodes in all major cities), after which the call is automatically transferred to the central computer hosting the TMN system, or dialling a London number for direct access. See Appendix B for the address and telephone number of TMN.

2.1.9 Multi-tasking

In an ordinary course about computer basics, it would be unusual to mention multi-tasking since this is an advanced feature. However, the topic is relevant to MIDI because as personal computers become ever more powerful, and MIDI applications ever more sophisticated, it is something which will become increasingly common.

A processor can do only one thing at a time, and traditionally computers have therefore run one application at a time. To change to a new application has meant leaving the original one and loading another. But human beings need to be able to switch tasks at will, and this is particularly true of the composer. He or she may wish to jot down an idea for a song while composing another, or suddenly wish to edit something in one song using a particular editor, while another is on the screen. By the time the current application has been left and the new one loaded, the idea may be lost. It is also often useful to be able to edit a sound on a synthesiser in the middle of a sequencing session, and/or switch between a sequencer and a score editor.

The answer is to have two or more applications running concurrently. This is perfectly possible, though the process eats up internal memory. The generic name for such a process is multi-tasking, but strictly speaking it is not always that. True multi-tasking means that the processor is constantly scanning all activities and spending a small fraction of a second on each, thus giving the impression of seamless concurrency. Task-switching, which is more common, means having one application active and the others ready in the background, already loaded into memory to be called up as necessary without the computer having to access the disk. It should be noted that true multi-tasking in MIDI can cause problems of timing, since some MIDI data may arrive at the precise moment when the processor is taking care of something completely different.

A third type of multi-tasking is where two processors are brought into play, running in parallel. This is the case when an intelligent MIDI interface such as the Roland MPU-401 is used. It has its own processor which can take care of such potential timing problems.

When different pieces of software are running under a multi-tasking system, they can be made to communicate with each other, provided that they conform to specific standards. The process is known as Inter-Application Communication (IAC) and many see the future of MIDI in this. MIDI was developed as a common standard between hardware manufacturers. IAC, if producers can agree on standards, could do the same for software.

2.1.10 Networking

LANs (Local Area Networks) are a means of connecting computers together which can then communicate with each other. There is no need for a modem in a LAN because the computers are connected directly by cables.

Many people are talking about LANs being important to the future of MIDI. It is certainly possible to incorporate MIDI applications in a LAN, and doing so gives advantages such as being able instantly to share data between computers, thus allowing more MIDI channels, for example. The result can be a very complex composition produced by a number of computers simultaneously. But here we will stick our neck out by saying that whereas sharing data between computers may be vital in business, it is not likely to affect many owners of home studios in the foreseeable future. Computers and networking hardware/software combinations cost a great deal, and the money can usually be better spent on upgrading other areas of the studio.

2.2 Makes of Computer

The word *computer* in a MIDI context means a *personal computer*. The term does not necessarily signify a PC in the sense of an IBM PC or compatible machine (even though the *PC* in *IBM PC* stands for *Personal Computer*) but rather a desktop or laptop computer as opposed to a large mini-computer or mainframe. This therefore includes the Atari ST, the Commodore Amiga, the Apple Macintosh, the Acorn Archimedes, and even computers based on what is now old 8-bit technology. *PC* on its own is normally used to signify an IBM PC or compatible machine.

Some computers are better suited to MIDI than others. Factors which play a part in determining their suitability are their power, and the extent to which they have made their mark in the world of electronic music – in other words, how many hardware add-ons and how much software is commercially available for them. We deal here with each family of computers, and judge them from the point of view of their use and potential use within the realm of MIDI.

However, in this context an important general point needs to be made. Computer retailers naturally wish to sell machines for which they are accredited dealers, and/or for which the profit margins are highest. This is not to disparage dealers, many of whom sincerely believe that the machines they sell are the best; and perhaps not surprisingly so, because there appears to be in all computer users – dealers and customers alike – an inordinately strong desire to convince the world that the machine they are currently using is either more powerful, more friendly, better served or better value than any other. In the domain of computerised music, the Atari ST, the Commodore Amiga, the PC and the Apple Macintosh each attracts a furious defence from its existing user-base, and so much so that it is virtually impossible to get an objective viewpoint. Perhaps there is no such viewpoint, and in any case we would not wish to stand under an umbrella while it is raining on other people: our own preference, revealed below, reflects our own prejudices.

2.2.1 The IBM PC, its Compatibles, and the PS/2

The biggest family of personal computers is based on the IBM PC. IBM – International Business Machines – has for many years dictated the industry standard. Its PCs have been widely cloned (copied) by other manufacturers, and huge amounts of software have been written to run on its operating system, MS-DOS. It remains even truer today than it did nearly a decade ago that (with the exception of specialised markets such as games) if a software house is going to write a program, it can hardly afford not to write an MS-DOS version of it.

This ought to be as much the case with MIDI as with other personal-computer applications, but the MIDI position is taking longer to clarify in the UK because the Atari ST, with its integral MIDI interface, from the start set a standard both in professional studios and for home use. History lingers on, and because of the relatively high prices of PCs when computer music began to take off, we still have a situation in the UK in which the Atari ST is the professional musician's computer. Indeed, it is surprising how few people are aware that a professional-standard PC system can cost little more than its equivalent Atari configuration.

It is therefore hardly surprising that we see so few innovations in the UK when it comes to the PC and MIDI. In the USA the situation is quite different. There, the PC has led the computer-music market for several years, and intense competition has resulted in some excellent innovations. These have in recent times become increasingly available in the UK, such that the PC can now be said to be very well served, and to be hard on the heels of the Atari.

We must admit that we are biased towards the PC, mostly because it is a world-standard professional machine, and because it offers the least expensive and widest upgrade path. But we should stress that this is in no way to denigrate the Macintosh, the Amiga, nor particularly the Atari ST. The latter has served and continues to serve MIDI and its users magnificently, but it is clear that the originally high price of the PC was responsible for keeping it out of impoverished musical hands, and though the influx of cheap PC clones from the Far East has changed this situation, the dominance of the Atari remains. For how long is an unanswerable question. It will not disappear overnight, for sure.

Two main types of PC are available, making up the XT and AT ranges. There are rules about which type of PC falls into which category, but common practice has it that an XT is based on the Intel 8086 16-bit processor, while the AT range is faster and generally more powerful, being based on an 80286 16-bit, or an 80386 32-bit processor. PCs come with various amounts of RAM from 512K to many megabytes, various amounts of floppy-disk storage, and various clock speeds from about 5 MHz upwards. ATs are often referred to as *286* or *386* to describe the machine by the processor it is using (though some people distinguish between an AT 286 and a plain 386). A 386sx is a 32-bit machine but limited to 16 bits for certain operations, and in general costs less than a full 386. Even faster are machines based on the i486 32-bit processor, though they are still rare.

The IBM PS/2 series (models 25, 30, 50, 55, 70 and 80) is essentially the same as the ordinary PC range, using same processors, clock speeds and so on. The difference is that, in models 50 and above, the PS/2 uses what is known as MCA (Micro Channel Architecture) in the expansion slots where cards can be fitted. MCA is faster than the standard architecture but there is only one MIDI interface which supports it, the Roland MPU-IMC. This has the same specifications as the MPU-IPC, which is the industry standard, but it has to be noted that the choice of interface on these PS/2 machines is limited to a single model and a single manufacturer.

Some PC clones, assembled in the West from parts manufactured in the Far East, bear the name of virtually unknown firms. Others are very well known and are of high quality, those from Compaq, Wyse and Wang being examples. Compatible models from known manufacturers to be found in UK High-Street stores come from Amstrad, Olivetti, Commodore, Atari and others (the Atari PC is not to be confused with the Atari ST, which is not a PC clone). Others, such as those from Elonex and Research Machines, are available through catalogues and often aimed at specific markets such as the educational sector.

The Yamaha C1

A PC clone deserving of a special mention is the Yamaha C1. This is a portable 286 machine, and is the most professional music computer so far manufactured. It comes with a built-in 8-port MIDI interface (giving 128 MIDI channels), advanced features for synchronising with tape recorders, and three music programs including a sophisticated 400-track sequencer.

The C1 was released in 1989, but it did not sell anything like as well as was hoped in the UK. It seems that a demand for a PC heavily oriented towards MIDI simply is not there, and though the machine has fared better in the USA where the PC music market is larger, it appears to have suffered from aiming at too specialised a sector.

2.2.2 Apple and the Macintosh

The Apple II was being used for music before MIDI was created. It is still a major machine in the USA where it is reasonably well served MIDI-wise, but is now used only rarely in the UK.

The Apple Macintosh, successor to the Apple Lisa, became the first professional music computer, because at the time of its release it was the only serious machine with adequate graphics capabilities to suit musical applications. It was faster than the IBM PC, and its graphically-oriented operating system appealed more to easy-going musicians than the rest of the command-based machines offered by the competition. Coupled with an Apple laser printer, it was for a while the only system offering anything approaching a viable possibility for professional music desktop publishing.

The Macintosh's lead world-wide over the PC in the field of MIDI resulted in a number of excellent pieces of software which are still available today, many in improved forms. However, with the price of PCs continuously falling, and the development of graphical user interfaces similar in appearance and usage to the Macintosh's interface, most of the good Macintosh software has been, or is being, adapted for other computers.

The Macintosh range of models includes some powerful machines such as the SE/30, the IIX, the IIcx, the IIci, and the IIfx, the latter having a clock speed of 40 MHz. All are able to address large amounts of RAM, and the numerous MIDI applications written for them tend to take advantage of this, as well as of their excellent operating system and multi-tasking abilities. The trend is likely to continue with the introduction of Apple's new operating system – System 7 – which is heavily oriented towards multi-tasking.

Current Macintoshes still have the internal stereo sound chip found on early models. It is not good enough for performances, but it can be used for editing purposes.

Feature for feature, the Macintosh has always been more expensive than its main rival the PC.

2.2.3 The Atari ST

Although business applications are available for it, the Atari ST range was initially launched principally for the games market. It nevertheless had a disk drive, a massive memory for its time, a 3-channel sound chip and a built-in MIDI interface. These features, and its low price, gave it an advantage in musical terms over all other home computers, and it virtually wiped out the competition.

Today, the cheapest Atari ST still costs less than most PCs, and that is not counting the free MIDI interface. But the Atari is not quite as cheap for serious MIDI applications as it might at first seem once the decision has been taken to upgrade the system. For instance, the average hard disk for the Atari costs twice as much as the average one for the PC.

Despite that, the Atari ST is still a viable option since in its basic configuration it is excellent value for money. It can be made to emulate the PC and the Apple Macintosh with special software, though so many high-quality MIDI products are available for the Atari that this not a significant consideration for those using the machine for musical purposes. In any case, emulated programs tend to run more slowly than on the machines for which they were originally written. However, it is worth noting that the Atari's 3.5 inch (720K) drive can read disks which have been formatted on a PC, so standard MIDI files produced on a PC can be read in directly.

The Atari ST comes in various models, such as the 520 STFM, the 1040 ST, the Mega ST2 and the Mega ST4, ranging in RAM size from 512K to 4 Mb, and all using a 16-bit processor running at 8 MHz and a graphical user interface (GEM – Graphics Environment Manager). The STE has enhanced sound and graphics, and easily expandable RAM. A laptop Atari model, the Stacy ST with 2 or 4 Mb of RAM, a hard disk and an LCD screen, is selling well and being used by musicians – indeed, it is targeted very much at them as a portable version of their existing Atari models. A new Atari machine, the TT, is about to be released in the UK at the time of writing. In its lowest configuration, the TT has 2 Mb of RAM, a hard disk, excellent graphics, and runs at an impressive 32 MHz.

The standard Atari 520, while capable of being used for many musical purposes, is unable to run a number of programs which require a large amount of RAM, and the 1040 is really now the only practicable Atari option as a starter machine for musical applications.

2.2.4 Commodore

Three types of Commodore computers can be used for MIDI: the CBM64 (or 128), the Amiga, and the CDTV.

The 64 and 128

The Commodore 64 (and later the 128) was and still is a very successful machine. It was first released in 1982 yet it is still going strong. There are MIDI interfaces and music software available for it, and indeed it was used for music quite extensively for a year or so before the appearance of the Atari ST.

The Amiga

The Amiga has become established as one of the best home computers for games, but its potential for more serious use is enormous. It has special chips for graphics, video and sound, and produces results which can approach professional standards. It has a 4-channel internal sound chip and stereo output. It uses the same processor as the Atari ST, though most models in the lower end of the Amiga range have a slightly slower clock speed (7.14 MHz). Their standard multi-tasking operation, however, more than makes up for this.

Although undoubtedly a more advanced machine than the Atari ST, the Amiga was a little late in arriving, was more expensive when it did arrive, and did not have a built-in MIDI interface, all of which affected sales in the music market. It is now increasing in popularity.

The Amiga has expansion slots for taking cards, and if an appropriate *bridge board* is fitted, it can run MS-DOS (the PC's operating system) which means that PC software and hardware add-ons can be used. Equally, an Apple Macintosh emulation card can give access to Macintosh hardware and software. However, these facilities have recently lost some of their importance for musicians who use the Amiga because the machine has been attracting its own musical hardware and software at a dramatic rate. There are now many MIDI products designed specifically for the Amiga, as well as numerous Amiga versions of products originally developed for other machines. A new product from the Commodore camp itself is AmigaVision, a powerful set of software tools for developing and running applications involving graphics and sound, with links to MIDI.

Some industry gurus believe that this is all coming a little too late for the Amiga to make a real impact in the musical world, that had it happened a couple of years ago it could have become *the* musical computer but that now the competition is too firmly entrenched. The PC has attracted so many users that it cannot be dislodged, the Atari ST is also firmly dug in, and the Apple Macintosh has its dedicated following. On the other hand, producers of MIDI equipment and software are cautious about entering a shaky market since development and promotional costs are so high, yet they appear to be entering the Amiga market in their droves, especially in the USA where there are myriad new products available which we have not yet seen in the UK. Time will tell.

Two basic Amiga models have been available for some time: the 500 (512K RAM) and the 2000 (1 Mb RAM). The newer 2500/30 runs at 16 MHz, and the 3000 and 3500 include models running at 25 MHz.

Commodore also offers a good but relatively cheap range of PC clones.

The CDTV

The Commodore CDTV, due for general release in the Spring of 1991, is not a computer in the usual sense of the word. It is a *multimedia* machine – a machine designed to handle a mixture of text, images, and high-quality sound, all held on compact disc. In its standard form it has neither keyboard nor monitor (a television set is used), and it is controlled by an infra-red remote control unit. The CDTV looks something like a home video recorder but contains an Amiga computer.

Commodore are clearly inviting MIDI applications to be written for it since they have built in a MIDI interface, and at the time of writing, a number of music titles are listed as being under development. There is also talk of an infra-red remote-control link to a synthesiser keyboard. The machine is aimed at the domestic market, and if it is successful it could open up the idea of multimedia applications to the public at large, whereas they are limited to a few enthusiasts at the moment, despite their huge potential in business, leisure, training and education.

2.2.5 Acorn

The BBC Micro

The BBC micro gets its name from the fact that when the government decided to put microcomputers into schools, the British Broadcasting Corporation was asked to provide a specification, and Acorn Computers landed the contract. The machine has appeared over the years in many models, the only ones now available (except second hand) being the BBC Master and the BBC Master Compact.

The BBC micro was equipped from the beginning with a 4-channel internal sound chip with instructions built into the machine to control it. It soon attracted a wealth of music software, and even began to be used by professionals (the machine is still found in some professional studios being used as a MIDI controller). In 1985, Hybrid Technology Ltd produced the Acorn 500, a piece of hardware which expanded the standard musical capabilities of the machine. The Acorn 500 used its own musical programming language called AMPLE (Advanced Music Production Language and Environment), a very powerful but rather daunting set of instructions and commands.

Today's successor to the Acorn 500 is the Music 5000, which offers 16 channels, paired to give 8-part polyphony. AMPLE is still the language used, but it is now much easier to handle since various user-interfaces have been added, including a computerised mixing desk. There are several other hardware add-ons in the same series, such as the Music 4000 keyboard, whose memory can be programmed using AMPLE, and the Music 3000 unit which gives a further 16 channels.

The problem with AMPLE, and the hardware on which it runs, is not in its power, sophistication or ease of use. Indeed, Chris Jordan whose brainchild it is, is a rare combination of musical talent, programming wizard and educational expert. Rather, it comes down to a question of standards, as it so often has done with the BBC micro. The machine is still the principal schools computer, even though schools now have a free choice, and it comes as something of a shock to pupils who have been brought up on it to find, when they leave school, that it is hardly used in the outside world when compared to the PC. When they go abroad, they find that nobody has even heard of the machine. There never was a more insular success in the world of computing.

AMPLE and the Music 5000 carry on that tradition, since they cannot be used without a BBC micro, but are nevertheless used for music education in schools. They represent better value for money, and are in many ways better and easier to use than MIDI hardware and software, but the likelihood of MIDI being displaced by them outside the school environment is remote.

The Archimedes

The latest Acorn computer, the Archimedes, has a 32-bit processor. Its RISC (Reduced Instruction Set Computer) architecture makes it into a fast, versatile and innovative machine.

Acorn are clearly interested in seeing it used as much for musical purposes as the BBC micro. It comes with a free program (Maestro) which allows music to be created in traditional notation on the screen, and to be played back either using the internal sound capability of the computer or a MIDI interface. It is really quite good as a piece of starter software.

The machine also has eight built-in sound channels any of which can be set to seven stereo positions. This alone ought to have attracted a wide range of sequencers and other software packages, but they have been very thin on the ground when compared to what is available on other machines. Indeed, the Archimedes would certainly be more popular than it is but for the fact that, yet again, it seems to be aimed principally at the UK market, and even as an upgrade to the BBC micro. It is virtually unknown in the USA, and being so usually means these days that a machine stands little chance of selling in any significant numbers, and therefore of being of major interest to important software developers.

2.2.6 The Yamaha CX5

MSX was an operating system close to MS-DOS which many Japanese computer manufacturers adopted for reasons of compatibility with each other. It generally failed to establish itself in the UK and the USA, and is dead or dying in other countries.

The Yamaha CX5, which belonged to the MSX standard, was the first home computer designed with the musician at heart, and it therefore represents a landmark even though it has generally fallen into disuse. It came with an integral MIDI interface, a synthesiser, stereo output, and a specially made silent music keyboard for input purposes which plugged directly into the MIDI interface. Although the machine sold well, the wider failure of the MSX range and the arrival of the faster Atari ST eventually made Yamaha withdraw it.

2.2.7 The NeXT Computer

This is a very advanced machine which uses an operating system designed for multi-tasking called Unix, and comes with significant built-in sound capabilities. It has a Digital Sound Processor, stereo outputs, a microphone input with an A/D converter for sampling at compact-disc resolution, and has sophisticated music software included in the (very high) price. Its standard user-interface is graphical: menus and windows controlled by a mouse, with superb monitor resolution (1120 x 832).

The machine has not yet made its mark in the world of music, but it has great potential to do so, and is already being used for research and experimental purposes in university music departments, and by serious modern classical composers.

2.2.8 The Amstrad PCW

The PCW, a computer intended principally for word processing, has become one of the best-selling machines in the UK. The fact that MIDI add-ons and music software packages are available for it at all is a testament to its popularity, because music was very far from the minds of its designers. The range of musical products is very limited, and it is certainly not worth buying a PCW specifically for music, but there are many people who make use of it for musical purposes.

2.3 Making the choice

Deciding on which kind of computer to buy for use with MIDI is not easy, particularly since there are elements of the choice for which no definitive general advice can be ever be given. Among these are factors related to personal taste – the 'feel' of a keyboard, the colour of a monochrome screen display, the aesthetics of the physical design of the machine – and more importantly, exclusivity or otherwise of use. Computers have succeeded in becoming an integral part of MIDI not just because of their powers, but also because people often already possess them before deciding to venture into the realms of computerised music. There is no such thing as an exclusively MIDI computer, only computers which happen to be used by some people exclusively for MIDI.

The fact that a personal computer can be used for numerous tasks is consequently an essential part of selecting one. A computer which is particularly suitable for music, and is well supported by software and hardware add-ons, may be less suitable for requirements in other areas, and vice versa. And this is intimately related to questions of compatibility. It may make little sense to buy an Atari ST if a PC is already owned and being used for purposes other than music.

All things being equal, we would recommend a PC, and preferably an AT, and we are aware of how contentious a statement this is in area where brand loyalty and the need to reduce cognitive dissonance are so strong. Despite the domination of the Atari ST in the UK, we would still maintain that the PC is a better choice when the long-term future is borne in mind.

2.3.1 Choice Checklist for Computers

In addition to cost, the choice of a computer for MIDI should also take into account (insofar as a beginner is able to foresee future needs):

❑ the level of professionalism aspired to

❑ the music applications specifically envisaged (composing, performing, printing musical scores).

❑ the importance or otherwise of portability

And the following questions should also be asked:

❑ What kind of compatibility is there with other machines?

❑ What is the availability and price of software, musical and otherwise?

❑ To what extent does the available software require an extension to the standard amount of RAM?

❑ What is the availability, compatibility and price of hardware add-ons?

❑ What is likely to be the re-sale value?

❑ What is the price of a complete system, not just the starter modules?

Finally, some advice which is often given because it is almost self-evident, but rarely heeded: never take advertisements at face value.

And remember that it was the majority which sent Socrates and Jesus to their deaths.

3

MIDI – the Theory

In Chapter 1 we briefly described the products required to set up a MIDI studio, and the principal extras available for it. MIDI itself is neither a product nor a piece of equipment, but a kind of connecting network holding the studio together. This chapter is concerned with the intricate structure and the workings of that network, that is to say the theory of MIDI.

It is possible to drive a car without knowing a thing about the engine. It is equally possible to use a MIDI studio without even knowing what MIDI is – that is the whole point of many pieces of commercial software. But the difference between driving a car and using MIDI is that making music necessarily involves a creative effort, and MIDI is there not merely to control a studio but also to assist in the intellectual process of creation. For this reason, having an understanding of MIDI theory can only enhance the practical use made of it.

Basics of MIDI Theory

MIDI is in many ways a language. Not a language like English or Japanese, because it is not spoken, nor a language like BASIC, Pascal, or any other computer language, because it is not possible to program in it. It is a language of modern musical instruments and other music-related electronic devices which allows them silently to communicate with each other.

But MIDI is also more than a language. It is both a hardware and a software standard.

The hardware standard, in conceptual terms, is relatively simple. It consists of a microchip which sends information between devices, plus what is called an *opto-isolator*, there to prevent mains electricity from damaging the circuitry. It also specifies how certain connections are to be made between devices.

The software standard is more complex. Take a basic piece of MIDI information, that of sounding a single note. The stream of MIDI data indicating this begins with an instruction that a note is to be played. This is followed by more instructions about the manner in which it is to be played – pitch and amplitude (loudness) being the main parameters. The stream ends with an instruction to stop playing the note, which also contains information about how to stop playing it, for example whether it should stop suddenly or die away slowly. And that is just the beginning. Much more information may be sent, about all manner of things which can affect the quality of the note: a change in the instrument sound (flute to clarinet, say), the amount of vibrato to be applied, and so forth.

3.1 The MIDI Software Standard

The MIDI software standard can be succinctly described as follows:

> *MIDI transmits and receives over 16 channels at 31.25 Kilobaud (Kb) using serial asynchronous communication.*

In order to understand this definition, each part of it has to be examined separately.

3.1.1 MIDI Channels

MIDI uses 16 different pathways, sent as an electrical signal down a wire. In the world of computers, these pathways are sometimes referred to as lines, circuits or links, but the word *channel* is the one normally used for MIDI. Each MIDI channel can control a single instrument or a group of instruments.

MIDI channels work more or less like television channels. Electromagnetic waves from all available television stations reach the aerial, but the television set tunes in to only one of them. In the same way, information for all MIDI channels is sent along a common MIDI cable. The various devices connected to that common cable pick up only the information related to the channel they are set to receive. Most pieces of data sent down the MIDI cable have a channel number tagged on to them. At the receiving end, each instrument or other MIDI device is tuned to receive data from only a certain channel, and to ignore the rest.

3.1.2 Kilobaud

In order for a computer to communicate with any electronic device, whether that device is another computer or a peripheral piece of equipment such as an electronic musical instrument, the two have to be set up so that they can understand each other. In other words, each has to be individually adjusted to a number of precise settings before communication can even begin. One of the most important of these settings in MIDI is the speed at which information is transferred.

In human speech, speed is not a critical factor: people can understand each other even if they are speaking at different speeds. There comes a point at which too fast or too slow a speed impedes meaningful communication, but the acceptable range is very wide. This is not the case with computer communications, since computers are not yet able to make the kinds of adjustments made by the human brain. A computer can communicate effectively with another electronic device only if both expect information to arrive at a precisely determined speed.

In order to get to grips with some of the reasoning behind such speed settings, it is necessary to understand some elementary arithmetical concepts.

The 0 to 1 of Binary

The arithmetic we use in our everyday lives is based on the decimal system: it works to base 10 (it was presumably developed because we have ten fingers).

When, in the distant past in the Middle East, Arabic people started writing numbers down, they created ten numeric symbols, that is to say the series 0 to 9. Using this system, which we have inherited, when we run out of symbols at number 9, we then use two of the ten available symbols, a 1 and a 0, to make the next number in the series: 10. We go on using two symbols until the number 99. At that point we again run out of symbols so we use three to make the number 100, and so on. The number 1358, reading from left to right, therefore means one thousand plus three times one hundred plus five times ten plus eight. It is what we all discovered when we first began to write numbers down at school, learning that each digit in a number is expressed as a power of 10 (each successive digit to the left of the decimal point represents a value ten times greater than the digit to its immediate right).

But base 10 is not the only possible arithmetical system. A hexadecimal system works to base 16, and we occasionally use this too in everyday situations, for example to measure weight. There are 16 ounces in one pound, which means that 17 ounces is one pound plus one ounce – the shift to a new column occurs at 15 rather than 9. In the pre-decimalisation days of shillings and pence (which some of us can still remember) we used a duo-decimal system (base 12) because there were 12 pennies to the shilling. This was very useful when working in dozens – if a dozen eggs cost three shillings, each egg cost three pennies. Decimalisation brought us back into line with those ancient Arabic people.

We shall later have to deal with some hexadecimal concepts because hexadecimal arithmetic is sometimes used within MIDI. For the moment, let us turn to the system used by modern computers.

Computers work with a binary system: base 2. This is because they are stupid. In fact, they can understand only one concept: whether an electrical state is on or off. Their power and apparent intelligence lie in being able to process long chains of On and Off states far more rapidly than any human being, but when all the dust has cleared, a computer can be reduced to a machine capable only of recognising whether something *is* or *is not*. The difference between a computer and Hamlet is that a computer cannot doubt.

If we wish to communicate directly with computers in their binary system, we use the first two of our ten decimal symbols: the 0 and the 1. This notation is called binary notation. Binary notation is unnatural to most of us, and for this reason computers have been designed to allow us to communicate with them not only in decimal notation, but even in something vaguely resembling English in the form of computer languages. The very first computer programmers did not have such luxuries, and they damaged their eyesight by writing out, and trying to check, enormous strings of 0s and 1s. Today, life is easier because the computer is made to do the hard work – it constantly translates human input into 0s and 1s. Nevertheless, it is important to understand binary arithmetic to get the best out of MIDI, because MIDI is based on it.

In a binary number, the right-most digit represents a decimal 1, the next a decimal 2, the next a decimal 4, and so it goes on: 8, 16, 32, 64, 128 ... In other words, each digit in a binary number is expressed as a power of 2, and therefore each successive position to the left of the binary point has a value of twice that of the digit to its right.

Here are some examples:

Binary	Decimal equivalent
00000001	1
00000011	3
00000111	7
00001010	10
00001111	15

One way of thinking about this system is that, working from right to left, you add together the value of each column. So, in the case of decimal 10, expressed in binary as 1010, you add together 0 + 2 + 0 + 8.

In a system which has only two symbols, you run out of them very often – in fact having counted up to 1 means having run out of them. It is not surprising, then, that as can be seen from the examples above, binary numbers which look very large to our decimal-trained eyes can actually be very small. The number 11 in binary is decimal 3, and 1000 binary is decimal 8. People who have £1000000 in binary notation are very far from being millionaires.

In computer terms, each 1 or 0 in the binary system is called a *bit*, standing for Binary digIT.

Bits are combined to make *bytes*, and a byte normally consists of eight bits. Each byte, depending on its combination of bits, can be made to represent a letter of the alphabet, one of the decimal digits 0 to 9, a punctuation mark such as a full stop, a space, or anything else seen on the keytops of a computer keyboard, and of course other information such as MIDI data. Let us stick for now, however, to text rather than musical information because, by definition, anyone reading this book understands the way in which text works.

Just as there is a MIDI standard, there is one for text called ASCII, the American Standard Code for Information Interchange. Take the letter upper-case Z. In ASCII this is represented in bit (binary) form as 1011010. We need not be concerned here why Z happens to be represented by this particular combination of bits. Suffice it to say that each letter of the alphabet is represented by its own unique combination. But eagle-eyed readers may have noticed that only seven bits are used for that upper-case Z. In fact, only seven bits are required to cover every character which can be generated from a standard English keyboard, leaving the eighth bit free for designating things like graphics characters and special printing codes. MIDI often uses the full eight bits, and on top of those eight bits, a couple more are added to each byte for special instructions which we shall examine in a moment.

Baud rate

The speed at which information is sent and received is measured in bits per second (bps). Now, assume that the speed is 300 bps. Since each byte consists of up to 10 bits, this is roughly equivalent to 30 characters (bytes) per second. And if we assume that the average English word is six characters long, a speed of 300 bps means in practice that textual data is being transmitted or received at a rate of about five words per second. That figure of 300 bps has not been plucked out of the air – it one of the standard speeds used in text communication between remote computers.

However, in the world of computer communications, people rarely talk about bps, but rather about *baud*. Some say this should be pronounced 'bowed' as in "He bowed to the audience". Others claim that it should be 'bowed' as in "His legs are bowed". Most people pronounce it like the word 'bored'. Since Monsieur Baudot himself was French, the latter two are the nearest etimologically accurate pronunciations.

Strictly speaking, baud is a measurement of the rate of change of a signal rather than a number of bits per second, and in certain areas of computer communications the difference can be significant. But for all practical purposes, and certainly with

MIDI, the baud rate can be thought of as the number of bits being sent or received each second.

The standard MIDI speed of 31.25 Kilobaud is a very much higher rate than the 300 baud rate we have mentioned. A Kilobaud (Kb) is 1,000 baud and the MIDI standard therefore means that 31,250 bits are transmitted and received every second, the equivalent in textual terms of about 520 English words, far faster than anyone can read, let alone type. The high speed is required because musical information, which includes not only the pitch and loudness of a note but also things like expression, is far more complex than letters of the alphabet. What is more, MIDI sends its data down 16 channels, and a high speed is required in order for it to be properly processed. For instance, even though the individual notes of a chord are sent one after another, they must sound together.

3.1.3 Serial Communication

Back to that sentence: *MIDI transmits and receives over 16 channels at 31.25 Kilobaud (Kb) using serial asynchronous communication.*

One way of making MIDI transmissions even faster would have been to use parallel communication, in computer terms the alternative to serial communication. In parallel communication, bits are sent simultaneously down a number of lines. In serial transmission, only one line is used. So, for example, a serial printer can work only like a typewriter, printing one character at a time, whereas a parallel printer is capable of handling several characters at the same time.

Although parallel transmission would have been faster and more efficient, serial transmission was chosen for MIDI for reasons of price. With serial transmission there is no need for multiple cables and multi-pin connections. A two-line electrical cable plus earth are all that is required, and the associated connectors are much cheaper to manufacture than parallel interfaces with multi-wired cables. In this way MIDI was made cheap enough to be available to the home market, an important reason for its success as a standard.

3.1.4 Synchronous and Asynchronous Communication

There is a final point to explain in the sentence: *MIDI transmits and receives over 16 channels at 31.25 Kilobaud (Kb) using serial asynchronous communication –* the word *asynchronous*. Transmission of computer data can be either synchronous or asynchronous.

In synchronous communication, data is sent in groups, usually called blocks. A block of data may contain many thousands of bits, and each block begins with a special set of bits enabling the receiving device to synchronise itself with the transmission. Essentially, what happens is that the receiver times the transmission as it is received and separates out the individual bits of information by dividing the

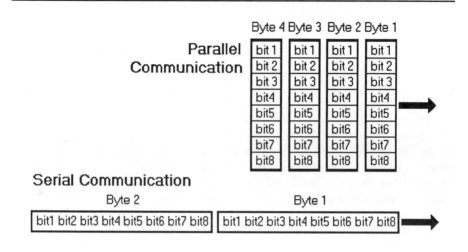

Figure 3.1: Serial and parallel communication

transmitted message into time intervals. Timing in synchronous communication is therefore critical.

In asynchronous transmission, bytes are sent one at a time, each identified by a Start bit and a Stop bit – the two extra bits added to each byte which we mentioned earlier. This type of transmission, the one used by MIDI, is said to be asynchronous (that is, unsynchronised) because the receiving device recognises each byte by its Start and Stop bits, regardless of when it arrived. In other words, the sending and receiving devices do not have to be synchronised, and bytes can be sent at irregular intervals. When a Start bit arrives, the receiving device knows that a byte is about to begin, and the Stop bit tells it that the byte has ended.

What actually happens in MIDI is that a device such as a MIDI musical instrument, when it is turned on, constantly monitors its MIDI In port. If the port is properly connected to another working device such as a MIDI interface, there is a stream of current – an On state, in other words the equivalent of a stream of 0s being sent. For this reason, a Start bit is always a 1, since if it were a 0 the receiving device would have no way of knowing that it was significant. As the 1 arrives, the current is momentarily interrupted, since a 1 represents an Off state. The receiving device therefore knows that a byte is about to begin and that the byte consists of the next eight bits. When those eight bits have been received, a tenth bit arrives – a 0 – to confirm that the byte has ended. This returns the current to its idling state, ready for the next Start bit to interrupt it.

Of course, all this happens very rapidly indeed, and is one of the wonders of the way in which MIDI turns all this activity into music.

3.1.5 A Word on Hexadecimal Notation

As we mentioned earlier, MIDI data is sometimes given in hexadecimal notation which works to base 16. It often appears in documentation (written simply as *hex*, or sometimes as a number preceded by an & character), and there can be instances when it has to be used rather than decimal notation, though they are few and far between.

Most human beings find binary notation far too difficult and tedious to handle on a day-to-day basis. Hexadecimal arithmetic is closer to binary arithmetic than decimal arithmetic, because as you double each number in binary by moving to the left, you produce numbers after 16 which are multiples of 16, that is to say 32, 64, 128, 256 and so on.

Base 4 (using only the digits 0 to 3) is not a real option because modern computers work with at least 8-bit processors. Octal arithmetic (base 8, using only the digits 0 to 7) was extensively used in the early days of mainframe computing before the invention of microprocessors. However, hexadecimal notation is now the preferred option when decimal notation is not used, partly because modern computers can handle 16-bit arithmetic directly, and partly because it produces faster code when programming. Apart from writing code in binary, the next step up is to write it in what is called *machine code*. Machine code uses hexadecimal notation for speed of execution: as will become clear in a moment, any number up to the maximum of decimal 255 for an 8-bit byte can be represented in hexadecimal by only two symbols. Hexadecimal notation is therefore a kind of shorthand way of representing binary digits.

Just as the decimal system works to base 10, and the binary system to base 2, so the hexadecimal system works to base 16. In other words, each successive digit to the left represents a value 16 times greater than the digit to its immediate right.

The symbols used in hexadecimal notation are the digits 0 to 9, plus the letters of the alphabet A to F. The letter A represents decimal 10, B is 11, C is 12, D is 13, E is 14, and F is 15.

So, 10 in hex is 16 in decimal, 20 hex is 32 decimal, A0 hex is 160 decimal, and FF hex is 255 decimal. After 255 decimal, three symbols are required in hex: 256 decimal is 100 hex.

3.2 The MIDI Hardware Standard

3.2.1 Sockets

Each MIDI instrument or other device can act as a transmitter and/or a receiver, and many modern musical instruments are equipped with special sockets for MIDI data input and output. MIDI uses ordinary DIN 5-pin (180 degree) connections, of the kind used in hi-fi equipment, though only pins 2, 4 and 5 are wired up (see Figure 3.2), with a shield on pin 2. There are three types of sockets:

MIDI Out: sending MIDI messages and data

MIDI In: receiving MIDI messages and data

MIDI Through: echoing out what comes through the MIDI In line. This is not the same as MIDI Out, because it is used for going to the next piece of equipment if devices are connected in series. More on that in a moment.

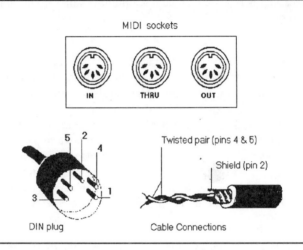

Figure 3.2: MIDI connections

3.2.2 Cables

MIDI uses shielded twisted cable pairs (see Figure 3.2), and cables must not be longer than than 15 metres, otherwise there are risks of a loss of signal and of unwanted time delays.

3.2.3 Connecting Instruments in Series

A number of MIDI devices can be connected in series to receive messages from a common source, using the MIDI In and MIDI Through sockets as shown in Figure 3.3. The process is known as *daisy-chaining*.

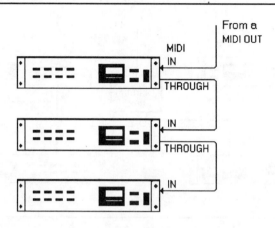

Figure 3.3: MIDI devices connected in a daisy chain

In order to avoid unwanted time delays, the usual recommendation in handbooks on MIDI is that no more than three devices should be connected in this way. However, musical equipment is improving continuously and today's MIDI instruments and other MIDI devices process information faster than those which were available when the MIDI specification was established. In practice it is often possible to get away with connecting more than three pieces of equipment in series, though the limit of three is always worth bearing in mind.

3.2.4 Connecting in a Star Shape

Unwanted MIDI time delays can in any case be avoided by using a distributor box called a MIDI Through Unit, as shown in Figure 3.4, producing a *star network*. This splits and amplifies the signal. See Chapter 4 Section 4.8.1 for more on MIDI Through Units.

3.3 MIDI Messages

The data used by MIDI consists of information about musical notes. All notes are numbered in MIDI in semitone intervals in the range 0 to 127 (decimal). In this range, the note Middle C is note number 60.

MIDI commands are normally referred to as *MIDI messages*, and their results as *MIDI events*. Note information is sent from the MIDI instrument to the computer (this is known as *record mode*) and back again (*playback mode*). There are all kinds of MIDI messages, carrying out a whole range of tasks from changing the

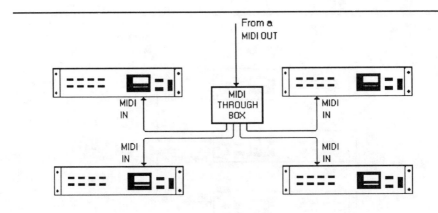

Figure 3.4: Star network

selected sound on a synthesiser to choosing a certain rhythm pattern on a drum machine, but the two most basic ones are:

❑ **Note On:** start playing – the equivalent of pressing a key on a musical keyboard

❑ **Note Off:** stop playing – the equivalent of lifting the finger from the key.

When a key is pressed on an electronic musical keyboard, whether or not it is a MIDI keyboard, a switch is activated which turns on a particular note. When the key is released, the note is turned off. This information is sent from the keyboard to the sound chip of the instrument, which then produces the sound.

Using a MIDI interface, these messages can be sent to a computer and back again. Pressing a key on a MIDI synthesiser keyboard causes a Note On message corresponding to that key to be transmitted out of the MIDI Out socket of the synthesiser and into the MIDI In socket of the interface. An instrument receiving a Note On message in the same way will sound a certain note in response (in other words, the instrument receiving the message will interpret it without having physically to be played). Equally, a Note Off message tells the receiving device that the note has finished.

In order to understand how this is achieved, first consider the following binary numbers:

    10010000, 00111100, 01111111

or in decimal:

    144, 60, 127.

If these numbers are sent to a synthesiser, they will make it play the note Middle C as loud as possible.

The first number denotes Note On. The second number indicates which of the notes in the decimal range 0 to 127 is turned on (in this case Middle C: decimal 60). The third number tells the synthesiser how loud the note should be played, again in the range 0 to 127 decimal (though MIDI actually uses the binary not the decimal numbers).

The same is true for Note Off messages. The Note Off message will turn off Middle C on any instruments tuned to receive the message on the channel along which it is sent. Here, for example, is the MIDI Note Off message for the note Middle C at maximum loudness:

Note Off	**Middle C**	**Maximum loudness**
10000000	00111100	01111111
(128)	(60)	(127)

The loudness of a note makes obvious sense with a Note On message, but what does it mean with Note Off? The answer lies in the fact that loudness depends on how hard a key is struck on the synthesiser keyboard (MIDI measures the strike velocity). So, releasing the key as quickly as possible gives the opposite effect – the sound will die away with maximum velocity. On the other hand, releasing a key slowly will give a fade effect. Thus, in the case of Note Off messages, maximum loudness in a sense does mean the reverse of maximum loudness in a Note On message.

Now for a closer look at at the first of the three binary numbers.

For MIDI purposes, it is made up of two parts. The first four digits describe what the message is, in this case Note On (1001) or Note Off (1000). The last four digits correspond to the channel number.

Channel numbers range from 0 to 15 decimal, which is sometimes a source of confusion because what should really be referred to as Channel 0 is by common practice referred to as Channel 1, since it is the first channel (this is also the way it is referred to in this book). Channel 2 is referred to in the byte as 1, Channel 3 as 2, and so on. The reason why 0 is used in the byte is that this is the only way of ensuring that all 16 channels can be catered for in four bits – in binary, four digits cannot represent more than 15 (1111 binary is equivalent in decimal to $1 + 2 + 4 + 8 = 15$).

In binary form, what all this means is that a Note On message transmitted on Channel 2 will start with the four digits 1001, and will end with 0001 (Channel 1 would have been 0000). The complete byte will thus be 10010001. On Channel 3 it would be 10010010, and so on. Here are some more examples:

> 1001 and 0000 = 10010000 Note On, Channel 1
> 1001 and 0001 = 10010001 Note On, Channel 2
> 1000 and 0000 = 10000000 Note Off, Channel 1
> 1000 and 0100 = 10000100 Note Off, Channel 5

In Note On and Note Off messages, the first byte is known as a *status* byte, the second and third as *data* bytes.

All this can be put more succinctly by saying that the first byte of a Note On or Note Off message always takes the form 1001nnnn, where nnnn is the channel number in binary.

The second byte, the data byte which specifies the note, needs only to reach the number 127, since all notes are handled within the range 0 to 127. In binary, 127 requires only 7 bits:

Bit number:	8	7	6	5	4	3	2	1	
Value:	0	+ 64	+ 32	+ 16	+ 8	+ 4	+ 2	+ 1	= 127

Therefore, the left bit of a Note On or Note Off data byte is always 0. And again, this can be expressed by saying that Note On and Note Off data bytes are always of the form 0nnnnnnn, where nnnnnnn is the note number in the range 0 to 127. A useful general rule which flows from this is that bytes in which the first bit is a 0 are data bytes, and bytes in which the first bit is 1 are status bytes.

The third byte (another data byte) in a Note On or Note Off message is the one concerned with loudness, referred to as *Velocity On/Off*. The word *velocity*, as with so many technical terms in MIDI, can cause some confusion. Velocity in this case means, for instance, how hard a key on a musical keyboard is pressed, or how quickly it is released – hence the term *velocity-sensitive* keyboards. So, Velocity On (or Note On velocity) indicates the speed with which a key is pressed at Note On, while Velocity Off (Note Off velocity) indicates how quickly the note is released at Note Off. The same also applies, of course, to how hard the strings of a MIDI guitar are plucked, how hard a MIDI saxophone is blown, and so on.

The so-called *default* value for Velocity On/Off is 64. This means that if the velocity has not been specified, as it would not be if you use a keyboard which is not sensitive to velocity, a middle-range velocity of 64 will be used by default (the word *default* is often used in this sense in the world of computers). 127 is the loudest (*fff*), 64 is *mp*, 1 is the quietest (*ppp*), and 0 is Off.

Such then, is the make-up of the two basic MIDI messages, Note On and Note Off. But that is just the beginning of MIDI.

3.3.1 Program Change Messages

Although there are many ways of playing an acoustic instrument (guitar, piano, flute, whatever) each of them can make only one basic sound – its timbre, which characterises it. Contemporary electronic instruments, on the other hand, can synthesise different kinds of sounds, and the most versatile among them is the synthesiser, with or without keyboard.

Sounds can be stored in one or more sound banks in the synthesiser's memory. They are given a number, and the desired sound can be selected from the internal bank of sounds by using buttons on the synthesiser. In MIDI, each of these sounds is referred to as a *program* and its number as a program number. MIDI can handle 128 program numbers, again within the range 0 to 127, and when a number is specified via MIDI, then sent to the synthesiser, this has the same effect as keying in the number directly on the synthesiser itself. A Program Change message received by the synthesiser through its MIDI In socket tells it to change its sound to another, as specified by the Program Change number.

Thus, if the list of sounds on a synthesiser offers (1) Piano (2) Organ (3) Strings (4) Flute and so on, a Program Change of 0 sets the sound of the synthesiser to Piano, and one of 3 sets it to Flute.

Notice once again the problem of MIDI message numbers being referred to as beginning with 1, while the messages themselves are numbered from 0, something which eventually becomes second-nature in dealing with MIDI. Certain equipment and software producers adopt a less confusing, but less natural, approach by using a 0 to 127 range rather than that of 1 to 128. It soon becomes clear which system is being used, and all that needs to be remembered is that even if a user is allowed to input 128 as a MIDI message parameter, the actual number transmitted in the MIDI cable is 127.

A Program Change message uses two bytes. The first byte is a status byte and is made up of two 4-bit segments. The first segment is always 1100 binary, and it denotes that this is a Program Change, while the second 4-bit segment denotes the channel number (0 to 15).

The second byte of a Program Change message is a data byte. The first bit is always 0 and the next seven bits denote the data in the range 0 to 127. A Program Change message therefore takes the form: 1100nnnn, 0nnnnnnn, where nnnn is the channel number in the range 0 to 15, and nnnnnnn is the Program Change number in the range 0 to 127.

3.3.2 Controller Messages

Part of what MIDI does is to define, in a machine-oriented language, the human art of playing musical instruments. Pitch, rhythm and loudness are the minimum parameters required in order to describe a performance. There are many others, like the use of vibrato, sustain and damper pedals, or pitch changes resulting from breath control or the stretching of strings (in MIDI terms, pitch bend). Some are uncharacteristic of acoustic instruments but are much in vogue with contemporary composers, and MIDI instruments and other sound-processing devices are capable of producing a wide range of them. They are handled in MIDI with the use of Controller messages.

Controller messages are three bytes long, and structured as follows:

The first byte is a status byte of which the first 4-bit segment is always 1011, denoting a Controller change. The second 4-bit segment specifies the MIDI channel (0 to 15) on which the Controller will have its effect.

The second byte is a data byte. The first bit is 0 and the next seven bits denote the Controller number (0 to 127). Some Controller numbers have become standard, while others are defined differently by different manufacturers and do different things on different instruments.

The third byte is also a data byte. The first bit is 0 and next seven bits denote the value of the Controller (in the range 0 to 127). With some Controllers, a range of values is applicable (for example, vibrato, or volume). With others, which are simply switches (sustain pedal, for instance), only the extreme values of 0 and 127 are used, and the rest are ignored.

Examples of common Controller numbers (in decimal) are 1 (modulation wheel, normally controlling vibrato), 2 (breath control), 7 (channel volume), and 64 (sustain pedal On/Off). See also below Section 3.3.6 for more Controller messages, and the classification of Controller numbers.

3.3.3 Finer Increments

Measuring a value on a scale of 0 to 127 is sufficiently fine-grained for most MIDI events, but others require much finer intervals so that an impression of a smooth change can be given. Pitch bend is a case in point, and it can be measured in MIDI on a scale of up to 16,384 increments (between -8192 and +8191).

Not all manufacturers of MIDI products necessarily use the full available range for pitch bend, but in any case more than 128 increments are always required, and a single byte cannot represent such a large number, the largest number which eight bits can represent being 11111111 or 255 decimal. If 0 is included, each 8-bit byte is capable of handling up to 256 different numbers, which means a maximum of 256 possible increments for each byte. But MIDI information is sent and received a byte at a time, so this poses a problem when numbers higher than 256 need to be sent. The solution is to apply a link between two data bytes, putting them side by side and therefore effectively making them into a single 16-bit byte. Putting two

8-bit bytes together gives a possible 16 bits, which are capable of holding 65,536 increments (if the number 0 is also used.)

As we have seen, each column (bit) in a binary number is potentially the value of its neighbour to the right, multiplied by 2. So, binary 1111 is decimal 15 because, reading from right to left, the first digit is 1, the second has a value of 2, the third is 2 multiplied by 2 = 4, and the fourth is 4 multiplied by 2 = 8. Add these together and the result is 15. By the time the left-most column is reached (that is, the eighth bit in an 8-bit byte), 64 is being multiplied by 2 to give 128, and therefore a maximum value for the byte of 255 when the 128 is added to the rest of the byte to the right.

Imagine adding another bit to the left to make a 9-bit byte. The maximum number it can now accommodate is 2 multiplied by 128, plus the maximum number already available in an 8-bit byte (255). So a 9-bit byte can handle any number up to 511 (256 + 255), or 512 increments including 0. If you go on adding more bits to the left, the highest possible numbers go on increasing, and at a dramatic rate. It is like the old question about whether you would prefer £100 or a penny doubled in value 20 times. By the time you reach only 16 bits, the maximum number a byte can hold has become 65,535. By the time you reach 20 doubled pennies, you can afford a fairly well-equipped MIDI studio!

The following table shows the maximum number which can be represented for each type of byte from two bits to sixteen bits.

Number of bits	Maximum available number
2	3
3	7
4	15
5	31
6	63
7	127
8	255
9	511
10	1023
11	2047
12	4095
13	8191
14	16383
15	32767
16	65535

Thus, a range of 0 to 65,535 can be specified with a 16-bit byte. But MIDI has then to understand that the two data bytes in, say, a Pitch Bend message are to be put together side by side. The pitch bend status byte tells it to do this, but it does it by a somewhat complicated process. It is worth understanding part of that process, for a good reason: it is sometimes necessary to know how to juggle pitch bend numbers, and while the process of putting two 8-bit bytes side by side is something which MIDI can do, or you can do yourself with a pencil and paper, the numbers you are juggling will not appear on a computer screen or other display in binary form but in decimal form (or perhaps as hexadecimal numbers). What is required, therefore, is a formula for making a 16-bit number from two 8-bit bytes, based on the way MIDI handles the problem, but in a form which is easier to handle than binary, such as our common decimal system.

The formula is derived by specifying one byte as the Most Significant Byte (MSB) and the other as the Least Significant Byte (LSB). The MSB contains a number which is to be multiplied by the maximum number of increments which can be represented by the LSB, including 0. If all eight bits are used for an LSB, the maximum number will be 256. The LSB contains a number which is to be added to that. Doing such a calculation produces the same result as putting together the two bytes and reading them as if they were one.

The formula for working this out is:

value = MSB x Z + LSB

where Z is the maximum number of increments which can be represented by the LSB + 1. In other words, with an 8-bit byte, Z is 256, not 255.

This is most clearly shown by an example. Suppose that all eight bits are being used, that the MSB contains the number 2 (in binary 10), and that the LSB contains the number 5 (in binary 101). Padding each binary number out to the left with 0s, so that each byte contains eight elements, then putting the two bytes together, gives a 16-bit byte as follows:

Bit number: 16 15 14 13 12 11 10 9 8 7 6 5 4 3 2 1
Binary Value: 0 0 0 0 0 0 1 0 0 0 0 0 0 1 0 1

The tenth bit is a 1, which means that the complete 16-element binary number would have the value 512 if all the values both to the right and the left were 0. But, to the right, the first three bits (101) make 5, so the complete binary number is 517 decimal.

Apply the formula: the MSB is 2, and 2 multiplied by 256 is 512. Add the LSB (5) and the result is the same: 517.

It is important to emphasise, however, that in some MIDI messages not all eight bits of a byte are used, so it is not invariably the case that the MSB is multiplied by 256. MIDI documentation sometimes specifies the MSB and LSB in a form containing a number of 0s followed by an indication of non-zero, such as: *MSB=0000nnnn* and *LSB=0nnnnnnn*. In these examples, the MSB is a 4-bit byte, thus giving the range 0 to 15, and the LSB is a 7-bit byte giving the range 0 to

127. In this case, the MSB would be multiplied by 128, since that is the maximum value of the LSB.

So far so good. But pitch can be bent up or bent down, an upward bend being represented by a positive number, and a downward bend by a negative number. Since no minus signs are available in MIDI, a negative number is represented by shifting the range upwards in such a way that the extreme minus becomes 0, thus giving positive values or 0 to the entire range. So, for maximum negative bend the LSB and MSB are both 0; for no bend at all the LSB is 0 and the MSB is 64 (the mid point of the range), and for maximum positive bend both the LSB and the MSB are 127. This is quite a complicated process, but it works out that for all negative values the MSB ranges between 0 and 64, and for all positive values between 64 and 127, which is the rule of thumb.

A Pitch Bend MIDI message consists of three bytes. The first, a status byte, is constructed of two 4-bit segments: a pitch bend identifier which is always 1110, and a second 4-bit segment, as usual denoting the channel number between 0 and 15.

The second and third bytes are data bytes. They both begin with a 0 followed by 7 bits, thus giving a range of 0-127. The first byte is the LSB of the pitch bend value: in more technical terms it is said to carry the Least Significant Bits. The second byte carries the Most Significant Bits.

Thus a Pitch Bend message denoting an upward bend of a value of 1,927 on Channel 1 would look as follows:

Byte	Value	Meaning
Status byte:	11100001	Pitch Bend on Channel 1
Data byte 1:	00000111	LSB containing the value 7, to be added to the result calculated in the next byte
Data byte 2:	01001111	MSB containing the value 79 (64 + 15), 15 to be multiplied by 128 = 1,920.

Note that the value of 64 contained in the second bit from the left in Data byte 2 is the negative section of the complete pitch-bend range.

3.3.4 Aftertouch /

Two further parameters related to synthesiser playing techniques have been assigned special MIDI messages. These are two different types of key-pressure aftertouch – the pressure applied to the keys of a synthesiser keyboard after the initial attack. Aftertouch can be assigned to control various parameters for the further development of a sound after it has been initialised, such as vibrato, tremolo and portamento. The two types of aftertouch are *polyphonic* and *channel*.

Polyphonic key-pressure aftertouch

In the case of polyphonic key pressure, each key on the keyboard can have its own aftertouch value.

The MIDI message for polyphonic key-pressure aftertouch is composed of three bytes: a status byte and two data bytes. The status byte is made up of a 4-bit segment which identifies the byte as polyphonic aftertouch – this is always 1010 – and a further 4-bit segment denoting the channel number. The second and third bytes are data bytes. They both begin with a 0 and end with 7 bits, thus giving a range of 0 to 127, as usual. The first of these data bytes indicates the note number, and the second carries the value of the aftertouch.

Channel pressure aftertouch

With channel pressure, the whole keyboard has one aftertouch value, even when more than one key is pressed at any one time (as in a chord). The Channel Pressure MIDI message consists of two bytes: a status byte and a data byte. The status byte is made up of a 4-bit segment denoting channel aftertouch (always 1101) and a second 4-bit segment specifying the channel number (range 0 to 15). The data byte starts with a 0 and is followed by a 7-bit segment (range 0 to 127) which carries the aftertouch value.

3.3.5 System-exclusive Messages

MIDI began life as a standard, and so it remains. But like all forms of communication it has developed its irregularities. All the MIDI messages described so far fall into a category which can be compared to basic human body language. No matter what the nationality of a person, raising the eyebrows indicates surprise, and smiling indicates pleasure. However, human beings also use different spoken languages, accents and dialects, and individuals even make up their own words.

Thus it is with MIDI. Manufacturers of equipment have evolved their own sub-languages within it, used to send messages which only their equipment will understand. These are referred to as System-exclusive messages. There is no point in bewailing the fact that MIDI has been unable to encompass all possible messages within a single standard, though this was certainly in the minds of those who first came together to invent it. Living languages change – indeed, if they do not change they are dead. The greatest grammarians who have ever lived have been unable to do much more than perhaps slow down a little the evolution of the spoken word. MIDI is also evolving, with additions to the standard continuously appearing, and non-standard additions (which may in time become standards) having to be accommodated.

A System-exclusive message can be used to do anything the manufacturer wishes, even some of the things covered by messages for which there is already a standard.

However, System-exclusive messages are mostly used for downloading (sending to the computer) or uploading (sending from the computer) information from and to the internal memories of synthesisers. (Note, in passing, the standard distinction between these two ideas in MIDI, since in some other areas of computer communications, there is occasionally hesitation between the two.) System-exclusive messages are also used to change individual sound (voice) parameters when editing the sounds of a synthesiser.

Despite the fact that System-exclusive messages are by their nature non-standard, there is nevertheless a standard to indicate that such messages are system-exclusive. They all begin with a byte containing the value 240. This is followed by a byte in the range 0 to 127 indicating the make of the equipment (the manufacturer's *identity code*). The next bytes contain the system-exclusive information itself, and a final byte containing the value 247 indicates that the message is complete. All bytes between 240 and 247 are in the range 0 to 127, that is to say that the first bit is 0 because they are data bytes.

In this context, it is worth mentioning that in buying MIDI hardware it is important always to consult the MIDI Implementation Chart, almost invariably found towards the end of the user manual. This contains a list of all the MIDI messages the unit is capable of transmitting and receiving. Parts of a typical Implementation Chart are reproduced in Chapter 6 Figure 6.6, and Chapter 7 Figure 7.9.

3.3.6 Classification of MIDI messages

It has not been our aim to explain all MIDI messages in this chapter, but rather to give an overview of some messages likely to be encountered when using MIDI and when deciding on MIDI products.

An overview of all MIDI messages appears in Appendix A, and they include certain messages which may be used in a direct manner only occasionally and in very specific circumstances, but which are fundamental to MIDI theory. In particular, some messages we have not so far mentioned are important not only for what can be done with them in practice, but also to a classification system which is as much a part of the MIDI standard as the messages themselves (see Figure 3.5).

There are two fundamental types of MIDI message: *channel* and *system*. Channel messages affect only a specific channel, and a number of examples have already been given: Note On, Program Change, Aftertouch (both varieties) and so on. System messages, on the other hand, affect the whole system independently of which channel an instrument is tuned to.

Channel messages

Channel messages are sub-divided into two types: Voice and Mode.

Voice messages are those so far treated in this chapter, again such as Note On, Program Change and so on, and most Controller messages.

Mode messages are a subset of Controller messages and affect a synthesiser's overall mode of operation. The subset is at the end of the set of Controller numbers 0 to 127, starting at 122:

122 is Local (Control) On/Off (see Chapter 6 Section 6.2.2 for an explanation of this feature).

123 is All Notes Off, which stops everything. Pressing Stop on a sequencer sends an All Notes Off message.

124 is Omni Mode Off. Omni mode means that the synthesiser will use all MIDI channels at the same time, rather an individual MIDI channel or set of channels.

125 is Omni Mode On.

126 is Mono Mode On, which instructs the synthesiser to act as a monophonic instrument.

127 is Poly Mode On, which is the opposite of 126 (polyphonic mode as opposed to monophonic mode)

System Messages

These are divided into three categories: System-exclusive messages, System Real-time messages, and System Common messages.

System-exclusive messages have already been mentioned above (Section 3.3.5).

System Real-time messages, as their name indicates, act in real time over the whole system and independently of any MIDI channel. They are concerned with various actions which need to be taken during a performance, such as checking for serious errors in MIDI connections. Examples are Continue, System Reset and Active Sensing (see Appendix A).

System Common messages are further subdivided into three: Song Position Pointers, Song Select and Tune Request.

(i) Song Position Pointers

When musicians rehearse a piece of music together, they do not necessarily have to start from the beginning of the piece: they can start at any point indicated on their individual scores and if necessary rehearse small sections of it. For this reason, musical scores often contain letters of the alphabet or other signs, and the musicians can count bars or beats from these marks onwards if they wish to start from some unmarked point. MIDI equipment and software have their equivalent way of indicating points in the score, that is to say Song Position Pointers. A Song Position Pointer is the number of semiquaver (16th note) steps which have elapsed since the beginning of a piece of music. Thus a tape recorder might send a message to a computer to start playing at step number 200. This means 200 semiquaver beats after the beginning.

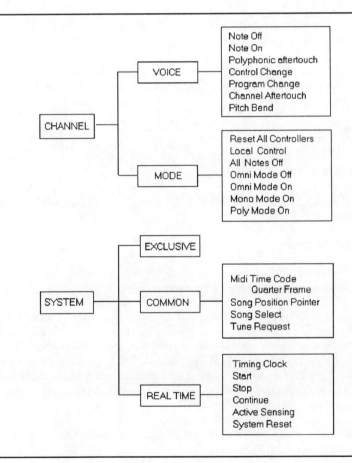

Figure 3.5: Classification of MIDI messages

(ii) Song Select

This message is used to choose a song in the range 0 to 127, and to load it into memory. Some drum machines and sequencers have a capacity to store many songs in their memory, which can be selected by pressing buttons on a panel. The Song Select MIDI message allows this to be done remotely from a computer or some other MIDI device capable of sending such a message.

(iii) Tune Request

A Tune Request message tells all connected MIDI instruments to tune themselves to a specific pitch, usually the note A as is done in an orchestra using an oboe as the standard. From this note, the MIDI instruments can fix the tuning of all their other notes.

4

MIDI Interfaces and MIDI Accessories

4.1 Interfaces, Specifications and Standards

A MIDI interface – the hardware which allows a computer to talk to MIDI instruments – can be internal, often in the form of an expansion card or board, external in its own box, or a mixture of the two. Some computers have a built-in MIDI interface. An add-on interface for other computers costs anywhere between £25 and £300, depending on the make of computer and on the sophistication of the interface.

The MIDI specification, outlined in the previous chapter, incorporates certain sets of rules about how MIDI messages and other data are to be transmitted and received. The hardware part of that specification is there to ensure that when two MIDI devices – musical instruments or other pieces of equipment – are connected together, what emerges from the MIDI Out sockets are copper-bottomed MIDI messages. It also ensures that connected pieces of MIDI equipment are automatically set to particular parameters, thus avoiding the common situation in non-MIDI data communications of having always to adjust settings so that two pieces of equipment can understand each other. A MIDI interface is the link between a computer and MIDI hardware, translating incoming and outgoing messages so that all the equipment is talking the same language without the intervention of the user.

MIDI is therefore envied by those who work in the area of general electronic data communications. Two electronic devices which can communicate properly with each other are said to *handshake*, and the difficulty of ensuring correct handshaking is one of the banes of the world of computer communications, where standards have sadly not been universally implemented. One of the main reasons for the success of fax machines over electronic mail is that a fax machine is as easy to use and understand as a photocopier, and this is so because a fax standard for handshaking has been established throughout the world. To send a fax to Australia, there is no need to adjust the baud rate, nor tweak complex parameters such as those used to set the number of data bits, Stop bits and error-checking bits expected by each machine, as must be done with electronic mail systems. It is simply a matter of dialling a telephone number and waiting.

So it is with MIDI. The communications specifications are hard-wired at the factory into MIDI devices, while at the computer end the MIDI interface acts as an intelligent interpreter. As explained in the previous chapter, MIDI is based on a 10-bit byte, including one Start bit and one Stop bit, and always transmits at 31.25 Kilobaud. Just as very few people who regularly use fax machines know the speed at which the device transmits its data, or even that a modem inside the fax machine is converting digital information into analogue information so that it can be sent down a telephone line, so many people use MIDI hardware without knowing about such niceties. True, the analogy cannot be taken much further because knowing about how MIDI works is a distinct advantage when it comes to using it, but the principle of a single standard, unalterably fixed into equipment, remains the major reason for the success of MIDI.

However, while the basic MIDI specifications are found on all interfaces, they have to be built to handle different makes of computer, and therefore do differ in their features. In practice, this means that it is not normally possible to use a MIDI interface intended for a particular family of computers with those belonging to another family (though a few interfaces can be used with almost any computer). It also means that some interfaces have advanced *intelligent* or *smart* features, while others are *dumb*. Intelligent interfaces are capable of working in either dumb or intelligent mode.

A dumb interface works only in what is known as UART mode. UART stands for Universal Asynchronous Receiver and Transmitter; as its name suggests, it is a device for enabling asynchronous computer communications (see Chapter 3 Section 3.1.4). As far as MIDI is concerned, all that a dumb UART interface can do is to receive and transmit data, without offering any extra facilities.

An intelligent interface, on the other hand, has built-in functions. For those who know about programming, an analogy might be the difference between writing a database program using dBase, with its built-in facilities for sorting, searching and file-handling, and writing one from scratch using BASIC. Intelligent interfaces, therefore, are able to carry out extra data processing which relieves the computer of some of its workload. They offer facilities such as filtering specified MIDI events, recording and playing from internal buffers (memories), providing a metronome beat, and handling tempo changes.

This would seem to be an obvious advantage, and with computers of low specification it certainly is. But personal computers today are far more powerful and work far more rapidly than those of just a few years ago. Thus, from the point of view of the user, the intelligence or otherwise of a MIDI interface is less important than it used to be, and is likely to diminish in importance in the future. There is one area of interface intelligence, however, which is very desirable, and deserves special attention: synchronisation.

4.1.1 MIDI Interfaces and Synchronisation

Synchronisation allows computers running sequencers and other music software, to play in precise time with external equipment such as tape recorders, video cassette recorders, and certain other devices. In more technical terms, it allows a MIDI performance to be *slaved* to a pre-recorded performance (that of an acoustic instrument or a human voice, for example) so that they can be played in perfect time with each other. A number of interfaces offer built-in synchronisation facilities.

Synchronisation is an important topic in its own right. Unless a computer is going to be used for work involving only MIDI musical instruments, or simply for score editing or running educational software, some kind of synchronisation will almost certainly be required. Many methods exist but three main types are widely available. We shall return to them from time to time in later chapters (especially in Chapter 10 Section 10.3 where some practical aspects of synchronisation are considered), but as far as MIDI interfaces are concerned, it is necessary to understand the following basic ideas about each of them:

Tape-sync

This is a special signal generated by the MIDI interface, usually as *FSK* – Frequency Shift Keying. It works by recording a code made up of two alternating pitches, at a rate which relates to the tempo of the music.

It should be said that the basic tape-sync method is somewhat unreliable. FSK code created by equipment from one manufacturer will not necessarily be understood by equipment from another. Furthermore, it will work only if the tape starts at the beginning of the synchronisation signal.

The problem of starting at any given point, however, is overcome in some MIDI interfaces with a *Chase Lock* feature, which allows the use of Song Position Pointers, ways of indicating particular points in a score so that a piece can start at any one of them (see Chapter 3 Section 3.4.2). So, a tape recorder might send a Song Position Pointer MIDI message to a sequencer, indicating that the computer is to start playing at a particular point. Of course, if the sequencer does not support Song Position Pointers, a Chase Lock feature is of no use. FSK with Chase Lock is sometimes called *smart FSK*.

Tape-sync code does not come out of the interface's Midi Out socket, but out of a separate tape-sync port.

Time code: SMPTE, EBU and Film

Some of the more expensive MIDI interfaces have a built-in Time Code Reader/Generator which supports three different international standards used for synchronising video and sound. They are used widely in the film and video industries, and are the state-of-the-art method of synchronisation in MIDI. They work by keeping track of hours, minutes, and seconds, but further sub-divisions are made into *frames* (because the time-code standard is primarily for film) and sometimes also parts of frames variously called *sub-frames* or *bits*. The latter are not to be confused with the bits making up bytes used in MIDI messages (see Chapter 3 Section 3.1.2). These bits are simply sub-divisions of a frame, and there are 80 bits to a frame.

Using this method, a precise time is stamped along a separate track of a tape recorder (a process known as *striping*). For instance, if a tape is stopped at a particular point, the time code might read *00:07:06:03:09*, meaning that this point on the tape is seven minutes, six seconds, three frames and nine bits from the beginning.

As a film runs in front of a projection lens, it does so at 24 frames per second, and this standard is called simply *Film*. For making movie soundtracks, therefore, this would be the time code to use. Other speeds have been standardised for video as follows:

❏ SMPTE (standing for Society of Motion Pictures and Television Engineers, and usually being pronounced *simpty*) uses 30 frames a second, though a sub-division of this standard, called *30 Drop Frame*, drops a frame at specified intervals to give approximately 29.97 frames per second

❏ EBU (European Broadcasting Union) uses 25 frames a second.

As far as synchronisation in MIDI is concerned, the code is generated (and read back) by the Time Code Reader/Generator. On playback, this device can convert the code to MIDI Song Position Pointers and send it to the sequencer, so that it will start playing. Despite the fact that the time code can be in any of the three formats as above, it is usually referred to as *SMPTE*, in the same way as certain brand names of goods have become generic (Hoover for vacuum cleaner, for instance), and Reader/Generators are usually called SMPTE Reader/Generators.

Over the last few years, SMPTE has proven to be the most reliable method of synchronisation, and is now the principal standard. Its general use was initially delayed by the high price of stand-alone SMPTE Reader/Generators (it is only recently that they have been incorporated in MIDI interfaces) but prices have now dropped from thousands of pounds to a couple of hundred or so, and they are still falling.

External SMPTE Reader/Generators do, however, have one disadvantage. Changes of tempo, including ritardandos and accelerandos, have to be programmed into the device, and these override any tempo changes programmed within the sequencer. This means programming tempo changes twice, once in the sequencer and once in the Reader/Generator. Few Reader/Generators can store more than one set of tempo changes, so if the score is like that of Listz's Hungarian Rhapsody, which starts slowly and gets gradually faster, external SMPTE devices are not the ideal synchronisation method. The solution is one which is built into a MIDI interface.

It is important to be aware that even if neither tape-sync nor SMPTE are available on a MIDI interface, this does not mean that synchronisation is impossible. Indeed, some methods of synchronisation found on certain pieces of MIDI equipment are superior to those found on many interfaces. What this does mean however, is that without a MIDI interface incorporating one or other of these functions, extra equipment will be required for synchronisation, and therefore extra cost will be involved.

MIDI sync and MIDI Time Code (MTC)

All MIDI interfaces can use *MIDI sync*. This comes out of a MIDI Out socket and keeps track of MIDI time. The MIDI clock ticks 24 times per crotchet (quarter note), independently of the tempo of the music. This is not to be confused with *ppqn* – pulses per quarter note – which is often used as a measure of the resolution of sequencers (usually 96 or 192, and nowadays even higher). MIDI sync is very useful for synchronising a sequencer to a drum machine, or one sequencer to another but, because of the electrical characteristics of the MIDI signal, it cannot by itself be recorded directly to tape. It has first to be converted to FSK by a MIDI-to-FSK device (costing about £100).

In 1987 a new method of synchronisation was incorporated into the MIDI specification, called *MIDI Time Code (MTC)*, and it has been hailed as the cleverest of them all. It incorporates time code, as in SMPTE, but divided into hours, minutes, frames, and quarter frames. Instead of being converted to Song Position Pointers (as happens with the sub-divisions of SMPTE) and sent to the sequencer, quarter frames are actually transmitted directly to the sequencer, which is left to make up its own mind about the position at which it should start. This method gives a better resolution than Song Position Pointers, and also solves the problem of ritardandos and accelerandos, though it is not yet widely implemented.

The sequencer and MIDI interface must, of course, be able to recognise MTC for it to work.

For synchronisation products, see below Section 4.10.

4.1.2 Beyond the 16-Channel Barrier

Very soon after the MIDI specification became established, it was discovered that 16 channels were really too few for serious musical applications. MIDI had been thought of initially as a standard for connecting electronic musical instruments, but it was soon being implemented on non-instrumental studio devices, for automating mixers and faders, changing parameters on effects units such as reverb and echo, and so on. These additional applications, and the development of channel-hungry multi-timbral sound modules, capable of producing the sounds of many different instruments simultaneously, made the 16 channel barrier a serious limitation.

Changing the MIDI specification to increase the number of channels was out of the question because of the way in which MIDI messages had been designed. The four bits denoting the channel number (see Chapter 3 Section 3.3), bundled as they are with another four essential bits to form the status byte of MIDI messages, were simply not enough to handle more than 16 channels because the maximum number which can be contained in four columns in binary notation is decimal 15, which with a 0 makes a maximum of 16.

One solution would have been to have a second status byte, but this would have complicated the messages and made MIDI slower. Far more importantly, it would have altered the very basis of the MIDI standard: the equipment already available for MIDI would not have worked with it, and the whole point of having a single standard would have disappeared. A general unwillingness to change the basic MIDI standard has been entrenched almost since MIDI began, and still remains in place today despite many pressures to deviate from it. It is a remarkable fact that for not far short of a decade – an eon in the world of computers and electronics – MIDI has remained fundamentally unchanged.

The only answer to the 16-channel limitation has been to keep the system as it was originally designed, and run more than one MIDI network. Consequently, some MIDI interfaces can be linked together to provide extra channel capability (obviously an expensive solution), and some provide more than one MIDI Out port, each port having 16 channels.

In the descriptions of interfaces which follow, a single MIDI In and a single MIDI Out port are assumed unless otherwise specified. It should also be noted that many of the cheaper MIDI interfaces come as part of a starter pack.

4.2 MIDI Interfaces for the IBM PC and Compatibles

This is an area which is generally more complicated than that of interfaces for other computers. The reason is that the PC is in itself unsuited for musical applications, but is the internationally accepted standard for personal computers, and has therefore attracted the widest range of interfaces.

4.2.1 The Roland MPU-401

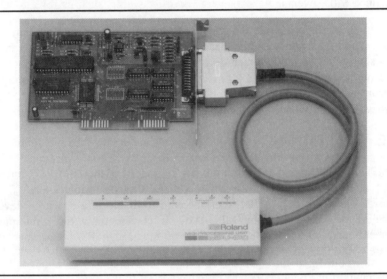

Figure 4.1: The Roland MPU-IPC interface Version 1.5A

The industry-standard MIDI interface for the PC is one released as far back as March 1984 by the Roland Corporation called the MPU-401 (MPU stands for MIDI Processing Unit). We would generally recommend this, or one of its clones, because a great deal of software is available for it, including shareware and public-domain (PD) software. Shareware is a way of selling software based on the honesty system of paying the author a small fee only if you like the product. PD software is free of charge if downloaded with a modem from a public online network, or very cheaply if ordered from a firm dealing with it.

At the time of going to press, the latest version of the MPU is the MPU-IPC Version 1.5A (as shown in Figure 4.1), which represents excellent value for money at the top end of price category B. It comes in two physical parts: a half-size card fits into one of the expansion slots inside the PC, and this connects to a small external box via a 25-pin D-shaped connector. On the box are four MIDI DIN sockets: a MIDI In, two MIDI Outs and a Roland DIN Sync for synchronising to various Roland devices, though for practical purposes this port is virtually redundant nowadays. There are also three 1/8 inch RCA-type sockets (small round sockets which take the jack plugs often found on modern earphones): a Tape-sync In, a Tape-sync Out, and a Metronome Out.

The MPU is a very intelligent interface. Using its own specialised commands, it can record into, and play notes from, its internal 8-track memory buffer. It has an internal clock with a timing resolution of between 1/24 and 1/192 ppqn. Using this clock it is able to provide an accurate metronome and handle tempo changes. Among its many other features, it has a MIDI Through facility, and it can filter out pre-defined MIDI events.

However, in intelligent mode the MPU will not handle MTC (MIDI Time Code) messages, and there has been a tendency for software developers to write programs for it using its dumb mode which does handle them. Nor does the MPU offer any expansion beyond the standard 16 MIDI channels. To get more, it is necessary to use more than one interface, and four of them can be connected to give a maximum of 64 simultaneous channels, though this is an expensive solution.

4.2.2 MPU for MCA

The MPU-401 will work only with models 25 and 30 of the IBM PS/2 range. For models above these, which use MCA (Micro Channel Architecture) for their expansion slots, the only MIDI interface card available is a specially developed version of the MPU-IPC, the MPU-IMC. It is essentially the same piece of equipment, and therefore allows owners of high-range PS/2 machines to run software written for the standard MPU.

4.2.3 Standard MPU-compatible Interfaces

The MPU has established itself as a standard in the world of PC music to such an extent that it has been cloned by other manufacturers, just as the IBM PC itself has been cloned. And as with PC clones, some MPU-compatible models are cheaper than the real thing and may offer fewer facilities, while others offer added facilities for a higher price. The principal producers of MPU clones are:

Music Quest

This is a Texan company whose MPU-compatible interfaces all work in intelligent mode and have features for adjusting parameters in case any hardware compatibility problems are encountered (for the technically initiated, the features are selectable port address and selectable Interrupt level).

The PC MIDI Card is basic, relatively cheap (price category B), and is often found bundled with various sequencers as a starter pack. It has no tape-sync facility, but recognises MTC.

The MQX-16 (price category C) offers Chase Lock tape-sync with MIDI Song Position Pointers, a feature not found on the MPU, and recognises MTC.

The MQX-16S is the same as the MQX-16 but with SMPTE (price category C/D).

The MQX-32 and the MQX-32M (both price category D) have 32 channels, SMPTE, and two independent MIDI Out ports. The 32M has two merged inputs, allowing simultaneous real-time recording from two instruments. A number of software packages can take advantage of the expanded channel facility, including Cakewalk Pro, Master Tracks Pro, and Texture (see Chapter 5 Section 5.11).

Both the MQX-16S and MQX-32M recognise and generate MTC.

Voyetra

Voyetra is a US company producing a wide range of MIDI basics and extras. Its MPU-compatible interfaces work in intelligent mode and have genuine Roland circuits rather than copies of them. There are differences, however: for example, the Voyetra interface metronome requires external amplification. As with Music Quest's interfaces, there are facilities for making adjustments in case of compatibility problems (though here for Interrupt levels only).

Voyetra interfaces have one MIDI In and one MIDI Out port, though this capability can be expanded to five with an accessory, the PC/Quadpad (price category A).

The V-4000 (price category C) is the basic model.

The V-4001 (price category C, though a little more expensive than the V-4000) has FSK sync.

The V-4001cs (price category C/D) has FSK sync and some extra synchronisation features intended for use with pre-MIDI equipment.

For other Voyetra PC interfaces, see below Section 4.2.4.

Dr T

Dr T is a firm particularly well-known in the world of the Atari ST, the Commodore Amiga and the Apple Macintosh. It does, however, produce one MPU-compatible interface, the Model 1 (price category B/C), which is a fairly basic card, with no tape-sync.

Midiers Land

The Midiers Land MD401 (price category A) is a budget MPU-compatible interface. The SM401 (price category B) has some interesting extras, such as some on-board sounds.

4.2.4 Non-MPU-compatible Interfaces

Yamaha C1

The MIDI interface in the Yamaha C1 music computer (unfortunately unavailable at present in the UK) is built into the machine and cannot be bought separately. We include brief specifications here, however, since the C1 may be re-marketed in the UK, and at the time of going to press is still available in continental Europe and the USA (from where it can be obtained directly).

It has eight independent MIDI Out ports of 16 channels each, two merged MIDI In ports (which means that two people can play in at the same time and the information mixed in a process known as *MIDI merge*), a MIDI Through port, SMPTE, and MTC. It is supported by a wide range of adapted versions of professional software originally written for the Roland MPU.

The C1 has also attracted some compatible MIDI interfaces, in particular from Voyetra. The V22 and the V24S (price categories B and D) have respectively two MIDI Ins and two MIDI Outs, and two MIDI Ins and four MIDI Outs, the latter with SMPTE. The V22M and V24M (price categories C and D) offer the same facilities, but are also MPU-compatible.

Midicard

This interface forms part of the PRO-MIDI Studio System by the US firm Systems Design Associates (price category E for the complete system). It has tape-sync, and includes one of the few sequencers which record direct to disk as opposed to RAM. Two cards can be used to give 32 channels.

The Midicard interface has a daughter card, the Midicard+ (price category B), which gives it MPU compatibility and thus allows it to run any software written for the MPU.

4.2.5 Interfaces Incorporating Sound

The lack of a proper sound source in the IBM PC and its clones still occasionally makes it a laughing stock among those who have not yet recognised its principal advantage: that of attracting myriad add-ons.

When the PC was first used for music, it became known as the giant which sounded like a mosquito, and no doubt partly because of such scathing criticism, IBM was not long in introducing its Music Feature Card (price category D), which simply drops into one of the PC's expansion ports. It is a single expansion card incorporating a MIDI interface and a Yamaha FB-01 sound module. It is not MPU-compatible.

Later on, Roland brought out its LAPC-1, which is a Roland MT-32 sound module on a card (price category D) capable of taking a special connector box called the MCB-1 (price category B) which acts as a full MIDI interface. The LAPC-1 on its own can produce sound only by receiving data from the PC in which it is installed, but the addition of the MCB-1 gives it the same capabilities as an MT-32 plus an MPU interface.

4.3 MIDI Interfaces for Apple Computers

Opcode Systems

The Professional Plus (price category B) has one MIDI In and three MIDI Out ports.

The Studio Plus Two (price category C) has two MIDI Ins and six MIDI Outs, as well as a switching mechanism for a modem and printer, allowing these to be used without having to change cables.

The Studio 3 is Opcode's top-of-the-range MIDI interface (price category D). It is a Studio Plus Two, but with SMPTE and MTC. The SMPTE facility is also available separately as the Timecode Machine (price category C).

All are external units and are available for the Apple II GS, and Macintoshes.

Passport Designs

Passport Designs, a Californian company, produces a basic MIDI interface for the Apple II GS and Macintosh models which can plug into either the modem or printer port, but which requires an optional external synchronisation box for tape-sync. At one time, it was available in the UK at under £100, but was then withdrawn.

However Passport's more advanced, professionally-oriented external interface, MIDI Transport (price category D), can be bought in the UK. It has One MIDI In, three MIDI Outs, and offers FSK, SMPTE and MTC. A version of MIDI Transport is also available for machines other than Apple (see below Section 4.7.1).

Mark of the Unicorn

Mark of the Unicorn, an established US MIDI company, produces the MIDI Time Piece (price category E) for the Macintosh. This is a rack-mounted advanced SMPTE interface cum MIDI merger, MIDI splitter, and MIDI patch bay (see Section 4.8 below). It has eight MIDI Ins and eight MIDI Outs (giving 128 channels), and it has advanced mute and channelisation features.

It can also be networked with three other Time Piece units (two on each of the Macintosh's serial ports) to provide a massive 512 MIDI-channel capability, though the only software which will support this number of channels at the moment is Mark of the Unicorn's own Performer sequencer Version 3.42 (see Chapter 5 Section 5.11).

Using even the 128 channels of a single unit, timing delays can become a serious problem, but this is a function of the Macintosh rather than the Time Piece, whose capabilities (it seems) have been introduced in view of the arrival of the new Macintosh IIfx.

J.L. Cooper Electronics

Sync Master (price category D) is a Macintosh MIDI interface/SMPTE synchroniser with two serial ports, for printer and modem, two MIDI Ins and six Outs. It generates all SMPTE formats and smart FSK.

The MacNexus Macintosh interface (price category A) is one of the cheapest on the market. It has one MIDI In and three MIDI Outs. At the time of writing it is not available in the UK.

4.4 The Atari ST

The Atari ST's MIDI interface is built into the machine. It is dumb, but has some interesting features. For example, a standard 5-pin MIDI cable normally uses only three of the pins: pins 4 and 5 carry the MIDI signal, and pin 2 is for the Earth, with pins 1 and 3 having been left by the designers of MIDI to leave room for future developments. The Atari uses pins 1 and 3 in the MIDI Out port to send a MIDI Through signal, though an adaptor is required to have both MIDI Out and MIDI Through.

Expansion boxes for the Atari MIDI interface.

A number of manufacturers produce pieces of hardware designed to overcome the limitations of the Atari interface such as only 16 MIDI channels and no SMPTE or tape sync.

The German company C-Lab produces the Export MIDI Expansion Interface, offering three independent MIDI Out ports giving a total of 48 channels. It also produces the Unitor MIDI Expander SMPTE/EBU Synchroniser (Figure 4.2). This has two MIDI Outs, plus two MIDI Ins which merge with the Atari's own MIDI In port to give a three-into-one merge for simultaneous live playing by three players. Combining Export's three MIDI Outs, Unitor's two MIDI Outs, and Atari's own MIDI Out, can give six independent MIDI Out ports, that is to say a total of 96 MIDI channels.

Figure 4.2: C-Lab's Unitor MIDI expander for the Atari ST

4.5 The Commodore Amiga

The range of external MIDI interfaces for the Amiga range is one of the widest and cheapest on the market. They connect to the computer via its serial port.

MicroMidi (price category A) available from Datel Electronics has one each of MIDI In, Out and Through. From the same firm, MidiMaster (price category A) has one MIDI In, three MIDI Outs and one MIDI Through.

From Trilogic, MIDI Interface I (price category A) has one each of MIDI In, Out and Through, while MIDI Interface II also has one of each kind, plus two additional ports which can be set to Out or Through.

Dr T produces the Model A (price category B) with one MIDI In and two MIDI Outs.

Kawai's FunLab music system for the Amiga 500 is a rather special product in that it is a complete system. It includes a MIDI interface with one MIDI In, two MIDI

Outs and one MIDI Through, a sequencer, a synthesiser editor, and a Kawai FS680 full-size multi-timbral keyboard, all for (just) within price category D. The interface can be bought separately in price category B, as can the the keyboard (price category D).

4.6 MIDI Interfaces for Acorn computers

BBC Micro

A number of software packages come with their own MIDI interfaces (see, for instance the UMI-4M sequencer, Chapter 5 Section 5.11).

Hybrid Technology's Music 2000 (price category B/C) is a MIDI interface forming a link between its Music System and MIDI (see Chapter 2 Section 2.2.5).

Another generally available interface is one produced by ElectroMusic Research (price category B). This has one MIDI In, two MIDI Outs, and tape-sync.

Archimedes

Among the comparatively wide range of MIDI interfaces for the Archimedes, the one produced by Acorn itself (price category B) has with one MIDI In, two MIDI Outs and one MIDI Through.

The PMI 4 interface (price category C) from Pandora is compatible with Acorn's interface and offers four sets of 16 MIDI channels.

The MIDI 4 Interface Card from ElectroMusic Research (price category B) has one MIDI In and three MIDI Outs. It will not fit the A3000.

4.7 Other MIDI Interfaces

4.7.1 Amstrad PCW and other computers

The two interfaces available for the Amstrad PCW come from EMR (ElectroMusic Research) and DHCP Electronics, both in price category B.

MIDI interfaces also exist for the Amstrad CPC, the Commodore 64 and 128, the Spectrum, and other home computers.

4.7.2 Generic Interfaces

Computers have one or more serial ports which are normally used for attaching a printer, a modem or a mouse. Many also have a parallel port, to which a parallel printer or other parallel device can be attached.

Both these kinds of port can be used for linking to a MIDI interface, and a number of generic interfaces connecting to them are manufactured for a whole range of computers. In most cases, serial MIDI interfaces will work with any computer equipped with an RS-232 or RS-422 port (these are standards for serial communication), therefore including the PC, the Commodore Amiga and the Atari ST (though the latter does not necessarily require an added MIDI interface). Parallel MIDI interfaces have attracted little attention, though we may see more of them in the future.

With the PC, a generic MIDI interface of this kind is worth considering for portable models with no expansion slots, for desktop models with no printer attached, or if expansion slots are in short supply because they are being used for other purposes and no modem or mouse is attached to the serial port. However, no currently available MIDI interfaces which connect externally in this way are MPU-compatible, so some software will not work with them.

Examples of generic MIDI interfaces are:

Midiator

The Midiator from Key Electronics is a serial interface which comes in three models, the MS-101, the MS-103 (three Midi Outs) and the MS-114 (four MIDI Outs). None has built-in tape-sync. At the time of going to press, they are not available in the UK.

Passport Design

A version of Passport's MIDI Transport for Apple computers (see above Section 4.3) is available in generic serial form (price category D). Although it is not MPU-compatible, it is well supported by software, for instance sequencers such as Master Tracks Pro, Prism, and Texture (see Chapter 5 Section 5.11) and score editors such as Encore and Finale (see Chapter 12 Section 12.6).

Eclipse

Eclipse's HRS-3000 (price category B) has three each of MIDI Ins and Outs, but no tape-sync. Its special feature is that it connects to a computer's parallel port. Once again, at the time of writing it is not available in the UK.

4.8 Choice Checklist for MIDI Interfaces

The following are some basic questions to be asked before buying a MIDI interface:

❏ Is an interface necessary? (This may seem an odd question, but we are assured that people occasionally try to buy a MIDI interface for the Atari ST, not realising that it has an integral one.)

❏ Does it work with the software the user has in mind?

❏ What are its synchronisation capabilities?

❏ How many MIDI channels does it have, or can it support if networked?

4.9 MIDI Accessories

4.9.1 MIDI Through Units

A MIDI Through socket on an interface is not essential, which is why so many interfaces offering such a port allow it to double as another MIDI Out.

If several MIDI devices are controlled from one sequencer (a MIDI orchestra, say, made up of ten synthesisers) it is theoretically possible to connect them in series via their MIDI In and MIDI Through ports (see Chapter 3 Figure 3.3). But not all MIDI devices are equipped with a MIDI Through socket, and in any case connecting more than three devices in this way can lead to problems of timing delays. The alternative is to connect them in a star-shaped network, for which an accessory called a MIDI Through Unit is required (see Chapter 3 Figure 3.4).

It is not unknown to try to achieve the same effect supplied by a MIDI Through unit by physically splitting the MIDI cable wires so that the signal can be sent to two devices. The resulting individual signals obtained with this method, however, may be deficient in electrical power, and may give poor results.

4.9.2 MIDI Merge Units

It is sometimes useful to be able to merge two or more signals into one, for example if two or more people want to play and record into a sequencer at the same time.

Since MIDI works by serial communication, the job of the MIDI Merge Unit is to ensure that MIDI messages from the various sources are merged properly – it waits for one MIDI message to end before allowing another one from a different source to join the main pipeline.

4.9.3 MIDI Patch Bays and MIDI Switches

A complex MIDI studio with many synthesisers, sound modules and other MIDI devices, may result in a situation in which a number of MIDI outputs have to be assigned to a number of MIDI inputs. Imagine, for instance, that a studio includes two keyboard controllers and five sound modules. It may be necessary to connect a keyboard controller to a sound module when its MIDI cable is at the time connected to another. What is required is a switching mechanism which allows this to be done without disconnecting and re-connecting cables. The answer is a patch bay.

A patch bay is a piece of hardware allowing the creation of a completely flexible MIDI network in which any of the inputs can be connected to any of the outputs. All the MIDI cables coming from and going to all the equipment of the studio are fed into the patch bay, and any routeing combination can be achieved either by pressing buttons on the front panel of the bay, or under software control.

Some patch bays also have facilities for MIDI split and even MIDI merge, so that one input signal can be divided between a number of outputs, or two inputs merged into one and then distributed into many. The price and sophistication of these units depends on the number of inputs and outputs they provide, whether the switching is done by mechanical means or electronic circuits, and in the latter case whether the patch bay has an internal memory so that particular set-ups can be stored for future use.

Stand-alone MIDI switches also exist which allow an input signal to be routed to an output without either merge or split facilities.

4.9.4 MIDI-to-CV Converters

These are devices which allow you to add MIDI facilities to pre-MIDI synthesisers which use Control Voltage (CV). The process of fitting out such a synthesiser is known as *retrofit*. For more on voltage, see Chapter 9 Section 9.1.1.

4.10 Products

SMPTE/MIDI synchronising devices

Producer	Product	Price	Features/comments
J.L. Cooper	PPS100	B	
Nomad	SMC1.0	B/C	
Roland	SBX-80 Sync Box	G	One of the very first SMPTE Reader/Generators. Now overpriced, though available much more cheaply.
Tascam	MTS-1000 MIDiiZER	G/H	Can be used to slave a tape recorder to SMPTE. Can also be plugged directly into a Tascam 238 8-track cassette recorder or the 644 MIDIstudio or, with an additional interface, to other tape recorders and videos with controllable tape-transport mechanisms.
XRI	XR300	C	
Yamaha	MSS1	C	
Yamaha	YMC10	B	MIDI to FSK converter

MIDI Through units

Producer	Product	Price	Features/comments
Philip Rees	V3	A	One In, three Out. Battery/adaptoroperated.
	V10	A	One In, ten Out. Mains operated.
Yamaha	YME8	A/B	Two sets of one In and four Outs.

MIDI Merge units

Producer	Product	Price	Features/comments
Groove Electronics	MERG	B	Two each of In, Out and Through. Extras include filtering out events,and adding split keyboard facilities.
Philip Rees	2M	B	One In, two each of Out and Through. Combines Pitch Bend messages into one.

MIDI Patch bays and Switches

Producer	Product	Price	Features/comments
Akai	XR400	C	Eight Ins, 11 Outs, 3-way merge.
Philip Rees	5 x 5 MIDI Switch	B	Connects any of five slaves to any of five masters.
	2S Switch	A	One to two.
	5S	A	One to five.
	9S	A	One to nine.
Roland	A-880 MIDI Patcher/Mixer	C	Eight Ins, eight Outs, programmable with 64 memories. Two merged Ins.
Yamaha	MJC8 MIDI Junction Controller	C	Eight Ins, eight Outs, programmable with 50 memories.

MIDI-to-CV converters

Producer	Product	Price	Features/comments
Groove	M2CV	B	Can control two mono analogue channels.
Electronics	M4CV	D	Can control four analogue channels, recognises pitch bend, velocity, aftertouch, and modulation wheel data.
Philip Rees	MCV MIDI to CV	C	Can control two mono analogue channels, recognises pitch bend and velocity.

5

Sequencers

A sequencer is so called from its ability to record a sequence of notes, store them, and play them back without the further intervention of the musician. Using a MIDI input device such as a synthesiser, different instruments can be recorded in real time, or programmed in step time, and the sequencer can play the whole arrangement by sending the performance information to attached MIDI instruments. The outputs of all the MIDI instruments are sent into a sound mixer, processed, and mixed down into a stereo signal which can be listened to or made into a master recording (the processes are described in Chapters 9 and 10). This can then be duplicated to other media such as cassette tape, or sent to a factory to make records and compact discs.

As is the way with so many tools of the computer trade, a sequencer was originally a collection of electronic parts contained in a very big box, but with the advent of the microchip, the required parts became small enough to be slipped into something more comfortable. The latest stage in the history of the sequencer is that it comes as a program on a floppy disk.

The Story of Sequencers

Sequencers began to be used extensively in the 1960s, at first with exciting results full of promise for the future. But by the end of the 1970s, when the novelty had begun to wear thin, they had come to be associated with a repetitive sound which many people rightly considered to be at best only on the fringe of artistic creation. Today, with the development both of modern sequencing software and the sophisticated hardware it handles, we are again back in exciting times.

Early sequencers worked with analogue synthesisers, that is to say synthesisers which used voltage controls to produce notes of different pitch, as opposed to digital synthesisers which deal only with numbers. The sequencers were covered with banks of knobs, and each knob was set to control a voltage path to the synthesiser, and thus a specific pitch.

These sequencers could remember a limited number of notes, and despite the fact that the music they produced lacked variation, groups like Tangerine Dream used them extensively. Indeed their repetitiveness was frequently exploited and became an essential ingredient of the music. Even musicians of a more conventional outlook of that period made use of them, but in a different way: by restricting their use to background chord arpeggios, they managed to restrict their repetitive presence.

One area where the idea of sequencing really took over was that of percussion, with the early success of drum (rhythm) machines which are still a major part of a MIDI studio. Here, the sequence is not made up of musical notes but drum sounds positioned at the correct points within one or more bars to form a pattern incorporating the desired rhythm. These machines are sequencers to all intents and purposes, but they are not usually referred to as such.

With the advent of microchip technology, sequencing facilities began to be incorporated into the synthesisers themselves. And shortly afterwards, MIDI arrived, allowing both internal and external sequencers to be connected to the MIDI instruments in the studio. It was now possible to *play* a sequence on a music keyboard connected via MIDI to a sequencer, as opposed to programming it step by step. The notes could be stored in the sequencer digitally, with the data denoting which key was pressed and when. What is more, the increased storage facilities which the microchip revolution brought with it meant that sequencers could store far more notes than their predecessors – hundreds, and soon thousands. This also meant that it was no longer necessary constantly to repeat sections in order to make up a song. A complete work could be stored in memory and the problem of enforced repetetiveness had disappeared.

The increased memory and enhanced processing power offered by microprocessor technology also meant that multiple instrument sequences could be recorded in a way similar to that used by multi-track tape recorders, and a complete arrangement could be stored. As we mentioned in Chapter 1, multi-track tape recorders were widely used in the 1970s to record an arrangement one instrument at a time, then to play them back all together, thus allowing one person to create the sounds of a complete orchestra. Today, big studios use tape recorders with 24 or more tracks, and even link two together if a particularly complex sound is required. But MIDI sequencers have limited the use of multi-track tape recorders to recording acoustic sounds only, that is to say those sounds which cannot easily be recorded directly using MIDI, such as the human voice and the sounds of natural instruments.

Of course, the basic idea of the sequencer – that of storing sequences of notes – is related to that of the tape recorder, and many sequencers use tape-transport icons in their graphics displays: Play, Record, Fast Forward, Rewind and Pause. But going a little beyond that basic idea, it can be seen that in the principles of the way it works, a sequencer is actually closer to a pianola – a piano which appears to play itself. A pianola uses rolls of paper punched with holes. The position and size of these holes, as the roll passes over the playing mechanism, determine whether a key is to be activated. In the same way, a sequencer's memory contains not the sound but data about the sound: keys pressed, loudness of note, and so forth. The process has its disadvantages when compared to storing patterns of magnetic particles on tape, because an analogue, continuous range of sound has to be converted in distinguishable increments if it is to be used on a sequencer. There are nevertheless also many advantages in digitising sound, the principal one being that it can be much more easily manipulated.

Software Sequencers

The first MIDI sequencers had LCDs and editing buttons, and they stored their data on cassette tape like the majority of home computers of those days (though current hardware models have integral floppy-disk drives). But it was clear that computers, via a MIDI interface and software, could provide cheaper and more powerful sequencing facilities. Memory is far less of a problem on a computer, even a comparatively unsophisticated one, and a full screen rather than a small LCD screen makes editing far easier. These factors eventually caused the move from hardware to software sequencers, a move paralleled in many areas of computing, where the ubiquitous micro can be made to do the work of many different pieces of hardware, thus generally making processes cheaper.

Dedicated sequencers are still readily available, however, and new models keep appearing, though in decreasing numbers. If anything, the trend in sequencers not intended for direct use on a computer is towards their incorporation into synthesisers. But the market for dedicated sequencers exists because they are more portable than a computer plus musical keyboard. Indeed, when travelling on the train, or staying in a hotel, a little musical keyboard with an integral sequencer is perfect for working out a new song. This is the electronic equivalent of using a napkin in a restaurant for jotting down ideas, which is how Strauss (it is said) jotted down the Blue Danube.

We shall nevertheless turn our attention principally towards software sequencers intended to run on personal computers, since these are now so common that the word *sequencer* has come to mean a software sequencer and, except in certain professional circles, a qualifier such as *hardware* or *dedicated* is often required to indicate the other variety.

A final general remark about sequencers is necessary at this point. Sequencers have been produced, as has so much MIDI material, with pop music in mind. The average pop song lasts only a few minutes, whereas a (so-called) classical piece can last much longer. Sequencers can handle only a limited number of MIDI events, and unless they write directly to a hard disk, are also dependent on the amount of available RAM in the computer. In many applications other than musical ones, files can be linked so that as one is finished, the next one is called up from disk. In music, this often results in an unacceptable period of silence as each file is loaded. Long pieces of music are therefore simply too difficult for many sequencers to handle, though as RAM gets bigger on computers, so this situation is easing.

Choice of Software Sequencers

Software sequencers fall into two principal types: *linear* and *pattern.*

With a linear-based sequencer, a piece of music is stored from beginning to end. There is no repeat feature, and if sections need to be repeated they have to be copied in their entirety.

With a pattern-based sequencer, sections of a piece of music are recorded or programmed in patterns, which then form the smallest units of the work. A single pattern is usually made up of a number of bars, and the final piece of music is a list of all the patterns and the order in which they are to be played.

Since a linear sequencer stores the entire piece of music note by note, it is obvious that its demands on memory are greater. But a linear sequencer is like a conductor's score – although individual tracks may contain repeats, they are reprinted, so that at any bar in the score it is possible to see every instrument which is playing. Linear sequencers devour memory, but they are therefore easier to use when orchestrating.

With a pattern sequencer, the memory problem is reduced. But the temptation to repeat sections is also greater, since it is such an easy thing to do. Consequently there is a bigger risk of a lack of variation in the final sound if the sequencer in question does not have facilities for incorporating variations into a repeated pattern. However, since the better pattern sequencers incorporate transposition and/or muting of certain instruments within a given pattern when it is repeated, and since in any case the question of boredom is something which is both subjective and easily avoidable in so many ways, a pattern sequencer is usually a better choice than a linear sequencer if memory is in short supply. Some sequencers, though they are few and far between, incorporate both linear and pattern characteristics.

5.1 Tracks

After the question of linear or pattern sequencers, the next most important factor in the choice of a sequencer is the number of tracks it can handle, and this is a subject which requires some detailed investigation because it has important effects for creating music.

Some sequencers are designed for a mere eight tracks, while some are capable of handling 3,000. The basic rules governing choice here are quite straightforward: (a) too few tracks can be a waste of time, and (b) the more tracks, the better. But, of course, price plays its part, and though there is a Golden Mean – an adequate (or optimum) numbers of tracks for particular purposes – the Mean is dependent with any given sequencer on how it handles its information.

Most commonly, sequencers record each instrument on a separate track, with the bare minimum of facilities available for each track being: a track name, a MIDI channel number, and an instrument number (a MIDI Program Change message). The optimum number of tracks depends on factors such as the way MIDI messages have been defined in the MIDI specification, and the design of the sequencer's editing functions.

In essence, the minimum requirement is the number of tracks which will allow information to be stored separately about each variable parameter of a performance up to the point of the final mixdown. An actual number can be found to suit particular requirements, according to a formula derived as follows:

It is important to keep the data for each instrument on a separate track of the sequencer, since this allows the greatest degree of flexibility. So, the most basic formula for calculating a required number of tracks is:

desired number of tracks = number of musical parts in the composition

All well and good. But many of today's MIDI devices are multi-timbral. A single synthesiser may be able to produce eight different instrument sounds simultaneously, using eight MIDI channels, in which case this one MIDI device alone will require eight tracks on a sequencer.

Furthermore, non-instrumental equipment may also require tracks on a sequencer. Many studio devices use MIDI to provide some form of automation – for example, sound-mixer faders (the sliding volume controls on sound mixers) can be controlled via MIDI messages, and recorded on sequencer tracks along with the actual musical score. A Yamaha DMP11 8-channel mixer has a total of 167 MIDI-controllable parameters, one for each of its functions. There is little likelihood of needing to change all these parameters at the same time, but a minimum requirement would be to control the volume of each channel on the mixer, and it would make sense to set aside a separate track of the sequencer for each one of them.

Sound-effect devices, such as those which produce reverbs and echoes, can also be controlled via MIDI messages, which can be used to switch from one effect to another or change the severity of an effect in real time. This data can also be recorded on sequencer tracks.

Drum machines contain many different percussive sounds. Although these are usually controlled on a single MIDI channel, with each sound being assigned to one MIDI note at a specific pitch, it is advisable to assign a separate track on the sequencer for each drum sound, so that subsequent editing is possible. For instance, the note which is two octaves below Middle C is normally assigned to a bass drum, and the note D above it to a snare drum. If the drum track has been recorded in real time, since both these sounds will originate from the same MIDI channel, they will be contained within a single track on the sequencer. And since sequencers' editing functions, like Note On velocity, work only at the level of the individual track, altering the loudness of one of these sounds separately means creating an extra track.

The basic formula therefore requires expansion to take into account the fact that modern MIDI devices are hungrier for tracks than their predecessors. Given this, we arrive at the following equation:

optimum number of tracks = total number of musical parts (including a part for each drum sound used) + number of MIDI parameters used by sound-processing devices in the studio and which need to be controlled separately in real time

In short: *opt tracks = tot parts + real-time param*

Putting some numbers to this formula, it can be said in a very general way that at today's MIDI specifications, 16 tracks is a minimum requirement, and between 32 and 64 tracks will be about right for most purposes. Do not spend money on many more than 64 tracks unless you are using a big MIDI studio or have definite plans to expand your MIDI equipment.

5.1.1 Other Track Considerations

Assigning tracks to groups

Some sequencers which offer large numbers of tracks include functions for grouping them into sections (as can be done on some sound mixers). This makes for easier manipulation of the tracks, for instance allowing a particular section of the orchestration such as the woodwind, the percussion or the strings to be heard separately.

Assigning tracks to channels

Usually each track is assigned to a single MIDI channel to control a single instrument. But more than one track can be assigned to the same MIDI channel so that two or more voices can be sent to the same instrument, and some sequencers allow a single track to be assigned to more than one MIDI channel so that it is possible to have more than one instrument playing the same music. There are even sequencers, though they are less common, which allow a single track to contain notes assigned to different MIDI channels. This means that data from a single track can be sent to more than one instrument, each playing a different musical part – in other words, the whole arrangement can be merged into one track. This, then, adds a further complication to our track formula, possibly reducing the required number of tracks, since if a sequencer does not have many tracks but allows them to be split in this way, it can still be adequate for some purposes. It should be said, however, that if many instruments are mixed down into one track, manipulating them can be a cumbersome business. In general, therefore, we would not recommend reducing the optimum number of tracks in this way.

Track-editing

The ability to edit tracks is a feature found on most sequencers, but there is considerable variance in the degree of flexibility available within the editing process. There are nearly always facilities to delete a track, move it to a different position, copy its contents to another track, and to insert a blank track between two which have already been recorded. But more sophisticated sequencers will also allow operations such as swapping two tracks, hiding a track so that it is not displayed on the screen, and sorting tracks by group, name or MIDI channel. These are useful features which can ease the composer's life, and thus help with the creative process.

5.2 Recording

The most common method of sending music into a sequencer is to play it using a MIDI instrument and record it – *real-time input*. Superficially, as we have seen, the procedure is identical to using a multi-track tape recorder, but here the instrument is wired into the computer's MIDI interface, no sound is recorded – only performance information – and the music is stored on disk not tape.

Some sequencers record directly to a track, while others record into a *phrase buffer* (an area of the computer's memory set aside for taking in musical phrases), the material being transferred to a track when the buffer is full or the music complete.

Notes can also be inserted using the computer keyboard (or mouse) or a musical keyboard, one by one, anywhere in the score – *step-time input*. Its main disadvantage is that the dynamic of each note has to be defined, otherwise the piece may lack feeling. Achieving a believable performance using step-time recording is an art in itself.

5.2.1 Time Signature and Tempo

Time signature and tempo must be set before recording takes place. If a time signature is not specified, the default signature (always $\frac{4}{4}$) will be used, as is usually the case with the default tempo of 120 beats per minute. The fact that the tempo can be set to a lower value can be a boon for those who are not accomplished players, since recording can take place at a slower tempo than the one intended for playback, thus allowing the mind more time to control the fingers.

5.2.2 Count-in

Almost all sequencers also have a count-in (lead-in) facility and/or an electronic metronome. Count-in is the equivalent of a band-leader's 'Four for nothing'. The sequencer beats out a number of bars before recording starts in order to give the player time to prepare, to feel the beat, and even to play before the recording begins.

5.2.3 Punch In/Out

A related recording feature which is common on sequencers is a facility for *Punch In* and *Punch Out*. With this, beginning and end markers are set, where recording will start and finish, and whatever is subsequently recorded is automatically inserted into that section. This is obviously useful not only for straight insertion, but also for recording over unsatisfactory sections of music without having to record an entire piece again. Even the most experienced instrumentalists make mistakes, and although these can be rectified using step-time recording, many people prefer to play – even a couple of bars – so that feeling is retained.

5.2.4 Other Recording Features

An important feature of any sequencer is its *clock resolution* (*timing resolution*), that is to say the smallest time interval allowed at which a note can be placed in a bar, and the smallest duration of a note. This is measured in ppqn (pulses per quarter note), the norm lying between 96 and 192 per crotchet beat, although some recent sequencers allow higher values. The higher the value, the closer the result will be to a human performance.

Recording features may also include facilities for recording from any place on a track not just the beginning, and for recording on more than one track at a time with each track assigned to a different MIDI channel. This latter feature is becoming increasingly common. It is needed if two or more people wish to record together, if a MIDI guitar is being used (most MIDI guitars use six channels, one for each string), or if it is necessary to transfer a score from one computer to another which uses a different disk format or runs a different program, by playing the music.

In addition to the above, some sequencers will filter out certain MIDI events during the recording process. Events such as pitch bend, aftertouch and some continuous controllers take up a lot of memory, and it may be desirable to filter them out while recording, especially if the sequencer does not have facilities for removing them after they are recorded. Good sequencers, however, will have a facility for thinning out such events at a later stage, something which is clearly very useful, and indeed which some composers find essential.

5.3 Play Features

Features available for playback are as important as those for recording, and as with record features, different sequencers offer different facilities. The most important ones to take in consideration when weighing up the plus points of a sequencer versus its price are:

5.3.1 Mute and Solo

These are common features, and essentially two sides of the same coin. *Mute* allows a track to be masked so that it will not be heard, while *Solo* allows a track to be played on its own. On more sophisticated sequencers the procedure can also be applied to groups of tracks, for example allowing all the strings or woodwind to be muted, or all the drums soloed.

5.3.2 Play Range and Loop Play

Play Range allows a beginning and end of section to be defined for playback purposes, and is obviously useful for listening to parts of a piece rather than in its entirety. Loop Play is an extension of Play Range, offering an automated way of hearing a section several times over. A range within a piece is defined, and the sequencer plays it back repeatedly until it is told it to stop.

5.3.3 Change Parameters while in Play Mode

Loop play is useful not only for practising a certain section before it is recorded, without having constantly to give Start and Stop instructions, but also for trying out different sounds when used in conjunction with a facility to change parameters while playing back. This latter facility is not implemented on all sequencers, though it can be an important factor in creating precisely the right sound.

Suppose that a studio has two or three synthesisers, between them offering about 20 different piano sounds. The exact sound required may not be known until it is heard to blend with the other instruments. The easiest way to set about choosing a sound in these circumstances is to record a part, set the sequencer to Play mode and, while it is playing, change the sound by pressing a key on the computer keyboard. In this way, it is possible to flip through hundreds of sound combinations in a matter of minutes.

5.3.4 Jukebox

A *jukebox* (sometimes called *song chain*) facility means being able to load and play a set of compositions one after another. It is particularly important when a computer is used on stage, or for demonstrations, or for long pieces of music which will not fit into memory. We should add, however, what experience has taught us: that care should be taken to ensure that there is no perceptible time lag between a file being loaded into memory and being played, something which can ruin a performance. This will depend on the way the jukebox facility is implemented, on the power of the computer and the way its operating system works, on the access time of the disk drive, and on the size of the files. The only safe general rule is to test everything out before a performance. It may be that no satisfactory solution is possible.

5.4 Edit Features

Most software sequencers worth their salt present a screen on which note information and other MIDI data are displayed for editing purposes. These screens differ in their presentation and functions from sequencer to sequencer, but their inclusion is important. It is not worth buying a sequencer which does not present such information on screen. The editing screen is what make a computer-based sequencer better than a dedicated box with a one-line LCD display, quite apart from the fact that the timing resolution (see below Section 5.5.2) in software sequencers is usually higher.

5.4.1 Displaying Events as Musical Notation

For a trained musician, the most obvious method of displaying music recorded in a sequencer is by traditional musical notation. But few sequencers do this because for really satisfactory results the process demands high-resolution graphics, large amounts of RAM, and a fast processor. For years, programmers have searched for, and found, alternative methods of displaying the recorded music.

As graphical user interfaces become the norm (in other words, as the Apple Macintosh interface becomes generally recognised as the best so far produced, and therefore even more widely copied and used than it is now), and as large amounts of RAM – many megabytes – become standard, we shall certainly see an increasing number of sequencers using the sticks and blobs of traditional musical notation. No matter how brilliant and logical the efforts of programmers to use a different kind of notation, they will not oust the traditional variety which has withstood the test of centuries. English spelling is difficult, inefficient, and often illogical, but all attempts to use a simpler system have fallen by the wayside. The same will be true of notation. While it is true at present that not everybody using computers to make music demands traditional notation, as an increasing number of musically trained composers begin to use them as well, so the demand is certain to increase.

However, until the new generation of really powerful computers becomes readily available at the equivalent price of today's machines (we would guess that this situation will not be reached until after 1993), standard musical notation within sequencers will for many people be either a luxury or a barely acceptable trade-off.

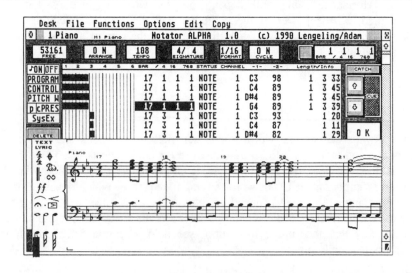

Figure 5.1: A sequencer screen using traditional notation

5.4.2 Displaying Events on a Grid

The best alternative to displaying traditional musical notation is a grid or graph where time is the *x* axis and pitch the *y* axis. Notes are shown as horizontal bars whose length corresponds to their duration.

This type of screen, if drawn using text-mode graphics, is faster and less demanding on computer memory than that required for traditional notation. It does not however show as wide a range of pitches as the traditional method of using more than one stave. A treble and bass double stave gives a range of four to five octaves. A 25-line text screen can offer at best about two octaves, and even a 50-line screen in high-resolution mode can barely manage four.

Nevertheless, while there is no denying that traditional notation gives a clearer overview of a piece of music, a good grid-edit screen can be invaluable when it comes to seeing what is happening while, for instance, slightly retarding the entry of every alternate chord. The effect is like listening with one's eyes. It is also possible with a grid to correct velocities instantly.

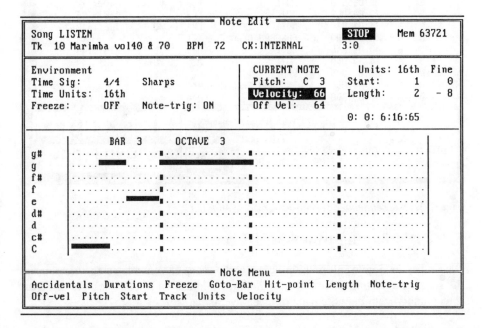

Figure 5.2: A sequencer screen using a grid

5.4.3 Displaying Events on a List

This is the least friendly way of presenting recorded information, and unfortunately the one adopted by many sequencers, especially those running on the cheaper computers. Events are listed on the screen, using four basic columns (though there are normally others). The first column displays elapsed MIDI time – bars, beats and clocks (ppqn) – the second displays the event type, the third the event value, and the fourth the event name (whether it is a Note On event, a Program Change, a Controller, or whatever).

The reason for the unfriendliness of this approach is that it gives no graphical representation of time. Time is just a number on the screen, and two adjacent

events on the screen can be as far from one another as a few bars or as close as at
the same time.

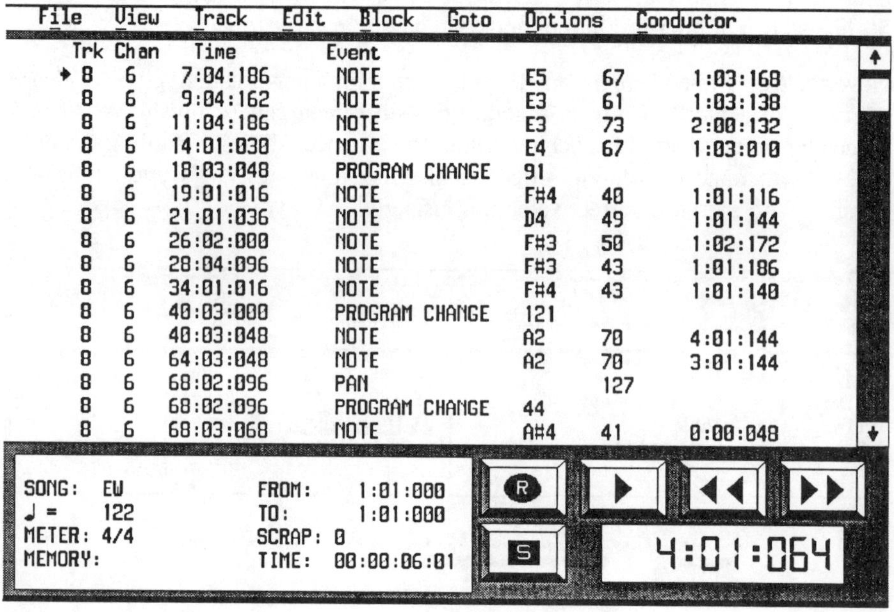

File	View	Track	Edit	Block	Goto	Options	Conductor	
Trk	Chan	Time	Event					▲
➜ 8	6	7:04:186	NOTE		E5	67	1:03:168	
8	6	9:04:162	NOTE		E3	61	1:03:138	
8	6	11:04:186	NOTE		E3	73	2:00:132	
8	6	14:01:030	NOTE		E4	67	1:03:010	
8	6	18:03:048	PROGRAM CHANGE		91			
8	6	19:01:016	NOTE		F#4	48	1:01:116	
8	6	21:01:036	NOTE		D4	49	1:01:144	
8	6	26:02:000	NOTE		F#3	58	1:02:172	
8	6	28:04:096	NOTE		F#3	43	1:01:186	
8	6	34:01:016	NOTE		F#4	43	1:01:140	
8	6	40:03:000	PROGRAM CHANGE		121			
8	6	40:03:048	NOTE		A2	78	4:01:144	
8	6	64:03:048	NOTE		A2	78	3:01:144	
8	6	68:02:096	PAN			127		
8	6	68:02:096	PROGRAM CHANGE		44			
8	6	68:03:068	NOTE		A#4	41	0:00:048	▼

SONG: EU	FROM: 1:01:000	ⓡ	▶	◀◀	▶▶
♩ = 122	TO: 1:01:000				
METER: 4/4	SCRAP: 0	Ⓢ		**4:01:064**	
MEMORY:	TIME: 00:00:06:01				

Figure 5.3: A sequencer screen using an events list

5.4.4 Displaying other MIDI data

Data other than note information is in nearly every case available for viewing on
the sequencer editing screen. It is sometimes found on a line at the bottom of the
screen underneath the note data, or as an events list.

5.4.5 Editing Individual Notes

Even the most experienced and talented instrumental players are capable of ruining
a performance, which would otherwise be immaculate, by playing a wrong note. It
is therefore important to be able to edit individual notes once the input to the
sequencer is complete.

Nearly all sequencers will allow this to be done, but when considering buying one,
high priority should be given to the presence of facilities for changing the pitch,
duration, start time and velocity of any note, as well as for inserting or deleting a
note using the computer keyboard, mouse or other input device.

5.4.6 Editing Individual MIDI Events

Being able to edit specific MIDI events is also important. A good sequencer will allow Program Change messages to be inserted or deleted so that sounds on a synthesiser or sound module can be altered at any point in a track. It should also be possible to insert, delete or change MIDI controllers at any point on a track so that parameters like volume, position in the stereo field, vibrato and so forth can be easily changed wherever the changes happen to be required.

Pitch-bend effects are a particular case in point, since they can be quite difficult to achieve successfully by an inexperienced instrumental player. A common error, for example, is to get the bending precisely as it is required, but to hold the fingers for too long on the control key. In this case, the Pitch Bend MIDI message will not end properly and will hang on to the next note, which of course will start bent, that is to say at the wrong pitch. For many people, it is therefore vital to be able to edit a Pitch Bend message and, where required, to insert a 0 value to set it to Off.

As a general rule, the more individual MIDI events which can be edited, the better.

5.4.7 Editing by Blocks

As well as being able to edit individual notes and events, and whole tracks, the ability to manipulate parts of the score containing a number of bars and a number of tracks is also useful. It should be possible to define a *block* (a section of music marked with a beginning and an end), and apply an editing function such as Cut, Copy, Transpose, or any other change or transformation which the programmers have been generous enough to include. The more such block-editing functions are used, the more indispensable they appear to become, and while it is common for beginners to think of them as advanced features which they can manage without, deficiencies very soon become annoying and the *if only* syndrome sets in.

Take the question of block definition itself. A beginner might well be satisfied with being able to define a block in terms of bars. Some sequencers, however, will allow the beginning and end of a block to be defined by finer time intervals, even by individual clocks. This is something which clearly gives more flexibility, but which may appear dispensable because it is possible, say, to move a block defined by bars, then adjust notes within those bars as required. The fact of the matter is that time and again it is necessary to split a bar when editing. Not to be able to do so can be very irritating, and irritation is not the best aid to creativity – except in the case of certain geniuses.

Insofar as it can be done, inexperienced users should therefore always be looking to the future in this way when assessing editing features on a sequencer, though of course these may have to be balanced off against other features. Only experience can determine precise requirements: no amount of the best advice available can be the perfect substitute for it. In the end, as with most activities, a beginner (and even an expert) should listen to advice, but has also to learn by mistakes.

5.5 Transforming MIDI Events

Transformation is not quite the same as editing. Editing is concerned basically with removing and adding, while transforming is concerned with making alterations to the performance information.

5.5.1 Pitch Transformations

These transformations change the pitch of notes in the recorded score. They can act over a section of a track, over a number of tracks or the entire piece.

Transpose

What is usually meant by a Transpose function in sequencers is the simple addition or subtraction of a given number of semitones to every note, regardless of the original key. Most sequencers include this feature, which is adequate for many purposes. However, for a proper musical transposition it represents too simple an approach, since manual adjustments have subsequently to be made in order to flatten or sharpen certain notes. A harmonic transposition function takes care of this problem.

Harmonic Transposition

Only advanced sequencers include this feature, which allows the overall pitch of a piece of music, or part of it, to be raised or lowered by a number of semitones, while keeping the same musical key. Depending on the sophistication of the sequencer, it may be possible to specify particular key changes, and even changes between musical modes as well as key signatures.

A simple illustration of harmonic transposition will clarify the way in which it works. Suppose you input the notes C and E, and ask for a transposition to the key of D minor. A straight transposition, raising the pitch by two semitones as is required from C to D, will produce the notes D and F#, the latter being two semitones higher than E. A harmonic transposition, on the other hand, will produce the notes D and F♮ , since in the key of D minor, the third note of the equivalent major key (F) is flattened by a semitone.

In addition, top-of-the-range sequencers will perform a check to ensure that by lowering or highering the pitch, the range of particular instruments is not exceeded.

Inversion/Harmonic Inversion

Inversion and harmonic inversion are other automatic functions which high-level sequencers provide in order to lighten the workload of the composer.

The term *inversion* as used in some sequencers does not have its normal musical connotations. As a standard musical term, inversion is used to indicate that the basic order of the notes of a chord have been changed. Here, however, it signifies a transformation of a sequence of notes to give its mirror image – the reflection of the note is the same distance in semitones as the original note is from a defined *pivot note*.

With straight inversion, the pivot note is selected and all music above this note is reflected below it, or vice versa. Harmonic inversion does the same but keeps the music in a specified key, working in the same way as harmonic transposition. Both are useful for rapidly creating accompaniment parts, because each note will harmonise with its inversion provided that the pivot note is acceptable (if not, it will in any case be rejected by the sequencer). To take an example of straight inversion, if the pivot note is C, and the original note is E above it, the inverted note will be G# below the pivot note. Given the same notes and a harmonic inversion, with a key signature of C major, the resulting inverted note will be an A and not a G#.

5.5.2 Other Transformations

Offset or Shift in Time

Only very basic sequencers at the lower end of the market will not include this function, which allows notes and other MIDI events to be shifted backwards or forwards in time. It is usually measured in divisions of a crotchet (quarter note).

It is used in a number of circumstances, typically if timing delay problems are being encountered because a slow sequencer, computer or synthesiser are being used, and a large number of tracks, but it can also be used creatively. It is very useful, for instance, for making a sound slightly thicker or creating echoes and delays. All that is required is to duplicate a track to another, then offset the copied track by a given time interval, depending on the effect desired. For thickening a sound, the interval will be short, of the order of a few ppqn. For echoes and delays it will be of the order of perhaps a semiquaver (16th note), though even semibreve (whole note) delays are not uncommon if the tempo is fast. For more on the subject of treating sounds in this way, see Chapter 9 Section 9.2.

In addition, offset can be used very subtly to alter the style of a piece of music, for example by sliding a snare-drum hit a few milliseconds ahead of or behind the beat. If ahead of the beat, the music sounds urgent and jazzy; if behind the beat, it sounds heavier or more laid-back.

Quantisation

Quantisation is the bad player's medicine, but it can also be a stimulant.

To *quantise* (*auto-correct*) means to round off notes to a nearest specified rhythmic value. For instance, the average player attempting to play four beats to the bar will place some beats slightly early and others slightly late, which is part of what gives music a human feel. But if the playing is so out of time as to sound incorrect, the notes can be quantised, that is to say shifted in time to the nearest specified value, say semiquavers (16th notes). In a nutshell, a Quantise function on a sequencer is very useful for players who have a problem with timing, and for those who do not but who require certain instruments to keep a very strict rhythm.

But quantisation can also be a compositional aid. It is possible, for example, to record a part, then try out different quantisation values, or to try two duplicate tracks with different quantisation values on each – one to demi-semiquavers (32nd notes), say, and the other to quaver (8th-note) triplets. The resulting poly-rhythms can be very interesting.

Extensive use of quantisation can nevertheless sometimes lead to mechanical music, so a number of recent sequencers include a function referred to as *humanising* or *random* quantisation. This allows a percentage value to be set, specifying how strict the computer is to be when it makes the quantisation transformation. It can work in one of two ways: either a percentage of the notes will be left unchanged, or they will all first be strictly quantised, then randomly adjusted by a small amount. The effect of each is slightly different, but in both cases the resultant sound is more natural than the very strict timing produced by straight quantisation.

Velocity changes

One of the commonest editing facilities required in a sequencer is the ability to alter the On velocities of notes in a recorded section or a track. Indeed, this is essential for assigning a different sound to music already recorded, the reason being that different sounds have different sensitivities to Note On velocity – recording a piece using a particular sound does not mean that the dynamics will remain the same when a different sound is assigned to that part. Changing Note On velocities, either by adding to or subtracting from their value, or by compressing or expanding their value by a specified factor, is the only way of adapting the dynamics of a score to match the velocity sensitivity of a new sound, unless the velocity sensitivity of the sound is edited in the synthesiser.

5.6 Graphs

Some sequencers will allow a range of events, such as Note On velocities, to be edited by graphical methods using a mouse. Instead of putting in individual values, or *min-max* (minima and maxima) ranges, the mouse is used to draw a graph on the screen and the computer fills in the values.

Graphical interfaces of this type boil down to a matter of taste. Those with some experience in using computers often prefer direct input to graphical representations, while beginners seem to handle graphical interfaces more confidently than direct input. But some old computer hands who have moved over to graphical interfaces now swear by them, and certain novices dislike them. The only advice for beginners which can be given here is to try before buying, and to be prepared for a change of mind.

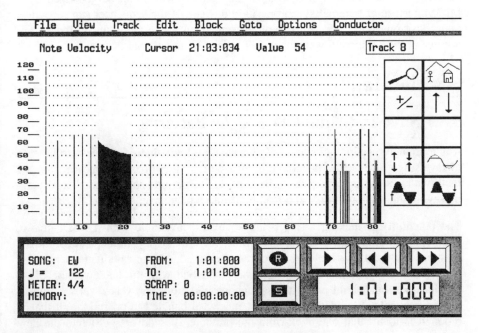

Figure 5.4: Using a graph to edit MIDI events

5.7 Tempo and Synchronisation

5.7.1 Tempo track

Many sequencers offer a dedicated tempo track – a track solely concerned with setting the speed of the music. Tempo is always a major consideration, and having such a track can make life considerably easier, since it allows accelerandos, ritardandos and jumps in the tempo to be set without having to examine tracks individually. It is especially useful to be able to change the tempo in fine time-increments rather than in steps of whole bars, and this is therefore a significant feature to take into account when choosing a sequencer.

5.7.2 External Synchronisation

It is also very important for a sequencer to be able to synchronise its performance with external devices such as tape recorders, so that acoustic instruments and human voices can be added, or music put to video or film.

There are different types of synchronisation, which are explained in detail in Chapter 4 Section 4.4.1, but the most important factor as far as sequencing is concerned is the question of Song Position Pointers which can be generated by a MIDI interface or external synchronisation devices. If the sequencer can recognise Song Position Pointers, it will be able to start playback at any point in the music, not just at the beginning, when acting as a slave to an external device.

5.8 File Handling

5.8.1 Save Individual Tracks or Patterns

It is extremely useful – in certain circumstances almost indispensable – to be able to save single tracks, and patterns in the case of a pattern-based sequencer. Such a facility allows tracks or patterns to be duplicated from one song to another, usually by saving the section to disk and reading it into a new song.

The potential for making music being so readily available with a MIDI studio, many people find that creating numerous versions of a single piece of music becomes almost a disease, with favourites being edited and re-edited for months, even years. Suppose that you are generally satisfied with the latest version of an arrangement, but would prefer the saxophone part from last year's version, which has been altered. Provided that the sequencer can handle the operation, all that is required is to lift that one track from the previous file and merge it into the new file.

More importantly, it should not be necessary to re-invent the wheel – MIDI is, or should be, there to make life as comfortable as possible for music-makers. Effects like timpani rolls, glissandos and trills can be very difficult to create realistically with synthesised instruments. Once a satisfactory effect has been achieved, it makes obvious sense to add it to a library of similar sounds, any of which can be inserted into new compositions as and when they are required. With the appropriate sequencer, it is a relatively simple matter to create such disk libraries.

5.8.2 Standard MIDI Files

In the early years of music programs for computers, each music software house had its own format for storing sequencer data. Soon came the need for transferring this data from one program to another: it needed to be transferred to music notation programs, two people using different sequencers needed to work on the same piece, a single composer wished to use two different sequencers because each had its advantages in specific circumstances. Such consumer demands led to the creation of a common format for storing sequencer data within the MIDI specification: standard MIDI files. The information stored in standard MIDI files includes performance data and track details, as well as any text, copyright notices and so forth.

In general, standard MIDI files store their information less efficiently than proprietary formats adopted in different makes of sequencer, something which held back their general acceptance for some time. They are now fairly widely implemented, having been approved by the MIDI Manufacturers Association at the end of 1988, though the effect of disagreements between software houses, and the different capabilities of sequencers, has resulted in there being three different formats:

Format 0. With this format, all data is combined into one track, and the original track numbers are lost. Thus, if a composition which uses all 16 MIDI channels takes up 30 tracks in sequencer A and is saved in Format 0, when this is loaded into sequencer B, the maximum number of tracks distinguishable (assuming that the sequencer has the ability to split tracks by MIDI channel number) will be 16.

Format 1. The original tracks are stored in separate areas of the file, each retaining its own number, though the tempo and time signature are always those of the first track.

Format 2. This is the same as Format 1, but each track can have its own tempo and time signature.

Most modern sequencers can handle standard MIDI files (any sequencer in price category C and above should be able to) but they vary in their ability to save and load particular formats. Format 2 is implemented in very few sequencers because it is not often required – a composition rarely has different tempi running on different tracks. The format is useful, however, for transferring drum machine patterns, which often do have different time signatures and tempi.

5.8.3 System-exclusive Information

The ability of a sequencer to record System-exclusive data is useful for storing the sound information of the instruments being used, together with the score itself. Via

System-exclusive messages, most MIDI instruments can dump (store) the data for a single sound, a bank of sounds, or their complete sound set-up. This can be recorded on an empty sequencer track or at a point just before the music begins, so that on playback the sound data will be sent to the instrument. The facility has an interesting knock-on effect:

Composers who write for acoustic instruments have always been limited in their ability to define a sound precisely. There is no doubt about the overall sound of a piano, but a Bechstein does have a different sound from that of a Steinway (this becomes clear when one is heard immediately after the other). The composer can specify variations in the way the instrument should be played, but not the exact timbre. With a synthesiser, things are different. A MIDI System-exclusive message can be used to store the exact timbre chosen by the composer.

Lovers of originality go to previously unheard of lengths in their attempts to recreate the sounds which composers of the past would themselves have heard as they listened to their compositions. Given a sequencer which allows instrument sounds and score to be saved together, the problem for future musicologists disappears. They may feel they have gained by this, though that of course assumes that they will be interested enough to search for the right instruments, or indeed want to re-create twentieth-century electronic music at all.

5.9 Other Sequencer Functions

5.9.1 Reverse in Time

This function will play a section of music backwards. It is of course interesting to experiment with the idea (among others, Mozart and the Beatles did so) but it is clearly not a crucial sequencer facility.

5.9.2 Arpeggios from Chords and Glissandos from Note Sequences

This function automatically converts chords to arpeggios, and creates glissando effects from a given note sequence. The relevant notes are defined together with the direction of the arpeggio or glissando (up or down) and the time interval for which it is to last. Some sequencers also allow the notes to be randomised.

5.9.3 Automatic Creation of Tremolos and Trills

Here, a note is defined, and the sequencer will split it into a selected number of notes of smaller duration, in other words allowing full control over the speed of a tremolo. The function is particularly useful for creating drum rolls.

For trills, the same process is used, except that two notes and the interval between them are also specified. Unfortunately, we know of no sequencer capable of creating trills which automatically increase in speed (note durations becoming smaller as the trill progresses) as expected in certain pieces of classical music. To accomplish such a trill, it is necessary to create a number of trills of decreasing note duration and add them together.

5.9.4 Notepads

Some sequencers provide on-screen notepads, even mini word processors, so that textual notes can be taken without leaving the software. If the sequencer works behind an interface which allows more than one application to be held in RAM, and providing of course that the computer has enough RAM left for another application when the sequencer is loaded, there is less need for a notepad facility within the sequencer itself. Even in this case, however, it can be useful to be able to bring up an electronic jotter at the touch of a key on the computer keyboard. In addition, an internal notepad can save textual notes inside the score, which is better than having two files.

5.9.5 Undo

An Undo function is a very handy utility. The last command given can be cancelled, and the screen is returned to the state the editing process was in before it was given. Not all sequencers offer this facility, but it is a big plus point, particularly for those whose fingers move faster than their minds. The ability to recall a track which has been deleted by accident after hours of work can seem miraculous.

5.10 Choice Checklist for Sequencers

The following are in our view the most important questions to bear in mind when buying a sequencer:

❏ Does it have an adequate number of tracks for its intended use?

❏ Is it pattern-based or linear-based, and which of the two methods suits the way you compose?

❏ Can blocks of music be moved around easily?

❏ Does it read Song Position Pointers?

❏ Does it have automatic Punch In/Out features?

❏ Does it allow editing at the level of individual MIDI events?

❑ How flexible is it when editing the Note On velocities of notes in a track? Can it expand or compress them?

❑ Does it allow MIDI events to be filtered out after recording?

❑ Does it allow MIDI events to be transformed in pitch and time?

❑ How good are its quantisation features?

❑ How fine is its clock resolution?

❑ Does it use graphical representations for editing purposes?

❑ Does it read and save using standard MIDI files, and which Formats are supported?

❑ Does it have an Undo feature?

5.11 Products

Sequencing software

Product	Producer/ Distributor	Computer(s)	Tracks	Price	Comments
Ballade	Dynaware	PC	9	C	For Roland MT-32 and CM range. EGA or VGA monitor required.
Bars and Pipes	Blue Ribbon	Am	64	C	Icon-based, using graphic Bakery display of pipes as an innovative way of displaying note sequences. Interfaces with AmigaVision (multimedia authoring tool)
Beyond	Dr T	Mac	64	C/D	32 MIDI channels.
Cakewalk	Twelve Tone Systems	PC	256	B/C	Editing features similar to Voyetra's SP4 series.
Cakewalk Professional	Twelve Tone Systems	PC	256	C/D C1:D	32 MIDI channels with Music Quest's MQX interface.
Cadenza	Big Noise	PC	64	C	32 MIDI channels with Music Software Quest's MQX interface. Excellent use of graphic editing of MIDI events. One of the best for the PC.
Creator	C-Lab	ST	64	D	96 MIDI channels, 384 ppqn. One of the best sequencers for the ST. See also Notator score editor (Chapter 12 Section 12.6)

Product	Producer/ Distributor	Computer(s)	Tracks	Price	Comments
Cubase	Steinberg Research	Mac, ST	64	E	16 Arrange windows, each with 64 tracks.
Cubeat	Steinberg Research	ST	32	D	As above but with 32 tracks perwindow.
Edit Track II	Hybrid Arts	ST	60	C	
- SMPTE Track II			60	E	Edit Track II, but with sophisticated synchronisation.
EZ Track Plus	Hybrid Arts	ST	20	B	Beginner level.
Genesis	Digital Music	PC	64	(TBA)	Runs under M/S Windows 3. Many pioneering features.
!Inspiration	Pandora	Archimedes	256	D/E	Full-featured, powerful, professional-level.
!nspire 1	Wild Rose Technology	PC	64	B	Good value – heavily reduced from original retail price.
KCS (Keyboard Controlled Sequencer)	Dr T	Am, ST	48	C	384 ppqn. Used on Madonna's 'Blonde Ambition' world tour.
KCS Level II	Dr T	Am, Mac, ST	48	D	As KCS, but with performance variations.
Master-Tracks	Passport				
- Jr		Mac, ST	64	B	240 ppqn.
- Pro		Am, Mac, PC, ST, Apple IIGS	64	D	As Jr but more features. 32 MIDI channels.
- Pro 4		Mac	64	D/E	Latest version with enhancements.
MIDI Studio	Ladbroke Computing	ST	20	A	New version (MIDI Studio Master) with 100 tracks (price category B) about to be released.
Music X	MicroIllusion	Am	250	C	Many extras including 16 x 16 MIDI patch bay, and four editors/librarians. Excellent value.
Performer	Mark of the Unicorn	Mac		D/E	Unlimited tracks, and Edit windows of several tracks open simultaneously.
Prism	Magnetic Music	PC	16	B	Good value.
Prodigy	The Digital Muse	ST	32	B	Starter version of Virtuoso.
ProMidi Studio System	Systems Design Associates	PC		E	Direct to disk sequencer. Number of tracks limited only by hard disk size. Uses its own interface.
Pro 24 III	Steinberg Research	ST	24	ST:B/C Am:D	Old industry standard.

Product	Producer/ Distributor	Computer(s)	Tracks	Price	Comments
Sequence	Yamaha	C1	400	–	Bundled with the C1. Many pioneering features, and one of the best ever produced.
Sequencer Plus Version 4	Voyetra	PC			Upgradable series.
- SP	Junior		64	B	Starter bundle with Voyetra interface is category C.
- SP4			500	C	Harmonic transpositions and inversions, universal librarian. Good value.
- SP4 Gold			1000+	D	Excellent. Some unique features.
Studio 24	ElectroMusic Research	Archi- medes	24	B	The only serious contender in sequencing software for the Archimedes.
Texture	Magnetic Music	PC	24	B/C	32 MIDI channels if used with Music Quest MQX interface, or 128 channels on C1. Used by Stevie Wonder.
Tiger Cub	Dr T	Am, ST	12	B	384 ppqn. Tiger (category B) is a graphic editor for use with any sequencer which can handle standard MIDI files.
Trackman II	Hollis Research	ST	32	C	
- System			32	C/D	With auxiliary MIDI interface for extra 16 MIDI channels, and programmable foot switch.
Trax	Passport	Am, Mac, PC, ST	64	B	240 ppqn.
UMI-4M	UMusic	BBC	16	C/D	Includes MIDI interface.
Virtuoso	The Digital Muse	ST	99	D	480 ppqn. Uses its own multi-tasking operating system.
Vision	Opcode	Mac	99	D/E	480 ppqn. Many excellent features. Used by Thomas Dolby.
- EZ Vision			16	B	Cut-down version.

Key

Am: Commodore Amiga
C1: Yamaha C1
Mac: Apple Macintosh
PC: IBM PC and compatibles
ST: Atari ST

Hardware sequencers

All disk drives for the following products are 3.5 inch. Timing resolution is 96 ppqn.

Producer/ model	Tracks	Notes	Disk	Price	Comments
Akai ASQ10	99	80,000	Y	F/G	Built-in SMPTE Reader/ Generator.
Cheetah MQ8	8	20,000	N	C/D	
Roland MC-300	4 + drums	25,000	Y	E/F	
- MC-500 MkII	8 + drums	100,000	Y	F/G	
Technics SY-MQ8	8	25,000	Y	D/E	Tape transport controls.

MIDI Instruments and other Input Devices

By input *in this chapter, we mean the action of entering a musical score or performance into a sequencer.*

Technology allowing, the MIDI market offers products wherever there is a demand, and even creates demand where only a latent desire may have previously existed. There is MIDI input equipment to suit almost every commercial need, and new methods of input appear with a frequency which is a clear indicator of both the volatility and the infancy of this market.

Such developments are of course welcome, but also complicate the musician's choice. There is a bewildering array of input devices, and for each type of device a substantial range of products. MIDI musical instruments, for instance, were originally restricted to keyboards. The current range of such keyboards is enormous, but now there are also MIDI guitars, MIDI wind instruments and MIDI string instruments. And for those whose only instrument is their own voice box, there are MIDI microphones and other devices for converting their voice into MIDI information, which can even then be used to play any MIDI instrument.

Most experienced musicians find it natural to input a performance into a sequencer by playing a musical instrument, whether keyboard or other. But even they may often turn to different input methods for specific purposes, methods such as direct input from a computer keyboard. Jean-Michel Jarre's specifically designed Laser Harp is a marvellous example of an instrument more intriguing to look at than it is to hear (today's audiences require imagery as well as sound). Jarre wears gloves with mirrors on the underside – these reflect the laser beams (the 'harp strings') back to a sensor, the length of the beam determining the pitch.

In this chapter we shall describe and discuss the various methods of input, and the devices which can be used for it, *though leaving aside for the time being the internal sound capabilities which such devices may possess – these are treated in Chapter 7.*

With any input device, especially those geared towards performance, the first consideration is always the variety of performance characteristics and nuances which the device is capable of translating into MIDI data. The more the better, and sound-producing features are not important in this context other than for monitoring the input. Far more important is how well the device will convert played dynamics, handle effects such vibrato, and generally convert as many as possible of the nuances of human playing into MIDI events. MIDI was originally conceived with keyboard synthesisers in mind, and they are still the most versatile input devices, but even they need to be checked for the scope of their MIDI implementation.

Therefore, before buying any MIDI input device, the MIDI Implementation Chart contained at the end of the user manual of such equipment should be consulted, in order to check which types of MIDI messages can be transmitted (see Figure 6.6 for a general example of a good Implementation Chart for MIDI input devices).

6.1 Computer Keyboard

Most sequencers and many score editing programs have facilities for entering MIDI note information directly from the computer keyboard or using a mouse. Entering notes in this way of course requires no playing skills whatsoever.

Typically, the cursor is moved to the desired position on a musical stave, or a grid of pitches, and a note is inserted, usually by pressing a key such as the Return key. Some programs, however, re-define the computer keyboard so that 12 keys are used like a musical keyboard to make up an octave, while two other keys are used to move up or down an octave. In other programs, the normal alphabetic keys (A, B, C and so on) are used. For each note entered, at least a duration and loudness (Note-On velocity) has to be specified, though most programs of this variety use a default value if no other value is entered manually.

Entering music using this method can be convenient when, for instance, a portable computer is being used while travelling, though doing so is really only for musicians capable of writing down music on paper while hearing the sounds in their heads as opposed to playing them on an instrument.

In any case, this kind of input is riddled with difficulties for most musicians, not least because expression is something which usually has to be played rather than thought out. Using numbers, something which most programs in this category require, it is really quite difficult to define interpretational deviations from the raw notes of a tune, even simple deviations such as those of timing and loudness. It can take months of practice, if not years, to establish perfect relationships in the mind between numbers and actual sound. It is similar to learning the exact tension required of your vocal chords to produce a given note at precisely the right pitch, without wavering or having just heard another note which can be used as a reference. Not impossible, and even easy for some people, but difficult for most mortals.

6.2 MIDI Keyboards

A MIDI Out socket is the only absolute requirement for a musical keyboard intended to be used for MIDI. Indeed, many composers use a keyboard which will not generate any sound itself but which is connected to a sound module. Of course, it is even possible to play a synthesiser without hearing any sound, the notes being sent directly into a sequencer, and with step-time input this option is not out of the question. Few people, however, find playing a silent keyboard silently a satisfactory input solution, whether in real or step time.

Keyboards without sound are called *controller keyboards* (or occasionally *master keyboards* or *mother keyboards*). They may be dumb in the literal sense, but are not necessarily any less smart when it comes to MIDI than keyboards with internal sound generators. In fact, not all that long ago it would have been true to say that silent keyboards dedicated to MIDI generally had better MIDI implementations than those with internal sound, but that is no longer the case. It now all depends on the price, the make, and how recent is the design of the equipment. In general, the cheaper controller keyboards do not offer a very wide range of functions, and if £300 or more is going to be spent on a keyboard, yesterday's higher-range model with sound is probably a better bet.

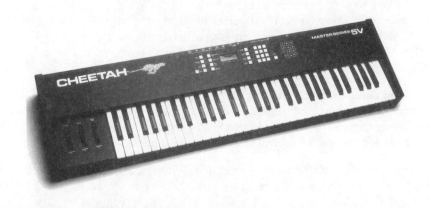

Figure 6.1: The Cheetah 5V controller keyboard

6.2.1 Facilities on MIDI Keyboards

Note On velocity sensitivity

All good keyboards have velocity-sensitive keys. The strike velocity is measured as a key is pressed, and the information is converted into a number between 0 and 127 which is sent to the computer after the Note On MIDI message. In this way, the dynamic is recorded with the note. Without this feature, all notes are recorded at the same dynamic level.

Some keyboards have only one interpretation of velocity sensitivity, while others allow a degree of control by offering different *velocity curves*. A velocity curve is the relationship between the velocity with which a key is hit, and the value of the Note On Velocity message which is sent – in other words it is the graph of points plotted using for one axis the velocity with which a key is hit, and for the other axis the value sent. A value of 0 is the lowest sensitivity of the key, and 127 is the maximum beyond which the key still sends the highest value.

Note Off velocity sensitivity

The Note Off velocity is the speed with which a key is released, and it therefore controls the cut-off characteristics of a note. Few keyboards – the expensive ones – incorporate this feature. It is certainly something worth having but, unless you are a professional, it is also something you can easily live without, since Note Off velocity is not as critical as Note On velocity, and it can of course be adjusted later on a sequencer. In any case, many sound modules do not have this feature, so even if it is recorded, it may not be possible to hear it. Keyboards which are not sensitive to Note Off velocity send the MIDI default value of 64.

Program Change

MIDI Program Change messages can often be triggered on a keyboard by buttons or dials on the top panel, and most synthesisers and keyboard controllers are equipped to handle them directly in this way. It is useful to be able to send Program Change messages by simply pushing a button, but once again this is not an essential feature even though it is a common one: adding such messages via a sequencer is a relatively trivial matter (unless the sequencer is question really needs to be thrown away).

Pitch Bend

A pitch bend wheel on a synthesiser is a very useful feature. By turning the wheel while holding down a key, the pitch of a note can be bent upwards or downwards depending on how far the wheel is turned and at what speed. Bending can be chromatic, that is to say in distinguishable semitone steps, or as a continuous glide.

Any keyboard priced above the top end of price category C should offer this feature.

Modulation

All keyboards except those we would categorise as toys have a modulation control, which usually sends vibrato or tremolo information. It may be in the form of a wheel or a joystick, though the term *modulation wheel* is often used generically to indicate modulation.

User-definable wheels

A user-definable wheel, found on some keyboards, is one which can be set to various parameters such as portamento, tremolo, or other Controller messages.

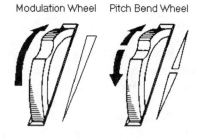

Modulation Wheel   Pitch Bend Wheel

Figure 6.2: Modulation and pitch-bend wheels on a synthesiser keyboard.

Aftertouch

Aftertouch – the amount of pressure exerted on a key after the initial strike – is a mid-range feature on keyboards and, if finances allow, it is preferable to opt for one which can handle it directly.

Aftertouch is a keyboard feature not found on acoustic pianos. When a key is pressed on a piano, the result is that a hammer hits a string or strings, and the note sounds until the key is released and the strings automatically damped by a felt pad, or (if the sustain pedal is pressed) until the note dies away. In other words, after the initial strike, the quality of a note cannot be altered except by controlling the release of the key. It achieves nothing to press the key harder after it has been struck.

On a synthesiser keyboard, matters can be far more flexible, since hammers are not involved. Electronic aftertouch sensors, if the keyboard is equipped with them, can sense changes in pressure after the initial strike of the key. For instance, alternating between an increase and a decrease in pressure can produce a vibrato effect. But MIDI Aftertouch messages can be set to control any number of parameters, from portamento and tremolo, to those which completely change the texture of the sound.

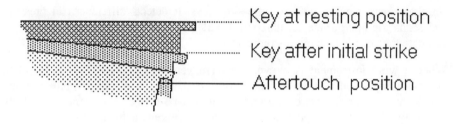

Key at resting position

Key after initial strike

Aftertouch position

Figure 6.3: Aftertouch

The most common form of aftertouch is channel or monophonic. With this, a common sensor underneath the keys gives a measure of the overall pressure. Polyphonic aftertouch is a rarer feature found only on professional-level keyboards. Here, a pressure sensor underneath each key sends a separate value for each keystroke. Thus, when playing a chord and applying different pressures with each finger, each note is treated separately.

Split keyboard

This fairly common feature gives the ability to define one or more points on the keyboard where a logical division can be implemented, with each group of keys assigned to a different MIDI channel. For instance, it is not unusual to have the keyboard split into two, so that the left hand can control one voice and the right hand another.

Local On/Off

With synthesiser keyboards (keyboards which can also produce sound), this function separates the keyboard section from its sound-producing circuitry. Thus, what is played on the keyboard is sent to the MIDI Out socket, while the sound-producing part of the synthesiser is controlled by an external source through the MIDI In socket. It is therefore possible to have the synthesiser's sound-producing section play a part coming from a sequencer while the keyboard is controlling a sound module, or being used to record an additional part in the sequencer.

The feature is found only on the newer mid- to professional-range multi-timbral synthesiser keyboards.

Breath controller socket

This is a socket for attaching an external breath controller accessory. A breath controller is a mouthpiece, with a sensor, into which you blow while simultaneously playing notes by pressing keys. It detects differences in pressure and sends the appropriate breath-control MIDI data to the synthesiser in order to simulate the sounds of wind instruments.

When a wind instrument is blown, there are very subtle modifications in pitch, volume, vibrato and tremolo which are due to changes in diaphragm pressure and embouchure (the tightness of the lips and the shape of the mouth and jaw). They are very difficult to synthesise accurately without actually blowing, so a mechanism attached to the synthesiser which lets you blow as you play the keyboard with your fingers can be very useful. South American Pan flutes, for example, can be very successfully synthesised with the process.

Breath controllers themselves are comparatively inexpensive accessories, though the keyboards with which they work tend to be in the higher price bracket (many Yamaha synthesisers, however, have a breath controller socket). An alternative is a dedicated MIDI wind controller, which is a multi-purpose wind instrument (see Section 6.5 below).

Foot pedals

Foot pedals used to turn Sustain on and off, and those used to vary the volume or any other MIDI parameter, are important for live performances. They can be bought as accessories, and most decent keyboards have a socket for them (why they are not given away free with all keyboards is beyond us).

On some of the earliest electronic organs, volume was controlled by a foot pedal, and it gave them a very distinctive sound, since the foot is not as sensitive as the fingers, and gross changes in volume together with too many changes were (and often still are) the result. On MIDI keyboards, too, foot pedals controlling volume have to be used with care.

6.2.2 Other Characteristics of MIDI Keyboards

Keys

Two sizes of key are generally available: mini and full size. Except for people with exceptionally small fingers, full-size keys are a must for real-time recording. On the other hand, for some people who are not keyboard players and do not wish to learn keyboard skills (which means that performances will be entered in step time) mini keys may be sufficient, though most keyboards with mini keys are not velocity sensitive.

Keyboards with weighted-action keys give (more or less) the feel of keys on an acoustic piano.

Note range

There should be a minimum of four octaves, and even this is sometimes too small a range. Most drum machines, and drum kits found on synthesiser keyboards, and some sound modules offering percussive sounds, use standard settings in which each sound is allocated to a different note on the keyboard. If a drum machine or sound module offers 64 percussive sounds, a four-octave keyboard with only 48 keys will simply not be able to play them all. With keyboards which do not offer a wide octave-range, a facility for switching playing to one or two octaves up or down is very important.

6.2.3 Choice Checklist for Keyboards

The following points should be borne in mind when considering a MIDI keyboard from the point of view of input:

❑ Velocity sensitivity

❑ The available built-in expression (through aftertouch, pitch bend, and so on)

❑ The number of keys

❑ The size of the keys

❑ The feel of the keys (weighted or not)

❑ The availability of additional expression through the use of accessories such as foot pedals and breath controllers

❑ The ability to set the Transmit MIDI channel to any of the 16 available, and to split the keyboard

❑ In keyboards with sound, a Local On/Off feature.

For controller keyboard products, see below Section 6.11.

6.3 MIDI Guitars

In the 1950s the electric guitar became the cornerstone of Rock n' Roll, and has since played a vital role in popular music. Not surprising, then, that given the pop-music orientation of MIDI, the guitar should be a natural target for manufacturers of musical instruments.

There are two types of MIDI guitar:

❏ At the lower end of the market, they are sound-producing synthesisers, but guitar-shaped and with notes triggered by guitar-string mechanics rather than keyboard keys. Really cheap guitars of this kind offer nothing more than MIDI Note On.

❏ At the middle and top end, they are electric guitars with various kinds of microphone pick-up designed to decipher nuances of guitar playing and convert them to MIDI messages. Such guitars have a normal guitar audio output, as well as a MIDI output which can drive external sound devices. Some expensive ones have special internal or external sound devices (guitar synthesiser modules) with matching MIDI implementation, for producing both guitar sounds and non-guitar sounds with guitar nuances of expression. If you have never heard a flute played like a guitar, the experience can be an ear-opener. And, of course, MIDI guitars are not restricted to the six-string variety: four-string MIDI bass guitars are also available.

Since many MIDI guitars are nothing more than ordinary electric guitars which can transmit MIDI data, an alternative to a dedicated MIDI guitar controller is a special Pitch-to-MIDI converter (see below Section 6.7). This can be attached with a microphone or a guitar pick-up to an electric or acoustic guitar, and the results can be quite satisfactory. Many guitarists, however, prefer to use a dedicated MIDI guitar for their MIDI work because it offers more flexibility.

However, there can also be difficulties with MIDI guitars. Experienced guitarists are likely to find that the response is not as fast as the response they are used to, and particularly with fast strumming, the result can be confusion. They also have a tendency to reproduce the higher *harmonics* of a note (overtones which give a sound its timbre – see Chapter 8 Section 8.6), sometimes producing in the lower registers a MIDI note which is an octave higher than the one intended. But they can be very good for monophonic (single-string) lead guitar playing, especially those in the mid and higher price range.

MIDI guitars range from the comparatively cheap Casio DG-20 (price category B) to complete professional guitar systems from Yamaha (the G10 with its sound module the G10C in price category F), Roland (the GR-50 with its sound module the GK-2, again in price category F) and Korg (the ZD3 with its sound module the ZD3, originally in price category G but now available in price category E).

Casio dominates the middle range with the MG-510, the PG-310 and PG-380. The latest (1991) model, the only one in production, is the PG-300 (price category E/F). This has an ordinary electric guitar output, and includes a synthesiser module (the VZ1) for extra sound production.

6.3.1 Choice Checklist for MIDI Guitars

In selecting a MIDI guitar, the following basic criteria should be borne in mind:

❏ The ability to use different MIDI channels so that each string can send information separately (pitch bend, for example)

❏ The ability to pick up velocity, that is to say how hard the string is plucked or stroked

❏ The ability to pick up pitch bend when the string is pulled with (normally) the left hand

❏ The speed of response to playing, especially with chord sequences

❏ The accuracy with which pitch is interpreted

❏ The actual guitar sound, since it may be played as a straight guitar.

6.4 Wind Controllers

Figure 6.4: Casio Digital Horn

Most digital wind controllers are general-purpose MIDI wind instruments – saxophone, oboe, trumpet and so on, all in one. Such a configuration often seems strange to trained wind players because wind instruments, apart from the common denominator of being blown, differ fundamentally from each other. Quite apart from the differences between brass instruments (sounded by vibrating the lips), reed instruments (sounded by vibrating a reed), flute-like instruments (sounded by blowing over a hole) and whistle-like instruments (sounded by blowing through a mouthpiece with a hole in it), wind players also perceive a basic distinction between, for example, a double-reed instrument such as the bassoon, and a single-reed instrument such as the clarinet.

But that common denominator of being blown, as opposed to being scraped or banged, is something which characterises the sound made by wind instruments, in that the breath is controllable only within certain limits. Listen to a melody line played on a keyboard synthesiser set to a trumpet sound, then listen to a real trumpet playing the same melody. No matter how complex the simulation of the sound in terms of its texture and the attack, sustain, decay and release of each note, there is a special quality about the real thing which comes from it actually being blown. A MIDI wind controller gets closer to the real sound than a synthesiser keyboard, unless it has a breath-control accessory fitted (even then, some wind players maintain that it is harder to produce a realistic sound with such an accessory as opposed to a wind controller).

The choice of MIDI wind controllers is comparatively limited:

❏ Casio's Digital Horn comes in three models: the DH-100 (price category B), DH-500 (in price category C, and the only one still in production) and DH-800 (price category C). All are breath-sensitive, all have built-in speakers, and offer a minimum of six pre-set sounds: saxophone, trumpet, synth-reed, oboe, clarinet and flute.

❏ Yamaha's WX7 and WX11 wind controllers are slightly more expensive than Casio's Horns, and are more serious pieces of hardware with very flexible MIDI implementations. They do not have on-board sound. The WX7 can work well with the Yamaha TX81Z sound module which accepts Breath Controller messages, and the WX11 also has its own special sound module, the WT11.

❏ The two Akai wind controllers are the most versatile in their range and MIDI implementation. The EVI 1000 Electric Valve Instrument and the EWI 1000 Electric Woodwind Instrument (both in price category D) are again silent. They have a range of over seven octaves, and accurate breath and lip sensors. The valve instrument uses a standard three valve fingering, like that of a trumpet. The woodwind instrument has basic saxophone fingering. The EWV 2000 sound module (price category C) for either (or both) of these instruments contains two monophonic synthesisers.

6.5 MIDI Drums

MIDI drums are played in exactly the same way as ordinary drums, though drummers often complain about a lack of skin response. As with MIDI guitars, there is a technique to be mastered.

The equipment consists either of a rectangular flat rubber area with pads which are hit with drum sticks, or a full-blown drum kit with each drum having a pad. Each of the pads triggers a MIDI note, and signals how hard it has been hit. The resulting MIDI messages are sent to a sound-producing device, which can be synthesiser, sound module or drum machine (see Chapter 7 Section 7.2.1). When the MIDI data is sent to a sequencer or a sound module, there is nothing in principle to prevent the notes being played as any instrument sound of which the synthesiser or sound module is capable, although the normal sound required would be percussive.

One of the best known drum pads is the Roland Octapad, which exists in various models (PAD-8, PAD-80 and so on, in price category E). They are stand-alone drum-pad units, split into 8 sections, as the name suggests. The latest version (SPD-8) also contains 39 built-in percussive sounds.

A cheaper version, without sound, is made by BOSS: the MPD-4 MIDI Pad (price category B/C). This can can control four external MIDI sounds, and has an additional three inputs for connecting external pads, giving a possible total of seven sounds.

Hand-hit MIDI drums are also available. The Roland PAD-5 Handypad (price category C) is specially designed for hand playing. It has five pads, and incorporates 14 pre-set rhythm patterns.

MIDI drum kits can also be bought as separate modules so that a system can be built up as required. The Casio DZ series is one such system. It consists of two types of pads – the DZ-20s (snare/tom-tom) and the DZ-30b (bass drum), both in price category B – a controller, and a Pad-to-MIDI converter (the DZ-1, in price category C). The latter can handle up to eight pads, so various combinations within this limit can be made up.

A more expensive system from Roland consists of the PM-16 Pad-to-MIDI converter (price category E), and three types of pads: the PD-11 (bass, in price category C), the PD-21 (snare/tom-tom, in price category B) and the PD-31 (Snare/tom-tom with four triggers, also in price category B). A frame stand system for the full kit (the MDS-2) is also available (price category C/D).

A complete drum-kit controller system comes from Cheetah, the DP5. This has five electronic pads with a stand, and in price category B/C represents excellent value for money. Units can also be bought separately.

Figure 6.5: The Roland PAD-5 Handypad

6.6 Alternative Instruments

In the MIDI Instrument Popularity League Table, and therefore in availability, keyboards are Number 1, drums 2, guitars 3, wind instruments 4, and trailing up the rear are so-called alternative controllers, such as MIDI violins. The idea that the string family is considered to be made up of fringe instruments may seem strange to the musician brought up on a diet of classical music in which the strings are supreme, but MIDI has always been heavily oriented towards the world of pop music, and a massed string sound can in any case be produced on a synthesiser keyboard. The single sound of a violin can also be synthesised, but of course it is very difficult, if not impossible, to simulate the precise sound of horsehair being drawn across catgut and steel. For this reason, there are a number of little-used MIDI instruments which provide what in MIDI terms are considered specialised sounds, string instruments being the prime example.

MIDI violins are rare but can be obtained in the USA, the best known one probably being the EV-5 from Barrett, which has the shape of a violin but with the entire sound-box missing. A real double-bass feel can be had from strange-looking objects called *fingerboard controllers* which are held like their acoustic equivalents. In some cases they offer a variety of alternative string tunings by having separate banks of them across the fingerboard, an example being The Stick from Stick Enterprises, again available only from the USA.

Farfisa offers a number of accordions with MIDI capabilities. A typical product is the MX12 (price category H) which has 41 keys, 120 basses, four canto voices, five bass voices, seven canto registers, seven bass registers. Hohner has two ranges: MIDI acoustic (price categories G to H), and MIDI electronic (about £5,000 to about £6,500).

Roland has recently released its PK-5 Dynamic MIDI Pedal (price category D). This is used to play bass lines with the feet – as is done with the bass pedals found on organs – but the PK-5 will work with any MIDI instrument. It has a 13-key pedal board and 13 levels of velocity sensitivity. It can handle Controller messages and has functions for controlling specific parameters on a number of modern Roland pieces of equipment such as the D-series synthesisers and sound modules (see Chapter 7 Section 7.7) and the Roland Intelligent Arranger (see Chapter 11 Section 11.2).

6.7 Pitch-to-MIDI Converters

These input devices are dedicated to picking up a sound, determining its pitch, and converting the information to a MIDI note. MIDI instruments such as wind controllers have one built in, but they can be bought separately for capturing the pitch of notes from acoustic instruments and the human voice. Some also have limited facilities for sending other MIDI messages.

Input of sounds into these converters can be direct, as when an ordinary electric guitar is plugged into one, or indirect by using a microphone. An orchestration can be built up by singing or playing parts separately, and letting the computer put them together.

When considering microphones and their use within MIDI, it is important to distinguish between those which capture the pitch of notes in this way, and those which are used for recording natural instruments and the human voice, either for adding to a MIDI score in analogue form, or for sampling. The latter are dealt with in Chapter 10 Section 10.1.

A Pitch-to-MIDI converter can be a box with sockets for a microphone and other inputs, or it can be enclosed in a (rather large) microphone. Those which come as a box usually have their own microphones which are not normally of very high quality.

Two products worth noting are:

(a) MIDI Mike by Digigram (price category C) which looks like a tall ice-cream cone, and allows non-MIDI instruments, such as electric guitars or old synthesisers, to be plugged in. It converts pitch to MIDI data in semitone steps or continuously, and has a range of four octaves.

(b) The Roland CP-40 (price category C) which is a box with microphone and guitar inputs, and will convert pitch to MIDI data from voice, brass and string instruments, or guitar monophonic sounds. It is also capable of implementing dynamics, pitch bend and tremolo, and has its own external microphone.

6.8 Data Entry Pads

These are special pads intended for facilitating the entry of notes. Typically, they have a couple of octaves of keys marked A to G, plus accidentals, octave up and down, aftertouch, hold, and so on. An example is the Roland CN-20 Music Entry Pad (price category B).

6.9 Digital Faders

Synthesiser keyboards have a volume control, but this does not necessarily send volume messages to a sequencer. A digital fader accomplishes this by allowing Controller number 7 (channel volume) information to be mixed with note information produced on a sequencer. The sequence is first recorded on, say, tracks 1 to 10; the sequencer plays back, and at the same time records volume messages on tracks 11 to 20; then tracks 1 to 20 are assigned to MIDI channels 1 to 10, so that on playback, the music on tracks 1 to 10 are affected by the volume messages on tracks 11 to 20.

Roland's CF-10 (price category B) will send both amplitude and panning messages on 10 channels. J.L. Cooper's Fader Master (price category D) also allows pitch bend, aftertouch, program change, note in, and continuous controllers to be assigned to eight faders and manipulated in real time.

6.10 MIDI Implementation Chart for Input Devices

A MIDI Implementation Chart, to be found at the end of the documentation accompanying MIDI devices, lists all the MIDI messages which the equipment is capable of transmitting and receiving. The Transmit column of a good Chart for input devices should look like the one in Figure 6.6 (see also Chapter 7 Section 7.5.1).

Notice that the Chart is divided into four columns. The left column lists the types of MIDI messages by name; the next two indicate whether the equipment will transmit or receive such messages; and the last column is reserved for any comments the manufacturer may wish to make. The standard way of denoting whether a feature is or is not implemented is a circle (o) for Yes and a cross (x) for No.

```
     [MIDI Master Input Device]                        Date:1-1-1991
       Model  SIGMA-1      MIDI Implementation Chart    Version 1.0
+-----------------------------------------------------------------------+
:                         : Transmitted  : Recognized  :    Remarks     :
:          Function...    :              :             :                :
:-------------------------+--------------+-------------+----------------:
:Basic     Default        : 1 - 16       :             : Memorised      :
:Channel   Channel        : 1 - 16       :             :                :
:-------------------------+--------------+-------------+----------------:
:          Default        : 3            :             :                :
:Mode      Messages       :              :             :                :
:          Altered        : **************:            :                :
:-------------------------+--------------+-------------+----------------:
:Note                     : 1 - 127      :             :                :
:Number    True Voice     : **************:            :                :
:-------------------------+--------------+-------------+----------------:
:Velocity Note ON         : o 9nH, v=1-127:            :                :
:         Note OFF        : x 9nH, v=0   :             :                :
:-------------------------+--------------+-------------+----------------:
:After     Key's          : x            :             :                :
:Touch                    : o            :             :                :
:-------------------------+--------------+-------------+----------------:
:Pitch Bender             : o            :             :                :
:-------------------------+--------------+-------------+----------------+
:                         : o            :             :                :
:  Control                :              :             :                :
:  Change                 :              :             :                :
:  0 - 121                :              :             :                :
:                         :              :             :                :
:-------------------------+--------------+-------------+----------------:
:Prog                     : o 0 - 127    :             :                :
:Change   : True #        :              :             :                :
:-------------------------+--------------+-------------+----------------:
:System Exclusive         : o            :             : Memory Data    :
:-------------------------+--------------+-------------+----------------:
:System   : Song Pos      : x            :             :                :
:         : Song Sel      : x            :             :                :
:Common   : Tune          : o            :             :                :
:-------------------------+--------------+-------------+----------------:
:System    :Clock         : x            :             :                :
:Real Time  :Commands     : x            :             :                :
:-------------------------+--------------+-------------+----------------:
:Aux  :Local ON/OFF       : o            :             :                :
:     :All Notes OFF      : o            :             :                :
:Mes- :Active Sensing     : o            :             :                :
:sages:Reset              : o            :             :                :
:-------------------------+--------------+-------------+----------------:
:Notes:     System exclusive details are not given on this table       :
:           They are given elsewhere in the equipment's manual.         :
+-----------------------------------------------------------------------+
Mode 1 : OMNI ON,  POLY    Mode 2 : OMNI ON,  MONO         o:Yes
Mode 3 : OMNI OFF, POLY    Mode 4 : OMNI OFF, MONO         x:No
```

Figure 6.6: MIDI Implementation Chart showing desirable transmit features for MIDI input devices

6.11 Products

Silent (controller) keyboards

For keyboards with sound see Chapter 7 Section 7.7. See also Chapter 11 Section 11.4.

All models listed here are velocity-sensitive and fully polyphonic. A circle (o) indicates that the feature is implemented.

Producer/model	Number of keys	Weighted keys	Channel aftertouch	Polyphonic aftertouch	MIDI merge	MIDI clock	Note Off velocity	No of velocity curves	Price
Akai MX-76	76	o	o		o	o		8	G
Cheetah MS7P	88	o	o		o	o		16	F
- V5	61	o					o	16	D
Elka MK55	61	o	o	o	o	o	o	19	E
- MK88	88	o	o	o	o	o	o	19	G
Kawai M-8000	88	o				o	o	4	G
Roland A-50	76	o	o	o	o			7	G
- A-80	88	o	o		o	o	o	7	G
Yamaha KX88	88	o	o		o	o	o	1	G

7

MIDI Output

Future historians of music will almost certainly categorise the twentieth century's contribution to the history of popular musical instruments into three: (1) the drum kit (2) the electric guitar (3) the electronic keyboard.

The order in not insignificant. Historically, it is the one in which their use spread among musicians, and from an evolutionary point of view it represents a trend from the acoustic to the electronic. Drums require a drummer, but the sound they make emerges from them in its natural state. An electric guitar falls somewhere in the middle in that it can produce an acoustic sound, but one which requires electrical amplification. A synthesising device such as a keyboard synthesiser is incapable of musical sound unless it incorporates or is connected to a loud-speaker.

7.1 Sound Synthesis

Sound can exist only in a physical form, as vibrations in air (or some other medium such as water). But it can be represented electronically in signals which can have two forms: analogue or digital. Analogue signals are often varying electrical currents, and digital signals exist as numbers or pulses. During its creation and manipulation in synthesising and recording equipment, sound is often converted from one of these three forms to another.

A microphone is an example of a device which converts acoustic sound into electrical analogue sound. A loudspeaker is an example of a device which does the opposite. As mentioned in Chapter 1, any device which converts an analogue electrical sound signal into a digital sound signal is called an Analogue to Digital (A/D) converter. One which converts a digital sound signal to an analogue sound signal is a Digital to Analogue (D/A) converter. Many MIDI devices have one of them, and some have both.

The reason why synthesising devices do not produce natural sounds is that there is a qualitative difference between the way in which they handle the process of sound production, and the way it is produced on acoustic instruments. Synthesising devices produce synthetic as opposed to natural sounds. Acoustic sound is life. Synthesised sound is a portrait of life, or an abstract painting.

To be able to paint a good picture, certain concepts have to be understood, concepts such as the relationships between colours, and spatial considerations such as perspective. Similarly, to be able to use synthesising devices to create new sounds or fine-tune existing ones, it is necessary to understand something of the elements which make up a sound. Even for those who will never wish to create new sounds, it is useful to understand a little about how a synthesising device works, and how it differs from an acoustic instrument.

With acoustic instruments, the player causes a physical object to vibrate: a violin string, a bassoon reed, a drum membrane, a vocal chord, whatever. In turn, these objects transfer their vibrations to the air, through which they travel like waves in a pool, before they reach our ears. The texture associated with the sound depends on the physical shape of the instrument, the material of which it is made, and the method used by the player to create the vibration. Hitting something makes a certain type of sound, rubbing something against something else makes another, blowing air into or across a hollow object makes another.

Acoustic instruments are therefore sometimes classified according to the methods used by those who play them to create sound. A harpsichord looks like a piano but can be classed with a guitar because its strings are plucked, not hit. The xylophone is often classed with drums as a percussive instrument, even though the basic layout of its keys is that of the piano – indeed, classical percussionists are expected to reach high levels of proficiency in playing such piano-like instruments as well as drums, cymbals and other percussive devices. Although the textures of the sounds produced by these families of instruments are very different from one another, there are similarities in the overall shape of those sounds. Most percussive instruments, whether glockenspiel, triangle or kettle drum, produce a sound which in terms of loudness starts sharply and reaches a peak very rapidly. Compare that with the sound of a flute, which tends to start slowly and take a comparatively long time to reach a peak.

7.1.2 Envelopes

The way in which the loudness of a musical sound develops in relation to time is called its *envelope*. An envelope begins at the moment of silence just before the sound is triggered, and ends at the moment of silence just after the sound dies out. Figure 7.1 shows examples of envelopes represented as graphs, where the vertical axis is loudness (volume or, in technical terms, *amplitude*) and the horizontal axis is time.

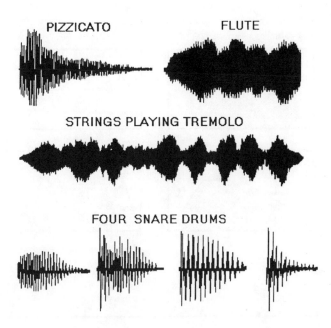

Figure 7.1: Natural envelopes

As can be seen, sound envelopes are not made of straight lines – they are usually rather complicated but nevertheless continuous shapes. Straight-line approximations, however, are generally used to simplify them in synthesiser sound definitions (see Figure 7.2). The straight lines represent:

Attack. This is the time taken for the sound to reach its peak value. It is measured as a rate of change, so a sound can have a slow or a fast attack.

Decay. This indicates the rate at which a sound loses amplitude after the attack. Decay is also measured as a rate of change, so a sound can have a fast or slow decay.

Sustain. The Sustain level is the level of amplitude to which the sound falls after decaying. The Sustain time is the amount of time spent by the sound at the Sustain level.

Release. This is time taken by the sound to die out. It is measured as a rate of change, so a sound can have a fast or slow release.

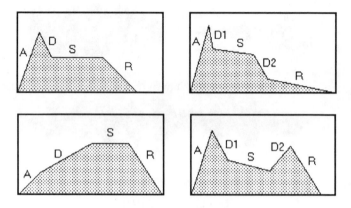

Figure 7.2: ADSR envelopes

The above measurements are usually referred to as *ADSR* (Attack, Decay, Sustain, Release) and a sound envelope is sometimes called an ADSR envelope.

It is clear, when measured in this way, why there is a distinct resemblance between the envelopes of (say) instruments which are all in some way hit, such as a piano, a xylophone or a drum, even though the textures of their sounds are entirely different. It is like icing a cake: whatever icing material is used to fill the icing bag, the shape of the decoration is determined by the shape of the nozzle, while the contents of the bag determine the taste and texture.

Similarly, the material characteristics of an instrument's vibrating parts create the sound waves which determine the texture and envelope of the sound. Two violins of precisely the same shape but made from different types of wood will produce sounds with differences in texture. A guitar will produce a different sound texture if fitted with nylon as opposed to metal strings.

7.1.3 Waves

The closest we can get to a graphical representation of a sound texture is the shape of a sound wave.

A simple sound wave starts at a neutral point of zero amplitude, rises to a peak, falls back to the neutral point, falls below the neutral point to form a trough, and rises again to the neutral point where it started. A second cycle, the next complete wave, then begins. The number of cycles (complete waves) per second is measured in *Hertz*, usually written Hz. One Hz is one complete cycle per second. One thousand Hz is a *KiloHertz* (KHz) – one thousand cycles per second. The number of Hz is the *frequency* of a sound.

We mentioned in Chapter 3 that a Tune Request MIDI message tells all the instruments to tune themselves to the note A, which is produced at a frequency of 440 Hz (only in this century was the number agreed upon, partly as a means of stopping the general rise in pitch which had been taking place over the ages). It can now be seen that to tune to the note A, a MIDI instrument fixes that note at 440 Hz, which then acts as a reference points for all other notes.

However, above and below the neutral point of a wave – before the peak or the low point of the trough are reached – the line may waver and make a more complex shape, even crossing the neutral point before a cycle is complete. The simpler the shape of the wave, the cleaner or purer the sound. A *sine wave* is the purest of tones. Some examples of musical sound waves are shown in Figure 7.3. It is worth mentioning here that so-called *white noise* (a random noise having the same amplitude at all frequencies) can be used to make up percussive sound textures.

A sound wave represents two essential elements: amplitude and pitch.

Amplitude. The louder the sound, the higher the peaks and troughs, that is to say the amplitude. A guitar string plucked hard will cause the wave to rise and fall further from its neutral position than if it is plucked lightly.

Pitch.   Pitch is determined by the *wavelength*, that is to say the length (the width in lay terms) of each complete wave, and therefore the frequency. Frequency is a measure of the number of complete waves per second, so as the wavelength increases, the frequency decreases. Longer strings, tubes and bars, larger areas of stretched material, and so on, create longer wavelengths and therefore lower notes. The string family, which includes the double bass, the 'cello, the viola and the violin, is characterised by instruments of very similar shapes but different sizes. As the instrument gets smaller, its pitch range rises, and its wavelength shortens (its frequency rises).

The variations in the regularity of a sound wave are caused by the fact that when an object vibrates, it does not do so at a single frequency. In fact, it produces a number of frequencies (harmonics), depending on the complexity of the sound. Each musical instrument produces different overtones, so each has a different timbre (for more on overtones see Chapter 8 Section 8.6).

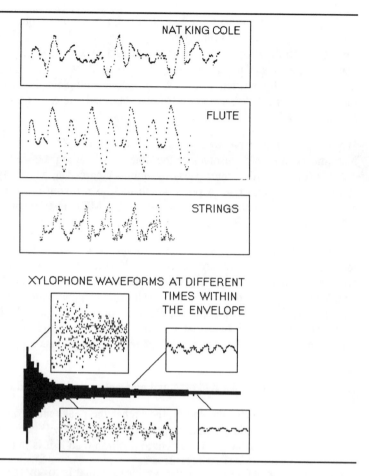

Figure 7.3: Examples of sound waves

In short, the vertical stretch of the wave determines amplitude, the horizontal stretch determines pitch, and the shape determines timbre. These parameters can be expressed as numbers, and a synthesiser calculates the numbers necessary to produce a given waveform. It then sends the numbers to a D/A converter, which converts the numbers into the voltages making up an audio signal to be reproduced on a loudspeaker (see Chapter 9 Section 9.1.1 for more about voltages).

We shall have to return to these ideas in the next chapter, concerned as it is with editing the sounds produced by synthesisers. For now, we take a closer look at the range of instruments capable of synthesising sounds.

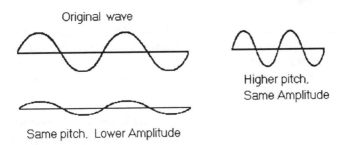

Figure 7.4: Waves showing differences in amplitude and pitch

7.2 Synthesising Devices

Almost all the output devices used in MIDI studios today are electronic. They come in the form of keyboard synthesisers, keyboard-less synthesiser modules, drum machines, and samplers. Whatever the shape, name, function or make of these pieces of equipment, they all take numerical data and convert it to sound.

What differentiates these devices are the methods they use to implement the process. They can be grouped into families according to type of synthesis or type of instrument. We shall use the latter classification, and treat different methods of synthesis later in this chapter. Products can be found in Section 7.7 below.

7.2.1 Types of Instruments

Keyboards with sound

A MIDI synthesiser keyboard with sound is a keyboard and sound-producing module in one. Each key on the keyboard is an electrical switch which turns on the relevant circuitry within the sound-producing module. This module can also be played externally, that is to say driven by another MIDI device or a computer which sends Note On data to it via the MIDI In socket usually found at the back of the instrument.

If a synthesiser keyboard is to be used for input (as it often is), the keyboard input facilities described in Chapter 6 Section 6.2 should obviously be taken into account.

Sound modules

Sound-producing modules similar to those found in synthesisers also come as separate units called sound modules or *expanders* (or *expansion modules*). And in this age of canned music, it is not surprising that there are canned musical instruments. The 1980s saw the introduction of a new type of electronic magic: a box called a *multi-timbral sound module*.

Multi-timbral sound modules contain one or more keyboard-less synthesisers. They are used to expand the capabilities of synthesisers (thus the name *expander*), and in particular to give them a thicker sound. The MIDI Out socket of a MIDI instrument is connected to the MIDI In socket of the sound module, and notes played on the keyboard are also sounded on the module. A single keyboard and nine sound modules replaces ten keyboards.

As computers and sequencers have begun to dominate MIDI, so the sound module has become the main sound-producing device, and these days synthesiser keyboards tend to be used only for input into a sequencer and for live performances.

Figure 7.5: The Roland MT-32 multi-timbral sound module

Drum machines and drum sound modules

Drum machines are devices dedicated to producing percussive sounds. They have large buttons to press, so that they can be used for direct input, and they have built-in step-time and real-time pattern-based sequencers for recording patterns.

Since the mid-1980s, drum machines have been using sampled sounds to re-create acoustic percussion. But a sampled sound is only a recording. It can be made louder or softer, but doing this will not accurately simulate the result of different forces being used when a drum is played, because not only the loudness but also the timbre of the sound changes according to how hard a drumstick hits a drum.

However, over the last year or so the Roland R-8 has set a new standard in drum machines with a feature which allows MIDI Note On velocity to alter the timbre of the sound, something which is easily achieved with synthesised sounds, but which has been a major problem in the past with sampled sounds. Now, by using multiple waveforms for each sound – in other words, sampling the sound at different levels of force – the different timbres can all be stored, and triggered according to Note On velocity. This results in an accurate simulation of the difference in sound between a snare drum being hit hard or tapped lightly, a cymbal being hit near the centre or the edge, and so forth.

The R-8 has 68 sounds and also contains the usual facilities found on drum machines such as being able to program patterns and put them together to make up a song. The R-5 is a cut-down version of the R-8, and the Boss DR-550 is a budget version.

Drum sound modules are boxes containing drum sounds. They lack the lack real-time playing pads and the built-in sequencer function, and can be played only by sending MIDI data to them from an external source such as a sequencer.

See also Chapter 6 Section 6.5 (drum pads), and for drum-machines and drum sound modules products, see below Section 7.7.

Workstations

These are super synthesiser keyboards. They consist of a keyboard, a sound module, a drum kit, and a sequencer, all in a single unit. They are stand-alone in the sense that they can be used for making multi-part music without the use of a computer/sequencer combination.

If you already have a computer, sequencer and MIDI instrument, buying a workstation means simply duplicating functions, though workstations can be handy as portable working studios. If you are not yet MIDI-equipped, a workstation is likely to prove a cheaper alternative than a studio consisting of a computer, MIDI interface if the computer requires one, sequencer software, synthesiser keyboard and drum machine. But it has to be said that cheaper also means less flexible.

Figure 7.6: The Korg M1 Workstation

7.3 Types of Sound Creation

MIDI music can be created from purely synthetic sound or from natural sounds, including the sounds of acoustic instruments and the human voice. The two types can be mixed, but the distinction between them is fundamental.

7.3.1 Synthesised Sound

As opposed to recorded natural sounds, synthesised sounds are created from scratch. There are many ways in which this can be achieved, but nearly all synthesising devices rely on sound-producing units called *oscillators* which vary the voltage of an audio signal, thus modifying pitch, amplitude and texture, so that a loudspeaker can react accordingly. Oscillators are so called because they produce the same effect as a sound wave passing from a vibrating object to the ear. The wave causes the medium (the air) ahead of it to be ever-so-slightly compressed as it moves, and leaves behind it a tiny vacuum (the air is said to *rarefy*). This compression and rarefecation is an oscillation.

What comes out of an oscillator is a continuous, steady and very simple sound. This is then enclosed in an envelope which gives it some shape. But the timbre of a single oscillator sound has a simple character which in itself is not sufficient for synthesising music except for effects such as in the theme tune from the original BBC *Dr Who* series. In order to vary the sound texture, signals from more than one oscillator are combined, something which is essential in building up the sounds of real instruments, most of which have complex timbres.

Analogue synthesisers

The first synthesisers were analogue, and they were used extensively in the 1960s and 1970s. With these devices, sound was both created and manipulated in analogue form, that is to say as an electrical signal. They are little used these days, though the term *Moog* lives on in the hearts of many people who used synthesisers in the 1960s. The first usable synthesiser was the RCA Mark I, which appeared in 1955 and which used punched paper tape to store its instructions – a system not that far removed, therefore, from the one used in pianolas. However, the Minimoog synthesiser – the brainchild of Dr Robert Moog, the inventor of the voltage-controlled oscillator – was the first commercially available synthesiser for the masses. The well-known album *Switched On Bach* was produced by Walter (Wendy) Carlos on a Moog synthesiser.

On an analogue synthesiser, the player would decide how signals from the oscillators were to be combined. Some models had panels full of sockets, and the player actually connected wires from one socket to another in order to create different routeing combinations for the electrical signals.

These synthesisers were also jam-packed with control knobs so that sound editing could be carried out as the instrument was being played. This real-time effect is missing from modern digital synthesisers, which expect a sound to be pre-defined before being triggered from the keyboard or via MIDI, and the only changes the player can make are pre-defined performance-related parameters such as vibrato, pitch-bend and aftertouch.

Polyphony on analogue synthesisers was limited. The very first were monophonic (but nevertheless cost the equivalent of a reasonably good piano). And the majority of them were not MIDI-equipped since they pre-dated MIDI.

However, because these instruments had a characteristic sound, which effectively has not as yet been reproduced by recent synthesisers, old analogue synthesisers are now being adapted for MIDI and sometimes sold at antique prices. This nostalgia has even prompted some manufacturers to release sound modules dedicated to the old analogue sounds, such as Oberheim's Matrix 1000 ("the synth with the 1000 sounds") and Cheetah's MS6. To hear the very distinctive sound of an analogue synthesiser, listen to Rick Wakeman's *Journey to the Centre of the Earth* or *The Six Wives of Henry the Eighth*.

Digital synthesisers

Here, sound is created by sending streams of numbers which are then converted to analogue signals. This has certain advantages, one of them being a cleaner sound. Other advantages are ability to process the sound with internal effects (reverb, echo, chorus and so on), to store the sound on cartridges, cards or disks, and to dump, load and edit sounds on a computer.

The aim of all modern synthesisers is to give as complex a timbre as possible, and different manufacturers have developed different methods of combining and processing the sound of different oscillators in order to achieve this aim. Each gives a different type of sound. Some of the methods used are ADD (Additive Digital Dynamics), AFM (Advanced FM), AWM (Advanced Wave Memory), DPM (Digital Phase Modulation), iPD (Interactive Phase Distortion), and VS (Vector Synthesis). The three most widely used categories are *Additive Synthesis*, *FM* (Frequency Modulation) and *LA* (Linear Arithmetic – see 7.3.3 below).

❏ **Additive Synthesis** has been used on synthesisers for some time. It consists of creating a complex waveform by adding together a number of simpler waves. It is still used by some manufacturers, and is widely found in sampling sound modules.

❏ **Yamaha's FM** method is different in that it divides its waveforms into two types. The interaction of two waves of different frequencies is called Frequency Modulation or FM (as in FM radio). The big waves are called *carriers* (they carry the signal) and the small waves are called *modulators* (they modulate the signal). The carrier frequency is the pitch of the sound, and the carrier amplitude is the volume. The modulator acts on the carrier to enrich its texture, and more than one modulator can act on the same carrier.

Yamaha calls its oscillators *operators*, and it has produced a number of FM synthesiser models, using between two and eight operators. The more operators available, the more complex the potential texture of the sound, but also the greater the number of potential combinations and therefore the more varied the range of available sounds. Two operators can be combined in only two ways, four can be combined in eight ways, and six in 32 ways. The different combinations are called *algorithms* (an algorithm sets out the logical steps to be followed in performing a task) and Figure 7.7 shows some examples.

7.3.2 Natural Sound by Sampling

It is theoretically possible to reproduce the sound of any natural instrument by purely synthetic means. However complex the sound wave, it can in principle be expressed in numbers which can therefore be built up to produce it. But in practice, synthesising almost any natural sound from scratch is an extremely complex operation.

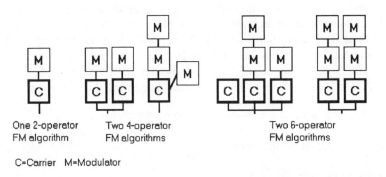

C=Carrier   M=Modulator

Figure 7.7: FM algorithms. Thick lines are carriers, thin lines are modulators

The alternative is to reverse the process by recording a natural sound and having a microprocessor in a MIDI device turn it into numbers – sampling. The sound waves are converted into voltages by a microphone which is attached to a sampling keyboard or sound module. The A/D converter inside the sampler converts the analogue electrical signal into numbers and stores them. The numbers (the sample) are then used to reproduce the sound every time a key is pressed on a synthesiser or a note message is sent to it. This is similar to what is done in digital recordings such as those produced on compact disc. The numbers pressed into the CDs can be read by a laser, which means that sound production is no longer dependent on physical contact between the disc and the pick-up arm.

Samples can also be bought from the manufacturers of samplers. They come ready-made on disk, on plug-in ROM cards, or on CD-ROM (compact discs containing data just as computer disks do, but which are read-only), and can contain whole libraries of sampled sound. As the sampler is made to play, the selected recorded sound is triggered.

Even though a sample has been recorded at a specific pitch, the sampler can alter that pitch by speeding it up or slowing it down, as on a tape recorder, so that the appropriate pitches are sounded as, for instance, the keys of a synthesiser to which it is attached are pressed. If you use a sampler to sample yourself singing a few words at Middle C, you sound like Donald Duck when the sample is played back an octave higher, and like Marvin the bored robot in *The Hitch Hiker's Guide to the Galaxy* when played an octave lower.

Sound sampling, then, is a sound photograph as opposed to the sound painting obtained with purely synthetic sounds. And sampled sound is the closest which can be achieved in MIDI to representing natural sounds, though exactly how close depends on the quality of the sound snapshot. The more pictorial information a photograph contains, the finer the detail and realism of the image. Defining a visual image with numbers – digitising it – means approximating the information to a set of co-ordinates on an imaginary grid placed over the picture. The finer the grid, the better the detail, but unavoidably, the more numbers required. And for a colour picture even more numbers are needed, since each box of the grid contains an approximation of the original colour selected from an available palette of colours. Again, the bigger the palette, the more true-to-life the image.

Sound is digitally defined according to the same principles, but spatial dimensions and colour are replaced by duration and amplitude, with the amplitude being selected from a palette of increments.

Sampling frequency

When a sampler records natural sound, it takes a sample at small time intervals and defines the amplitude of that sound numerically. The number of measurements taken in one second is called the *sampling rate* or *sampling frequency*, and the higher the sampling frequency, the finer the resolution of the sound, in other words the higher the pitch which can be recorded. The sampling rate is measured in Hz, and for best results samplers need to take their samples using at least twice the frequency of the highest pitch required.

The full reason why this is so would lead us into complexities which are both unnecessary here, and beyond the scope of this book, but it can be explained in simple terms using an analogy:

A film samples images at a given number of frames per second. Filming a wheel with its spokes turning at a rate which is faster than the visual sampling rate produces a curious effect which everybody has seen: the wheel appears to turn backwards, and can waver between apparent backward and forward movement (with a special disc, the phenomenon can be used to set a gramophone turntable to the correct number of revolutions per minute).

The same kind of interference patterns are produced as sound is sampled, occurring as so-called *aliases*: additional frequencies. The higher the sampling rate, the higher the frequencies at which the aliases occur, and when a sound is sampled at twice its basic frequency, they occur at levels which are higher than the frequencies which make up the sound. They can then easily be filtered out.

Compact discs are produced by sampling at 44.1 KHz, which means that the highest frequency they are capable of reproducing is about 20 KHz – a very high pitch. The ability to hear very high-pitched sounds decreases with age. It is thought that babies in the womb may actually be able to hear ultra-sound devices used for amplifying their heart beats, but few people outside the womb can hear frequencies above about 20 KHz, so the sampling used for compact discs is more than adequate. The fact that a frequency is not heard, does not mean that it does not affect the part of the sound which is heard – for example, very low frequencies may be felt as vibrations in the body even though they are too low to be heard with the ears, and extremely high frequencies beyond human hearing can still affect a sound's timbre. Nevertheless, most people would agree that CDs give high-quality reproductions of natural sounds.

A really expensive MIDI sampler can be made to sample at frequencies higher than those used for CDs, but even a sampling frequency of only 15 KHz can give acceptable results in some circumstances, and anything above 32 KHz will give good quality. Most samplers give a choice of sampling frequencies.

Sampling resolution

The accuracy with which amplitude is measured during sampling is called the the *sampling resolution*. This is measured in bits (binary digits – see Chapter 3 Section 3.1.2 for details of bits and binary numbers). Early samplers were 8-bit and therefore had a maximum of 256 increments, that is to say that amplitude was measured in the range 0 to 255. Today, it is more common to sample amplitude at 16-bit resolution with 65,536 increments (CDs are also sampled at this resolution) so that finer differences in dynamics can be detected. However, again unavoidably, the finer the increments, the larger the amount of data required, which means that samples may have to be stored on a hard disk or on floppy disks of high capacity.

PCM

It should be mentioned that sounds produced digitally are sometimes referred to as being created by Pulse Code Modulation (PCM). It is not uncommon to see sampled sounds referred to as *PCM sounds*, though PCM sampling involves storing data serially rather than in parallel, meaning that PCM-sampled sounds cannot be transposed to a different pitch.

The cost and value of sampling

Sampling is an expensive way of creating polyphonic sound because of the equipment required to achieve acceptable results. Natural sounds have a quality of their own which is difficult and, given the current state of the art, often impossible to reproduce satisfactorily. Except for the really dedicated (or rich), generally speaking there is better use for money elsewhere in the studio. What is more, samples are not easy to manipulate because they have to be so large. They sound realistic only at an interval of about half to one octave above or below the sampling pitch. So, to sample a piano, for example, a separate sample has to be taken at least every two octaves to get a workable result, something which makes manipulation even harder, and uses up valuable memory.

However, sampling is used for human voices and other effects which cannot be created by sound synthesis, and is therefore sometimes indispensable. It is also worth noting that a sampled sound mixed with a synthesised sound can sometimes produce amazingly original results. One composer known to us recently mixed the growl of a cheetah (the real animal, not the make of equipment) into a snare drum, with astounding results.

For sampling products, see Section 7.7 below.

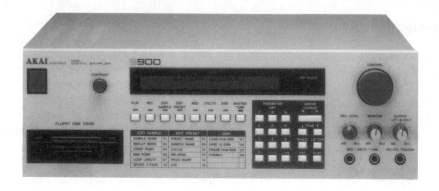

Figure 7.8 The Akai S900 sampler

7.3.3 Chipboard Sounds

While Yamaha was enjoying success with its FM synthesis method, and other manufacturers (such as Akai) were making inroads into sampling or getting stuck in the mud of analogue synthesis, Roland engineers were working on yet another approach to producing sound. The result was *LA* – Linear Arithmetic.

This method combines sampled sound and synthetic sound, just as veneered chipboard used in cheap furniture has an expensive outer cover and cheap glued wood-mush on the inside. LA synthesis uses (in terms of memory) expensive samples of real sound envelopes, combined with a cheap filling of an oscillator-created synthetic mush of sound. The result is a fairly realistic acoustic sound, close in quality to sampled sound but considerably less demanding on memory and thus considerably cheaper. Because of its synthetic characteristics and smaller data size, it is also easier to manipulate, making it easier to create new sounds.

LA synthesis used on the Roland D series of synthesisers is still a very successful formula, and has forced other manufacturers to adopt similar ideas.

7.3.4 A New Generation of Synthesisers?

In 1989 a US company called Peavey released its DPM3 workstation keyboard, a 16-note polyphonic 16-note multi-timbral synthesiser, with a built-in drum machine and 9-track sequencer.

But the really unusual feature of this synthesiser is that it incorporates an off-the-shelf Digital Signal Processing (DSP) programmable chip, instead of the traditional Application Specific Integrated Circuits (ASICs) contained in other synthesisers designed to handle only one specific type of synthesis. The chip in an FM synthesiser can handle FM sounds, and the one in an LA synthesiser LA sounds. A DSP, on the other hand is programmable, and can be made to behave as an FM synthesiser, an LA synthesiser, or whatever type of synthesis is required.

Although at the time of going to press this synthesiser is sold already programmed with a sample-plus-synthesis method, new programs are expected to appear within a short time and the success of Peavey's offering could change the standard ways of producing synthesisers – though as with all things in the world of electronics, it should be added that the crystal ball can be awfully fickle.

7.3.5 Acoustic Sound

So far in this book, we have concentrated on MIDI and its uses with electronic devices. But it is not used exclusively with them – it can also be used with traditional mechanical instruments, and not just by sampling their sounds.

It is possible not only to sit down at a normal acoustic piano, fitted with a reproducing system, play Rachmaninoff's Piano Concerto No 2 (or anything else), and have the performance recorded in a computer in MIDI form, but also to have the computer play it back on the acoustic piano. This is achieved by using very accurate linear motors and sensitive robotics technology – the keys are hit using a complex mechanical system, and the music is generated just as if a human player were sitting at the piano, or as if it were being controlled by a pianola mechanism but far more flexibly.

There are two major makes of piano robots: The Austrian Boesendorfer and Yamaha's Disklavier.

The Boesendorfer – the ultimate in pianolas – is not a new product but has recently been adapted for MIDI. It uses its own extended MIDI resolution for Note On velocity (by making use of MIDI Controller 68). MIDI uses 128 steps to record dynamics and an on/off toggle for pedal effects. The Boesendorfer uses 564 steps for dynamics and 256 for pedal positions, a range decided on after carrying out extensive measurements of real performances. It will convert its particular form of data to standard MIDI data for playback by other instruments if necessary. Prices in the UK start at a frightening £61,000.

The Yamaha Disklavier is a similar product. It does not have the extended MIDI resolution, its pedals are either on or off, and it costs a fraction of the Boesendorfer: a mere £16,000 for the 6-foot grand version.

7.4 Polyphony and Multi-timbrality

In previous chapters we have touched on the idea of polyphonic music (music in which different parts, or *voices*, are sounded at the same time) and that of multi-timbrality (the ability to sound more than one timbre or instrument-sound simultaneously) in devices such as multi-timbral sound modules. It is important to be aware of the difference between these two notions, since they are distinct but can also be inter-dependent.

When used of a musical instrument, the term *polyphony* indicates the number of notes it can handle simultaneously. A flute or the human voice (normally) sound only one note at a time, whereas a piano can simultaneously sound as many notes as it has keys.

Keyboard synthesisers come with keyboards of different sizes – typically having 48, 61 or 88 keys – but even for someone with 48 fingers it would not be possible to sound 48 keys simultaneously, let alone the 88 keys making up a full-size keyboard. This is because in electronic instruments each note is created by a dedicated piece of circuitry and, mostly for reasons of price, their number is limited to the number of notes likely to be needed for practical purposes.

Since most synthesiser keyboards are designed to be played live as well as being used with a computer, the polyphony of the majority of them has traditionally been limited to eight notes because players rarely use more than eight fingers simultaneously. However, many are now 16-note polyphonic, and some top-of-the-range models have 32-note polyphony. A polyphony greater than 8-note can be useful in allowing duets to be played on the same keyboard, but much more importantly in offering a wider range of multi-timbrality, as explained below.

As well as being polyphonic, most modern synthesisers are multi-timbral, that is to say that they can handle different musical parts on different MIDI channels at the same time. If a synthesiser is 8-part multi-timbral, it sends MIDI information on eight independent MIDI channels, and therefore acts like eight separate synthesisers.

But there is always a balance to be struck between polyphony and multi-timbrality. On a multi-timbral instrument, a player can allocate a number of notes to each timbre. So, if eight separate timbres are selected on an 8-note polyphonic 8-timbre synthesiser, each timbre can then be only monophonic. If four timbres are selected instead of eight, each timbre can be 2-note polyphonic; or some other combination within these limits can be implemented, such as 5-note polyphony for one timbre and monophony for each of the remaining three. It can be seen that with 16-note polyphony, the range of multi-timbrality is increased accordingly.

When a player runs out of polyphony, one of two effects is felt. Take the example of a 4-note polyphonic synthesiser keyboard. Four keys pressed simultaneously will produce four notes. As soon as a fifth key is pressed while the first four are held down, either the fifth key will not sound at all or – and this is usually the default condition – the fifth key will play but the sound of the first key will be lost. This affects the sustain of notes and can create a dry sound, and glissandos become virtually impossible. When a glissando is played on a piano with the sustain (loud) pedal pressed, each string continues to vibrate while the others are hit by the hammers. In other words, the complete range of notes sounding at the same time is heard. A glissando on a synthesiser is of course limited by its maximum polyphony.

As a general rule, therefore, the amount of polyphony required is that of the greatest number of notes which may have to be sounded together. But, in any case, the more polyphony the greater the flexibility available to the player, and the better the chances of reproducing the sounds of natural instruments. And the rule has to be tempered by other factors, since high polyphonic values may not always be needed.

The sounds of monophonic acoustic instruments, like those of the woodwind and brass families, in themselves require no polyphony, though with polyphony, chords can be produced (something which avant-garde players of acoustic wind instruments are fond of doing). Furthermore, if the desired sound is that of, say, a clarinet with some echo – as would be produced if the instrument were played in an empty cathedral – some polyphony will be required, since one note is still sounding while the next note is being articulated.

If only single-note string parts are envisaged, 2-note or 3-note polyphony will probably be sufficient. For a full guitar sound, 6-note polyphony is adequate, though 8-note is better: one for each string and two extra for enriching sustain effects. For a piano, an organ or a harp sound, the more polyphony the better, and 16-note polyphony is really the minimum for anything like realistic effects. If a full piano sound is required as part of a complete orchestration, a minimum of 32-note polyphony will have to be the order of the day.

So, to play back a full orchestration, the composer or arranger allocates an amount of polyphony to each instrument, ensuring that the total does not exceed the maximum amount of polyphony available on the synthesiser. The amount of polyphony on any one MIDI channel can be set up in a *performance memory*, which is described in the next chapter, Section 8.4. But some multi-timbral instruments allocate their polyphony to the various timbres automatically, a process known as *dynamic allocation*. This is best explained by an example.

Take an 8-note polyphonic synthesiser which is being sent MIDI data from a sequencer on four MIDI channels, with each channel having been set up to receive 2-note polyphony. If the synthesiser is not capable of dynamic allocation, and a third note is sent on any one channel, that third note will not be sounded even though there is spare polyphonic capacity in other channels, which may not even be sending any MIDI data at all at that particular time. Notes will be sounded in this case on a first-come first-served basis as they arrive at the synthesiser, the note which is not sounded depending on how the sequencer has organised the sending of its data.

However, if the synthesiser is capable of dynamic allocation, it will borrow some polyphonic capability from a channel which has spare capacity, and the third note will be sounded with the other two. Notice that the third note will not be re-allocated to another channel, but added to the two original notes in their channel, which temporarily will be allowed 3-note polyphony. This example is of course a very simple one, and in practice there can be a complex interaction of polyphony and channels when dynamic allocation is active.

Dynamic allocation is clearly something to be desired and should therefore be a serious point to consider when buying a synthesiser, especially with second-hand instruments which may have many good features but lack the ability to handle polyphony in this versatile way. Most of the latest synthesisers are capable of dynamic allocation, which can be overridden if required.

7.4.1 Polyphony and Multi-timbral Sound Modules

It might be expected that multi-timbral sound modules (keyboard-less synthesisers), which are destined to be played remotely and are perfect for computer performances, would offer more polyphony than their keyboard equivalents. Unfortunately this is not the case. Sound modules are usually plain rack-size versions of existing keyboard synthesiser models, containing basically the same circuitry but in a different box, and having the same polyphony as the keyboard versions. Only recently have the first 32-note polyphonic sound modules emerged.

7.5 Choice Checklist for Output Devices

The following features should be taken into account when considering any MIDI output device:

❑ The amount of polyphony and multi-timbrality

❏ The availability in a multi-timbral device of separate audio output sockets for each timbre (important if sounds are to be further processed before recording)

❏ On-board sound effects such as reverb, echo and chorus

❏ Extras which can replace certain pieces of equipment, such as a set of drum and percussion sounds which can obviate the need for a drum machine

❏ The ability to edit sounds. Some output devices can handle only their own pre-set sounds

❏ The ability to handle alternative tunings (see Chapter 8 Section 8.6)

Above all, listen to the sounds an output device produces, and only then decide if they are what you require.

7.5.1 MIDI Implementation Chart for Output Devices

As with input devices, always consult the MIDI Implementation Chart of the equipment before buying (see Figure 7.9, and also Chapter 6 Section 6.10).

Note that it is obviously not enough for input devices to be able to send MIDI messages concerned with expression and dynamics if the sequencer is unable to record them, and the synthesisers and sound modules unable to respond to them on playback. The MIDI Implementation Chart will show the ability of the output device to respond to velocity sensitivity, volume, pitch bend, vibrato, aftertouch, breath control and other MIDI messages used in recording a performance.

7.6 MIDI Lighting

Pink Floyd use sophisticated systems of laser lights under computer control (and Computer-Assisted Design programs to plan the layout of their equipment on stage). Jean-Michel Jarre's stage even expanded over the city of Houston whose sky-scrapers were used for a multimedia spectacular, with lasers, fireworks and music, watched live by 1.3 million people – we wonder how long it will be before the first rock spectacular takes place in space. Most of us are not in the same league – our resources will always be grounded, and in any case do not stretch to a crew of over 100 support staff for a stage performance. But mere mortals can nevertheless afford MIDI lighting equipment which can be used to synchronise lighting effects with music. Two typical rack-mounted products (from Groove Electronics) are:

MIDI Lite Controller (price category D). Lamps are plugged into this device which can control separate channels using Note On messages – a lamp is lit for a definable time when a Note On message is received. The unit also incorporates an internal sequencer which can synchronise with MIDI clocks.

```
    [MIDI Output Device]                              Date:1-1-1991
      Model  SIGMA-2        MIDI Implementation Chart  Version 1.0
```

Function...	Transmitted	Recognized	Remarks
Basic Default Channel Channel		1 - 16 1 - 16	Memorised

Mode   Default
    Messages
    Altered
		1, 2, 3, 4	

Note Number True Voice		0 - 127 0 - 127	
Velocity Note ON Note OFF		o v=1-127 x	
After Key's Touch		x o	
Pitch Bender		o	

Control   1
       2
       4
       5
Change   7
       8
      10
      11
     64
     65
     66
		o
		o
		o
		o
		o
		o
		o
		o
		o
		o
		o
			Modulation
			Breath Control
			Foot Controller
			Portamento time
			Volume
			Balance
			Pan
			Expression
			Sustain (Hold1)
			Portamento
			Sostenuto

Prog Change : True #		o 0 - 127 0 - 127	
System Exclusive		o *	Memory Data
System : Song Pos : Song Sel Common : Tune		x x x	
System :Clock Real Time :Commands		x x	
Aux :Local ON/OFF :All Notes OFF Mes- :Active Sensing sages:Reset		o ** o o x	

```
Notes: *  System exclusive details are not given on this table
          They are given elsewhere in the equipment's manual.
       ** Desirable, if equipment is a keyboard
```

Mode 1 : OMNI ON, POLY	Mode 2 : OMNI ON, MONO	o:Yes
Mode 3 : OMNI OFF, POLY	Mode 4 : OMNI OFF, MONO	x:No

Figure 7.9: MIDI Implementation Chart showing desirable response features for MIDI output devices

MIDI Gate (price category C). This unit is an add-on for a professional lighting desk. It has six output triggers (0 to 10 volts output) and gives varying brightnesses of the lamps by using Note On velocity, and varying durations using Note Off messages.

7.7 Products

Synthesiser keyboards

Silent (controller) keyboards can be found in Chapter 6 Section 6.11 (see also Chapter 11 Section 11.4). Here, we list the output capabilities of synthesiser keyboards rather than advanced controller functions.

All models listed here have velocity sensitivity and, unless otherwise specified, channel aftertouch. A *w* in the Action column means weighted-action keys. In the Extra storage column, *Mcard* means Magnetic card (RAM or ROM), *FD* means 3.5 inch floppy disk, and *Cart* means Cartridge.

Producer/model	Keys	Action	Polyphony	Multitimbality	Sounds	Type of synthesis	Extra storage	Price	Comment
Casio VZ-1	61		16	4	196	iPD	Mcard	D/E	Rack-mounted version is VZ-10M.
Ensoniq VFX	61		21	12	120	DC	Mcard	G	Microtuning. Includes drum-kit (see Glossary).
Hohner HS-2	61		16	4	196	iPD	Mcard	D	Casio VZ-1 clone.
Kawai K1II	73	w	8-16	9	96	AS	Mcard	F	Includes drum kit.
- K5	61	w	16	8	96	ADD		F	Rack-mounted version is K5M.
Roland D10	61		8-32	9	128	LA	Mcard	F	Includes drum kit. No after-touch. Rack-mounted version is the D110
- D50	61		16	2	128	LA	Mcard	G	Rack-mounted version is the D550.
- D70	73	w	30	6	119	LA	Mcard	G	Advanced LA sounds.
Yamaha DX7	61		16	1	32	FM	Cart	D/E	Will have its place in books on the history of twentieth- century music.
- DX7II	61		16	2	64	FM	FD	G	Microtuning. Rack-mounted version is the TX802.

Drum machines and drum sound modules

Producer/model	Price	Comment
Drum machines		
Akai XR-10	D	
- MPC-60	H	Sampling drum machine and sequencer.
Alesis HR16	E	
Boss DR-550	C	Budget version of the Roland R-8
Cheetah MD16	D	
Kawai R-50E	D	
Korg DDD-1	C	
- S3	F	75 editable sounds, effects, and SMPTE.
Roland TR-808	C	Old favourite (back in fashion).
- R-8	F	See above Section 7.2.1, Drums
- R-5	E	Cut-down version of the R-8
Yamaha RX120	D	
- RX8	D/E	
Drum sound modules		
Akai XE-8	C/D	32 sounds, eight outputs.
Kawai XD-5	E/F	64 sounds, eight outputs.
Roland R-8M	E	68 sounds, eight outputs, rack-mounted, sound capabilities of the Roland R-8. Can access three cards simultaneously (an excellent feature).
Yamaha EMR-1	C	37 sounds, two outputs.

Workstations

Producer/model: Korg M1
Keyboard: 61 keys, velocity-sensitive, aftertouch
Sounds: 16-note polyphony, 8-part, 100 sounds, 44 drum sounds, four Outs
Effects: 33 (two simultaneously)
Sequencer: 8-track, max 7,700 MIDI events
Price category: G
Comments: Very popular. Korg M1R is a rack version of the M1 with no keyboard – price category F)

Producer/model: Korg T1, T2, T3
Keyboard: T1 – 88 weighted keys; T2 – 76 keys; T3 – 61 keys. Velocity sensitivity, aftertouch
Sounds: 16-note polyphony, 8-part, 200 sounds
Effects: 33 (two simultaneously)
Sequencer: 8-tracks, 56,000 MIDI events, two MIDI channels
Price categories: G and H
Comment: Expensive

Producer/model: Peavey DPM3
Keyboard: 61 weighted keys, velocity sensitivity, aftertouch
Sounds: 16-note polyphony, 16-part, 100 sounds and five drum kits
Effects: 39 (four simultaneously)
Sequencer: 9-track, 20,000 MIDI events
Price category: G
Comment: Revolutionary architecture

Producer/model: Roland D20
Keyboard, sounds and effects: As Roland D10 keyboard (see above)
Sequencer: 8-tracks plus drums, 35,000 MIDI events
Price category: G

Producer/model: Roland W30
Keyboard: 61 keys, velocity sensitivity, aftertouch
Sounds: 16-note polyphony, 8-part, 128 pre-set sounds or sample your own at 15 or 30 KHz
(max of 14.4 at 30 KHz), eight Outs, connects to Roland CD-5 ROM player
or an external hard disk for loading and saving samples
Effects: None
Sequencer: 16-track (eight for internal sounds, eight for external instruments), 15,000 MIDI
events
Price category: G
Comment: The only sampler workstation

Producer/model: Yamaha SY77
Keyboard: 61 keys, velocity sensitivity, aftertouch
Sounds: 32-note polyphony, 16-part, 128 sounds
Effects: 44 programmable effects (four simultaneously)
Sequencer: 16-track, 16 MIDI events
Price category: H
Comment: Cut-down version exists as the SY55 (price category G)

Producer/model: Yamaha V50
Keyboard: 61 keys, velocity sensitivity, aftertouch
Sounds: 16-note polyphony, 9-part, 200 LA/FM/analogue sounds plus 61 drum sounds
Effects: 32, all editable
Sequencer: 8-track plus percussion track, 16,000 MIDI events
Price category: G

Synthesiser sound modules

Producer/ model	Polyphony	Multitimbrality	Audio outputs	Price	Comments
Casio VZ8M	8	3	2	C	256 iPD sounds. Can be set to work from a keyboard, guitar, or wind controller.
- VZ10M	16	4	4	D	192 iPD sounds. Rack version of VZ1 keyboard.
- CSM-1	16	4	2	B	100 sounds. The cheapest 16-note polyphonic sound module on the market.
- CSM-10P	16	1	1	B/C	Module with sampled piano, harpsichord, vibraphone and pipe-organ sounds.
Cheetah MS6	6	6	1	C/D	416 analogue sounds. Very good.
Evolution Synthesis EVS-1	16	8	2	D	100 sounds. Four methods of synthesis, including FM, and combinations of them.
E-mu Proteus 1	16	8	6	F	As Proteus 2 but half the sound capacity.
- Proteus 2	32	16	6	G	8 Mb of memory memory. Best simulation of the sounds of a symphony orchestra.
Korg M3R	16	8	2	E/F	100 sounds, 33 effects. Sound module of the M1 workstation but with four times the memory.
Oberheim Matrix 1000	6	1	1	E	1,000 analogue sounds.
Roland MT-32	8-32	9	2	C	128 LA sounds. Drum kit with 32 sounds. Internal reverb. Classic.
- CM-32L	8-32	9	2	D	As MT-32 but drum kit with 64 sounds.
- D-110	8-32	9	8	D/E	Professional version of MT-32.
- D-550	16	2	2	G	128 LA sounds. Internal reverb, parametric EQ, and chorus effects.
- P-330, MKS-20	16	1	2	D/E	Modules with specially synthesised piano, harpsichord and vibraphone sounds.
Yamaha FB-01	8	8	2	B/C	336 simple FM sounds. Crude microtuning.
- TX81Z	8	8	2	C	160 FM sounds. Microtuning. Good for wind controllers.
- TX802	16	8	10	F	256 6-operator FM sounds. High-resolution microtuning.
- TG77	32	16	12	G	128 sounds, drum kit with 61 drum sounds, 44 programmable effects (four simultaneous).

Sampling keyboards

All the keyboards listed here are velocity-sensitive.

Producer/model: Akai X7000
Keyboard: 61 keys
Polyphony; multi-timbrality: 6-note; 6-part
Sampling resolution; rate; time: 12-bit; 4 to 40 KHz; 0.8 to 8 sec.
Outputs: One (six, with optional adaptor)
Disk drive: 2.8 inch
Price category: C/D

Producer/model: Casio FZ-1
Keyboard: 61 keys, aftertouch
Polyphony; multi-timbrality: 8-note; 8-part
Sampling resolution; rate; time: 16-bit; 9, 18 and 38 KHz; 29.1, 58.2 and 116.5 sec.
Outputs: One stereo, eight mono
Disk drive: 3.5 inch
Price category: F

Producer/model: Ensoniq EPS
Keyboard: 61 weighted keys, aftertouch
Polyphony; multi-timbrality: 12-note at 52 KHz, 20-note at 31 KHz; 8-part
Sampling resolution, rate and time: 16-bit; 6.25 to 52.1 KHz; 4.9 to 41.3 sec.
Outputs: Two (optional further eight)
Disk drive: 3.5 inch
Price category: G
Comment: Includes 8-track sequencer, 80,000 MIDI events

Producer/model: Ensoniq Mirage
Keyboard: 61 keys
Polyphony; multi-timbrality: 8-note; 8-part
Sampling resolution, rate and time: 8-bit; 8 to 33 KHz; 2 to 8 sec.
Output: One
Disk drive: 3.5 inch
Price category: E
Comments: Includes 8-track sequencer, 333 MIDI events per track. Has historic value. Much loved

Producer/model: Roland S10
Keyboard: 49 keys
Polyphony; multi-timbrality: 8-note; single part
Sampling resolution, rate and time: 12-bit; 15 and 32 KHz; 4 and 8 sec.
Output: One
Disk drive: 2.8 inch
Price category: C/D

Sampling sound modules

Producer/model: Akai S900,
Polyphony; multi-timbrality: 8-note; 8-part
Sampling resolution; rate; time: 12-bit; 7.5 to 40 KHz; 11.75 to 63.3 sec.
Outputs: Eight
Internal memory: 720K
Disk drive: 3.5 inch
Price category: F
Comment: Widely used

Producer/model: Akai S1000
Polyphony; multi-timbrality: 16-note; 16-part
Sampling resolution; rate; time: 16-bit; 22.05 and 44.1 KHz; 11.5 and 23 sec. stereo
Outputs: Two pairs of stereo and eight mono
Internal memory: 2 Mb
Disk drive: 3.5 inch
Price category: H
Comments: Stereo. Hard disk model also available

Producer/models: Casio FZ-10M, FZ-20
Polyphony; multi-timbrality: 16-note; 8-part
Sampling resolution; rate; time: 16-bit; 9, 18 and 38 KHz; 29.1, 58.2 and 116.5 sec.
Outputs: Two stereo and eight mono
Internal memory: 2 Mb
Disk drive: 3.5 inch
Price category: F (FZ-10M), G (FZ-20)
Comment: FZ-20 can take a hard disk

Producer/model: Cheetah SX16
Polyphony; multi-timbrality: 8-note; 16-part
Sampling resolution; rate; time: 16-bit; 6 to 48 KHz; 2.7 to 43 sec. stereo
Outputs: Eight
Internal memory: 512K
Disk drive: 3.5 inch
Price category: F
Comments: Stereo. Compatible with Akai S900 and S1000 series

Producer/model: Ensoniq EPS
Polyphony; multi-timbrality: 12-note at 52 KHz, 20-note at 31 KHz; 8-part
Sampling resolution; rate; time: 16-bit; 6.25 to 52.1 KHz; 4.9 to 41.3 sec.
Outputs: One stereo, optional eight mono
Internal memory: 480K
Disk drive: 3.5 inch
Price category: H
Comment: Includes 8-track sequencer, 80,000 MIDI events

Producer/models: Roland S-550 and S-330
Polyphony; multi-timbrality: 16-note; 4-part
Sampling resolution; rate; time: 12-bit; 15 and 30 KHz; 7.2 and 14.4 sec.
Outputs: One mix and eight individual
Internal memory: 1.5 Mb
Disk drive: 3.5 inch
Price categories: H and G
Comments: S-330 almost the same as S-550, but half the internal memory. S-550 has
optional SCSI (Small Computer Systems Interface) port for connecting to
Roland CD-5 (CD-ROM player with sound library)

Producer/model: Roland S-770
Polyphony; multi-timbrality: 24-note; 32-part
Sampling resolution; rate; time: 16-bit; 22.05, 24, 44.1 and 48 KHz; 10.35 to 22.5 sec. stereo
Outputs: One stereo and six mono, plus digital Input/Output
Internal memory: 2 Mb
Disk drive: 3.5 inch, plus 40 Mb hard disk
Price:: About £5,000
Comments: Stereo. Optional Roland CD-5 (see immediately above) and Roland MO-7 (540 Mb magneto-optical disk)

Producer/model: Simmons SDX
Polyphony; multi-timbrality: 48-note; 16-part
Sampling resolution; rate; time: 16-bit; 11, 22 and 44.1 KHz; 88 to 352 sec. mono
Outputs: One stereo and 16 mono
Internal memory: 8 Mb
Disk drive: 3.5 inch, plus 20 Mb hard disk
Price: About £11,500
Comments: Capable of stereo. 9 inch built-in monitor, 64-track sequencer with 32 MIDI channels

Producer/model: Yamaha TX16W
Polyphony; multi-timbrality: 16-note; 16-part
Sampling resolution; rate; time: 12-bit; 16, 33 and 50 KHz; 6.74 sec. stereo
Outputs: One stereo and 8 mono
Internal memory: 1.5 Mb
Disk drive: 3.5 inch
Price category: F/G
Comment: Capable of stereo only at 33 KHz

Sample players (cannot record)

Producer/model: Akai S1000PB
Polyphony; multi-timbrality: 16-note; 16-part
Outputs: Ten
Price category: G
Comment: Playback version of Akai S1000

Producer/model: Roland CM32P
Polyphony; multi-timbrality: 31-note; 6-part
Outputs: Two
Price category: E
Comment: Digital reverb

Producer/model: Roland U-110
Polyphony; multi-timbrality: 31-note; 6-part
Outputs: Six
Price category: E/F
Comments: Digital chorus and tremolo, 99 pre-set sampled sounds, more on RAM card

Producer/model: Roland U-220
Polyphony; multi-timbrality: 31-note; 6-part, plus drums
Outputs: Six
Price category: F
Comments: 128 pre-set sounds plus chorus/flanger and reverb/delay effects. U-20 is keyboard version (61 keys, velocity-sensitivity, and aftertouch)

Producer/model: Yamaha TG55
Polyphony; multi-timbrality: 16-note; 16-part
Outputs: Four
Price category: E
Comments: 64 pre-set sounds using Yamaha's AWM2, 61 drum sounds and 34 sound processing effects

Creative Sound

New sound has always been the aim of composers and arrangers, but originality combined with beauty is an elusive goal. If we are to believe the makers of the film *The Glenn Miller Story*, Glenn Miller spent endless hours of searching for a way of producing the exact sound he had in his mind. He finally found it for his first hit *Moonlight Serenade* by eliminating the traditional baritone saxophone from his front line and replacing the lead alto saxophone with a clarinet, which then shared the melody with the lead tenor saxophone. Whatever the fact behind the film fantasy, the combination gave that special Miller sound.

But creating a new sound with acoustic instruments is obviously limited by the range of instruments available. Generations of musicians – classical, swing, jazz – have all but exhausted the possibilities, and only the geniuses among them have achieved something outstanding with new combinations. Realistically, there is little mileage in this method for the average modern composer.

Some of today's composers may demand abnormal sounds from traditional instruments, such as a normally monophonic wind instrument sounding two notes at once, or piano strings being hit with a drum stick. Some may juxtapose solo instruments in unusual joint concertos – if Mozart could do so for the flute and harp, why not the triangle and the tuba? Some, of the John Cage persuasion, may make a composition out of a pianist not actually playing a piano at all, but sitting silently on the piano stool for 4 minutes 33 seconds while the audience listens to itself coughing and shifting in its seats (hearing such a performance of a work by Cage is an experience never to be forgotten). However, the chances of finding a unique formula for natural instruments, which the world will recognise as a master stroke, are slim to say the least.

In the last 20 years or so, synthesised sound has modified the problem and opened new vistas. For the first time in the history of music, the sound made by an instrument does not necessarily depend on its physical shape and material characteristics, but rather on variable combinations of numbers.

Cynics reading this may wonder why pop groups, nearly all of which use synthesisers, all sound alike. They are right to wonder, but the fault lies not with the potential of the technology; it lies with how that potential is used.

Of course, pop-music fans may well say that all classical music sounds the same to them. Modern pop music is nevertheless a conveyor-belt product carefully monitored by market-research people. Production time is costly and cannot be given over to experiment. If a formula is in fashion and sells, it is repeated until it sells no longer. What is more, very few of the original creators of a song have any artistic control over the final result, which is left to technicians and marketing personnel. The sounds used are the factory-set parameters which come with a device, and which are usually nothing more than imitations of acoustic instruments. Good synthesisers and sound modules can sound amazingly like real flutes, clarinets, strings, organs and so on. It seems that the temptation to use such life-like reproductions is too strong to be resisted.

Yet programmable synthesisers can create a vast number of sounds which are not imitations of acoustic instruments, and it should be the aim of modern composers to take advantage of their capabilities. But, in order to do that, the composer must be able to program them and edit their sounds. And therein, perhaps, lies the real problem when it comes to pop music. Mostly for reasons of price, editing facilities on electronic sound-producing devices are not easy to use. Most synthesisers and sound modules will allow their sounds to be edited with adjustments of the controls on their panels, but more often than not such on-board editing facilities consist of a single-line LCD and a limited number of buttons. Friendliness and flexibility can hardly be said to characterise such features.

However, a number of newer synthesising devices, although programmable, have no internal editing facilities. Their sounds can be edited only via a computer and MIDI, and a sound editor program running on a computer is far easier to use than the editing facilities to be found on most synthesisers and sound modules. Such programs are also much more powerful and flexible, though getting the best out of one takes some knowledge and practice.

8.1 Sound Editors

Sound-editor programs, sometimes called *synthesiser voice editors*, are available as generic programs which will work with several makes and models of MIDI instruments, and as separate programs which will work only with a particular model.

They usually display all their editing facilities on a single computer screen, and the cursor keys and/or a mouse can be used to move around the screen and invoke them. Diagrams and graphs often allow a sound to be shaped by drawing the desired wave or the lines of an envelope with a mouse, while the program calculates the numeric parameters from the drawing.

Such programs also allow the user to create sounds at random, to create sounds of varying texture by specifying a start sound and an end sound and having the program fill in what is in between, to convert sounds from one synthesiser format to another, to make up libraries of sounds capable of holding much more than can be held in an instrument's memory, to sort sounds by name and texture, and to control a host of other things affecting the manipulation of sounds. Indeed, such programs are so versatile that it comes as a surprise to many people using them for the first time that they have not dominated MIDI. The reason is that sequencers have become so much a part of the standard MIDI studio that they have tended to push other sound-controlling software into the background. Yet sound editors running on computers remain virtually the only fully usable set of tools available to MIDI musicians for creating new sounds, unless they are willing to persevere with unfriendly internal synthesiser editors.

Sooner or later, they are bound to come into their own, and the impetus of a big market will then push them forward to new frontiers. Indeed, already beyond the drawing board are sound editors incorporating techniques of Artificial Intelligence, and guiding the composer towards creating a sound by using natural-language descriptions: bright, soft, brassy, thick, stringy, strident and so forth. At the time of writing, we know of no commercially-produced software which will do such things, but it cannot be long before programs of that ilk become readily available. When that happens, music may well take a giant leap. For the moment, it is a question of manipulating numbers, and a good deal of trial and error.

8.1.1 Sound Editors at Work

Modern digital sound-producing devices such as synthesisers and sound modules store as numbers in their internal memories anything between a few dozen sounds and (on sophisticated instruments) a couple of hundred. These sounds, held in banks (sets), can be sent as System-exclusive messages to a computer in a process is known as a *MIDI dump* or *bulk dump*. The dumped data can be read straight into a sound-editing program, or stored on disk for later editing. A dump can consist of a single sound, but is more usually a bank of sounds, and even the entire contents of the memory of a synthesiser or sound module.

As with all software, different sound-editing programs have their own methods of presenting information, but a typical program handling a dumped bank starts by listing the names of the sounds on the computer screen. By moving the cursor keys, or using a mouse, a sound can be highlighted as *active*, that is to say that it becomes the current sound. At this point, it can be heard when the synthesiser's keys are pressed, or it can be played when editing the sounds of a sound module. It is possible to go through all the sounds in a bank and simply listen to them, or change their positions in the bank, copy selected sounds, delete others, and so on. More importantly, however, the parameters of any sound can be altered.

The active sound is edited on an Edit screen (or Edit window within the main screen) where all the data for that sound is displayed in cells, sometimes with accompanying graphs (see Figure 8.1). Again, using the cursor keys or a mouse, it is possible to jump from cell to cell, just as in a business spreadsheet program, and change the contents of any of them. The new set of values is sent back to the synthesiser or sound module so that the changes which have been made can be heard. Once the required sound has been achieved, it can be saved on disk, or sent back to the memory of the synthesiser or sound module where it can be stored.

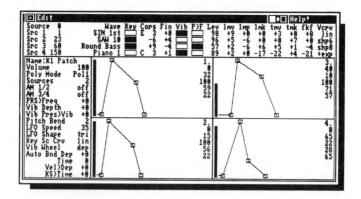

Figure 8.1: A typical synthesiser voice editor screen (Sound Quest)

Simple enough, and certainly infinitely friendlier than changing sounds on synthesisers themselves. But sound is a very complex matter, and the skill required to build up a sound demands an understanding of its components beyond that already explored in the previous chapter. The Attack, Decay, Sustain and Release patterns of sound envelopes are only four of a number of parameters used to define a sound. What is more, it is also necessary to know how particular synthesisers and sound modules create their sound by combining their oscillators. This is less daunting a prospect than might be imagined, since manufacturers are fond of over-defining the methods of synthesis they use in order to appear innovatory, when in reality there is a good measure of common ground between all the methods. Nevertheless, the differences cannot be ignored if a sound editor is be used to best advantage.

8.2 Finding the Right Combination

In the world of sound, things are never what they seem. Most people, unless they have looked into the subject, would tend to think that the sound of an individual instrument is a single sound element. It rarely is.

Consider the simple example of the sound of a gong. It is in fact made up of at least two basic sounds, not one: a short initial bang (the stick hitting the gong) which dies away rapidly, and a long *woooosh* which dies away very slowly (the gong vibrating and its energy being dissipated). The bang sound continues (perceptibly, though only just) after the woooosh sound has begun. To produce a single note, an electronic instrument has to use at least one oscillator, but at least two will be required to synthesise a gong-like sound. In other words one oscillator is needed for each component of a sound.

In addition, the sound of each oscillator has to be shaped using an ADSR envelope. In the case of the gong, the oscillator used for the bang will have a very fast attack, and a very fast decay so that it dies away very rapidly, while the oscillator used for the woooosh will have a slow attack and a slow decay, and die away very gradually.

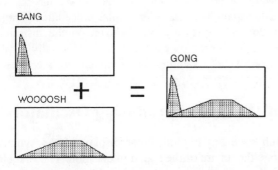

Figure 8.2: Two envelopes for simulating a gong-like sound

But that is not all: the sound of two oscillators alone is not complex enough to produce the timbre of a gong sound. Therefore, the two oscillators used to create the two basic sounds associated with a gong have to be treated independently by other oscillators to produce the required textures for the bang and the woooosh. In practice, up to four or more oscillators acting on each other may be required to synthesise a realistic gong sound, even though they are dealing with only a single note. And, clearly, the greater the number of oscillators, the fuller the sound.

Some sound-producing devices offer a choice of how many oscillators are to be used in a sound, while others restrict the process to a fixed number. Compare, for instance, two common sound modules: the Roland MT-32 and the Yamaha FB-01. Each has 32 oscillators (Yamaha, as noted in the previous chapter, calls them *operators*, while Roland calls them *partials*, but no matter). With the Roland MT-32, the composer can decide how many oscillators – between one and four – are to be used for any particular sound. With the Yamaha FB-01, each sound is allocated four oscillators, whether or not they are all used.

It is worth noting in passing that the distinction directly affects the amount of polyphony of which each device is capable. The Yamaha FB-01 can be only 8-note polyphonic, while the MT-32 is theoretically capable of 32-note polyphony if each sound is created by only a single oscillator. But, as we have seen, sounds created by single oscillators are not as rich in texture, or as accurate when imitating natural sounds, as those created by multiple oscillators. Four are usually required, so the apparent flexibility of the Roland MT-32 is not the important advantage it at first may seem to be. What is more important is the maximum number of oscillators available for each sound, and this is four in both cases.

Most synthesisers and sound modules offer a choice of how oscillators can be combined in order to produce a sound. These are the *algorithms* of Yamaha's FM synthesis method: the FB-01 has eight, while the DX7 has 32. In Roland's LA synthesis, the combinations are called *structures*, and the MT-32 has 13. Other methods of synthesis from other manufacturers offer similar procedures. Graphical representations of the algorithms/structures are often shown on the instrument's display panel (and briefly explained in the user manual) and are usually displayed on screen in sound-editing software. Examples of combinations are shown in Figure 8.3.

8.2.1 Assignment of the Sound-producing Oscillators

It is possible to adjust each oscillator on the screen-display of the synthesiser editor, and therefore to change the nature of the sound in question. The first step in making such adjustments, and therefore of creating a sound, is to think about it in terms of dividing the oscillators into two, according to their function within the sound. We shall call them Type A and Type B oscillators.

Type A oscillators produce the sound: they are the *carriers* of FM synthesis, as described in the previous chapter. Piggy-backed onto them are the Type B oscillators, those which are assigned the subsidiary role of modifying the Type A variety. These are the *modulators* of FM synthesis.

Type A oscillators normally affect the sound as follows:

❑ Their volume is directly proportional to the volume of the sound

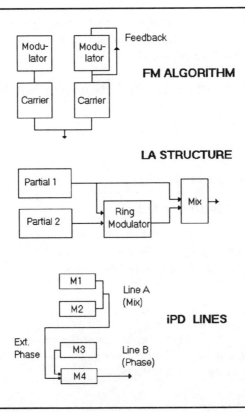

Figure 8.3: Combining oscillators in FM, LA and iPD synthesis

❑ Their frequency generally affects the pitch of the sound

❑ Except in FM synthesis, their waveform plays an important role in the texture of a sound: smooth waveforms create smooth textures (flutes, organs); coarse waveforms create coarse textures (brass); random waveforms create noise (pitchless sounds)

❑ Their envelope characteristics are roughly the envelope characteristics of the sound

❑ Their sensitivity to MIDI Note On velocity dictates the amplitude of the sound, that is to say the extent to which the loudness of the sound will be affected by (for instance) how hard the keys of a synthesiser are pressed.

Type B oscillators normally affect the sound as follows:

❑ Their volume affects the brightness of the sound

❑ Their envelope modifies the basic texture of the sound

❏ Their sensitivity to MIDI Note On velocity dictates the extent to which the brightness of the sound will be affected by (for instance) how hard the keys of a synthesiser keyboard are pressed.

8.2.2 Other Parameters Affecting the Sound

Sound performance settings

These settings, which can also be adjusted on screen, affect the sensitivity of the sound being edited towards performance characteristics such as vibrato, tremolo, portamento, breath control and pitch bend.

Low Frequency Oscillator (LFO)

The word *Frequency* as represented in the acronym LFO is not used to indicate pitch directly, but the speed of oscillation. An LFO is often used to act on an entire voice or an entire instrument, and it affects pitch and/or amplitude by being set to a certain speed and depth of variation, as is required in tremolo (amplitude) and vibrato (pitch).

With a low LFO *speed* (say, 5 on a scale of 1 to 100)) overdoing the LFO *depth* acting on pitch (say, 90) will create either ghost-like or machine-like sounds, while with a fast LFO *speed* (say, 100) the same pitch *depth* will produce a hiss as in wind, storm, seashore and similar effects.

Keyboard Scaling

With some sound editors, it is possible to choose whether sounds will get louder or softer as, for instance, the player moves up or down the keyboard. And with some, it may also be possible to define whether envelopes will get shorter as notes rise in pitch, and longer as they fall. As a rule, in natural sounds high notes die away more rapidly than low notes, and this facility will allow the effect to be reproduced automatically.

8.3 Editing Samples

Samplers do not use any fancy methods of sound synthesis. The numbers representing a sound are simply a map of it, though the map can hardly be called simple, and many numbers are required. A sound lasting just one second, sampled at 44.1 KHz, will take up 44,100 bytes at 8-bit resolution; at 16-bit resolution using an 8-bit processor it will take up 88,200 bytes (getting on for a million numbers), though actually editing samples does not involve working at that level of detail.

As with synthesised sound, some editing programs allow envelopes, and in this case also waveforms, to be drawn on the screen with a mouse, which the program then converts into sample data. It is therefore feasible to create sounds from scratch and send them to a sampler, though the usual way of using sound-editing programs with samplers is to edit an existing sampled sound.

Editing a sample can involve cleaning out any hiss, changing its dynamic range, applying ADSR envelope shaping, and so forth. But where a sample-editing program really comes into its own is in providing help with *looping*, and re-shaping samples using Cut and Paste.

Looping is one of the most important of sample-editing functions, and also one of the most difficult things to achieve. In terms of memory, the most expensive commodity on samplers is sampling time – it is simply too wasteful of precious memory to record a note ten seconds long. The solution is to sample a short section, then repeat it by looping it. However, for a loop to work there must be a precise match of the waveforms at the beginning and end points of the looped section, and the amplitude of the sample at these two points must also be at very similar levels. If these two conditions are not met, the loop does not join smoothly and a thumping noise is heard.

However, a good editor program can search for perfect looping points or, if it is unable to find them, can help to edit the waveforms and envelopes so that a good loop can be achieved. And Cut and Paste functions allow sections of the sample to be moved around and re-shaped in such a way as to allow good looping points to be joined.

8.4 Editing Multi-timbral Settings

Modern electronic instruments do not merely store data about sounds. They also memorise parameters about performance configurations (see Figure 8.4), tuning settings, alternative tuning scales (see below Section 8.6), MIDI channel numbers, note allocation of drum sounds (in other words, which MIDI note represents which percussion sound) and so on. Most of these settings can be edited with comparative ease, on the instrument's panel if desired – except for one group of them: performance memories, which can sometimes hold almost as much data as a set of sounds.

The term *performance memory* is used to describe the way in which the sounds of multi-timbral sound modules and synthesisers are configured. An alternative term is *patch setting*, a *patch* being a piece of jargon originating from the time of analogue synthesisers when so-called patch cables were used to pass the signals from one individual component of the synthesiser to another. A patch is now used to indicate the parameters making up an individual sound, as well as all the sounds in a performance memory. The buttons on a synthesiser allowing different sounds to be called up are sometimes called patch buttons, just as sound editors are occasionally referred to as patch editors.

PERFORMANCE NAME	Another song							
PART	1	2	3	4	5	6	7	8
MAX. NOTES (0-8)	3	1	1	2	1			
INSTRUMENT (A1-B64)	A2	B8	B8	A7	B63			
CHANNEL (1-16,OMNI)	1	2	2	3	3			
LOWER LIMIT (C-2 – G8)	C-2	C-2	C-2	C-2	F4			
UPPER LIMIT (C-2 – G8)	G8	G8	G8	E4	G8			
TRANSPOSE (-24 – +24)				+24	-12			
DETUNE (-50 – +50)		-8	+7					
VOLUME (0-127)	127	110	110	78	95			
OUTPUT (MIX, L – R)	MIX	L	R	MIX	L			

Figure 8.4: Multi-timbral performance settings

A multi-timbral device can receive information on more than one MIDI channel, and thus act like a number of synthesisers working simultaneously. A performance memory specifies how each of those synthesisers will behave, *viz*:

❏ which MIDI channel will be used for each musical part

❏ which sounds, and from which bank in the synthesiser's memory, will be allocated to that part

❏ the maximum number of notes allocated to that part for polyphonic purposes

❏ the volume of the part

❏ to which of the audio outputs the part is allocated (usually left or right, but occasionally a bigger range since some sound modules have multiple outputs)

❏ the upper and lower note limits of the part

❏ whether the part should be transposed (in semitone or whole octave steps)

❏ whether the part should be de-tuned slightly up or down

❏ which extra effects such as reverb and echo (if the module is capable of them) will be applied to the part.

Most multi-timbral sound modules and keyboards can store a number of performance memories, typically 16, 32, 64 or 128. They are useful for working on several musical pieces at the same time because it is a fairly easy matter to switch from one to the other, just as when writing letters on some word processors it is possible to keep separate files containing the information about different formats (paper size, sign-off messages and so on) for different kinds of letter.

Performance memories are also useful, especially on stage, for combining different sounds in real time to create a thicker texture, in which case the process is known as *dual mode* or *sound layering*, that is to say a set-up in which two or more different timbres are assigned to the same MIDI channel, so that when the keyboard is played they sound at the same time.

8.4 Librarians

Synthesisers and sound modules use ROM and RAM cartridges or cards to store extra sounds (ROMs cannot be altered, RAMs can). None of these comes at a bargain-basement price: a single cartridge holding a mere 16 voices, or a card holding 128 voices, can cost over £45. But for the price of about four of them, a Universal Editor/Librarian can be bought, which will not only allow the sounds of most available MIDI equipment to be edited, but also whole libraries of sounds stored on disk to be compiled.

This is not only a cheaper solution but also a more convenient one because librarians allow you to work with single large databases of sounds rather than lots of small banks limited to the memory size of the equipment. With large banks, sound scan be sorted, searched for, and so on. It should be said, however, that the situation is in flux. Some of the newer top-of-the-range synthesisers and sound modules are fitted with 3.5 inch floppy-disk drives.

8.5 Editors for Non-instrumental MIDI Equipment

Editor programs are available for other pieces of equipment which are controlled via MIDI and need to be programmed using sets of numbers, but which do not in themselves produce sound. These include effects units, MIDI mixers and audio patch bays, all of which pieces of hardware are treated in Chapter 9.

8.6 Alternative Tuning

We have concentrated in this chapter on the way in which certain tools can be used to create new sounds, something we believe to be a worthwhile goal. However, it is far from impossible to achieve sonic originality with existing instruments sounds, particularly with tuning scales different from those traditionally found in Western music. Chinese, Arabic, Indian and other so-called ethnic music, sounds qualitatively distinct from ours, because it not only uses different instruments but also different scales.

Western music splits an octave into 12 semitone steps, with each step divisible into a 100 *cents* making a total of 1200 cents in an octave. For the last couple of hundred years or so, these steps have become hardened into our way of hearing music, and all the structures of our music are based on them. But they are not the only possible steps, and in former times a number of other scales were used in the West. Indian music of today has a scale of 22 steps, Indonesian music scales of 5 and 7, ancient Arabic of 17, and although modern Arabic music uses a 12-step scale, the steps are not the same as the 12 semitones of Western music. It is a kind of arrogance on our part to refer to any scale which is not composed of the 12 semitones we know so well as *microtonal* (indicating that the spaces between the semitone steps are used), as if these semitones were the only applicable standard. Nevertheless, the word is commonly used to describe music which is not based on the Western system.

The subject of microtonality is extremely complex, encompassing psycho-acoustics and mathematics, and a whole host of difficult concepts and formulae concerning frequencies and harmonic ratios. Many books on the physics of music contain sections on it, and there are books entirely devoted to it. For those who wish to explore the area, we would recommend *Tuning In – Microtonality in Electronic Music* by Scott Wilkinson (Hal Leonard Books, 1988), not only because it is a practical guide to alternative scales on modern electronic instruments, but also because it is (more or less) understandable by the lay person. Here, we shall confine ourselves to a few basic notions.

The steps on a piano keyboard, with its keys for practical purposes permanently set to produce a particular pitch, are a compromise known as *equal temperament*. This means that the tuning of each key is set as one of the 12 equal steps (semitones) in an octave, but in order to sound in tune with each other in every musical key they have to be *tempered* (adjusted) so that each is very slightly out of tune with its neighbours. The reason for this lies in the composition of musical notes.

A musical note produced by an acoustic instrument or the human voice consists of a *fundamental*, which is the lowest frequency (the one which gives the note its perceived pitch) and other higher frequencies called *overtones*, which give the sound its timbre. A clarinet produces a mellow sound from an abundance of lower overtones, while an oboe lacks them and produces a sharper sound. Overtones can occur in a *natural harmonic series*, in whole-number ratios to the fundamental: halves (2:1), thirds (3:1) and so on. They are then called *harmonics*, or *partials*, the latter because in order to produce a note of the same fundamental frequency as the original fundamental, a vibrating string or tube would have to be half its original length (2:1), a third (3:1) and so on – partial strings or tubes would have to be used. Harmonics can sometimes be heard faintly if an acoustic instrument is listened to very carefully. Instruments which give sounds of indeterminate pitch, like drums and cymbals, produce overtones with frequencies outside the natural harmonic series.

When a note of a given pitch is played together with a note whose pitch belongs to one of its own harmonic series, they harmonise. When the same note is played with another which is outside its own harmonic series, the result is dissonance. An interval of a second (C and D played together, say) sounds dissonant. An interval of a third (C and E) harmonises.

The problem is that dividing an octave into 12 equal steps does not produce whole-number ratios for intervals. A pure or *natural* interval of a third is fine when played in one key signature, but sounds dissonant when played in another. It is not practicable to retune a piano every time it is to be played in a different key because it takes such a long time to do so. The tuning of a piano is therefore tempered so that it can be used in any musical key. An interval of a third in equal temperament is 14 cents wider than its natural counterpart (the overtone produced in the harmonic series). An interval of a fifth is two cents narrower. It is for this tuning that Bach wrote his celebrated *The Well-Tempered Clavier*, preludes and fugues in all keys.

Electronic keyboards, of course, can be tuned without the physical barriers associated with tuning pianos. Notes are by common practice produced at specified frequencies defined according to the equal-temperament standard. For example, with the note A at 440 Hz (as it is now agreed world-wide), the note Middle C falls at 261.63 Hz, the D above it 293.66 Hz, and the E above that at 329.63 Hz. But in principle there is nothing stop a synthesiser manufacturer allowing players to define their own scales. The only reason why this is not usually done is one of demand: obviously, Western musicians tend to create Western-style music.

A few years ago, however, as part of its bid for originality Yamaha made such a feature available to the middle-of-the-road musician, where before it had been used only in experimentalist university music departments. A number of Yamaha's keyboard instruments in the TX and DX range allow the tonal intervals of an octave to be re-defined. They also include some pre-set alternative tunings for the whole keyboard, such as quarter-tone scale and an eighth-tone scale. Other manufacturers producing similar instruments include Ensoniq and Kurtzweil.

These are the electronic extension of experiments with microtonal instruments in the nineteenth century, huge keyboards with 40 or more keys per octave laid out in rows or other combinations for use with different key signatures. The difference is that such instruments were produced for perfect intonation within the accepted musical framework of the time, not for originality. Technology now allows us to use 12 keys to produce many more steps within an octave. It is unfortunate that today's middle-of-the-road musicians do not appear to have reached the relevant pages in the manuals of the modern instruments capable of alternative tunings. Unfortunate, because such tonal flexibility is another path in the search for originality.

8.7 Products

Facilities vary enormously in sound editors. Some are basic, while others have advanced features, such as advanced graphical user-interfaces, memory-resident librarian modules, global editing of combinations of similar parameters, simultaneous editing of several synthesisers, and so on.

Editor/librarians for particular synthesisers

Producer	Cmptr	Price	Synthesisers/comment
Bacchus	PC	B to C	Yamaha DX7, TX81Z, TX802. Not for CGA monitors.
C-Lab	ST	B	Roland MT-32; Oberheim Matrix 1000; Korg M1.
Dr T	Am, Mac, PC, ST	B	Casio CZ, VZ series; Roland D series; Yamaha DX, TX series; Kawai (all); Oberheim 6/1000, E-mu Proteus.
Gajits	Am, ST	B	CMpanion for Roland CM series. 4DCompanion for Roland D series.
Geerdes	ST	B	Yamaha DX7, SY77; Kawai K1, K4/R: Roland U-110, U-20, D5/10/20/110, MT-32, D-50; Prophet VS; Korg M1/R, M3/R.
Newtronic	Am, ST	A to B	Yamaha FB-01, DX, TX series, SY77; Roland D series, MT-32; Korg M1, M3; Kawai K1; Ensoniq VFX. They include free sounds.
Opcode	Mac	B to C	Yamaha DX, TX series, FB-01; Casio CZ series; E-mu Proteus; Korg M1; Oberheim 6, 12, 1000; Roland D-series, MT-32.
Poke	PC	A/B	Very wide range – too long to list.
Sound Quest	Am, PC, ST	B	Even wider range.
Steinberg Research	ST	B to C	Yamaha DX, TX series, SY77; Korg M1/M3; Roland D-10/110/20/50, MT-32; E-mu Proteus; Kawai K1.
Voyetra	PC	B	Yamaha DX, TX series; Roland D-50, D-550; Korg DW-8000, EX-8000.

Universal Editors/librarians

Product	Producer	Computer(s)	Price
Gen Edit	Hybrid Arts	Mac, ST	Mac: D ST: C
Galaxy	Opcode	Mac C	
X-OR	Dr T	Am, Mac, PC, ST	C/D
MIDIman	Hollis Research	ST	B
Midi Quest	Sound Quest	PC	C
Midi Master	Computer Business Associates	PC	C

Sampler Editors

These programs work with most samplers, but check before buying.

Product	Producer	Computer(s)	Price	Comments
Alchemy	Blank Software	Mac	E/F	Digital EQ.
Avalon	Steinberg Research	ST	D	Edit eight samples simultaneously and, with optional D/A converter, monitor edits without need to transfer data back to the sampler.
Computer Music	Composers Desktop	ST	B	One of the first on the Atari. Price is for the system, with additional modules in price categories A to B.
FDSoft	Lyre	PC	C	
GenWave	Hybrid Arts	ST	C	
Sample-Maker	Dr T	ST	C/D	
Sample Vision	Turtle Beach	PC	D	Intelligent looping.
SoftSynth	Digidesign	Mac, ST	C/D	Does FM synthesis too.
Sound Apprentice	Passport	Mac	D	
Sound Designer	Digidesign	Mac, ST	Mac: D ST: C/D	
Sound Designer II SK	Digidesign	Mac	E	Stereo, disk-based, digital EQ.
Sound Designer II	Digidesign	Mac	F	SMPTE, supports Sound Tools digital recording and editing (see Chapter 10 Section 10.6.)
Turbosynth	Digidesign	Mac, ST	D	

Key

Am: Commodore Amiga
Mac: Apple Macintosh
PC: IBM PC and compatibles
ST: Atari ST

Practical Sound

Thus far in this book we have looked at the different ingredients which can convert bytes composed of 0s and 1s into meaningful musical sounds: a computer, a MIDI interface, input devices such as synthesiser keyboards, sequencers for arranging combinations of notes, and output devices like sound modules. The moment has now come to leave talk of basic ingredients, to think about adding spice and seasoning, and doing some real cooking. And if the meal is to be of gourmet standard, a mixer is necessary – a sound mixer.

9.1 Sound Mixers

If more than two musical instruments are used in a MIDI studio (including acoustic instruments) a sound mixer is a necessity. The reason is that human beings (along with most tape recorders) have only two ears. In the end, all music played via MIDI is funneled into two signals (the *mixdown*), usually to be recorded, amplified, and listened to via a stereo speaker system. Enthusiasts of quadraphonic sound would say that this does not have to be so, but the fact remains that stereo sound is the present standard, and is likely to remain so.

A MIDI studio may have many sound modules, both synthesiser and sampling, synthesiser keyboards, and other sound-producing devices. The audio signals from all these pieces of equipment are fed into a sound mixer, where they are processed, then mixed into a stereo signal which can be recorded to tape.

Mixers, then, are electronic devices used to mix a number of sound sources into a number of sound destinations, and these numbers in both cases vary with the flexibility of the unit. An *8:2* (eight into two) mixer, for example, accepts eight inputs and gives two outputs. A *16:8:2* (sixteen into eight into two) mixer accepts sixteen inputs and can give either eight or two outputs, the eight outputs being used perhaps to send separate signals to an 8-track tape recorder.

A mixer can easily be recognised in a MIDI studio, however jam-packed it is with equipment. The mixer is the piece of hardware with the most knobs and/or sliders (called *faders*). It comes in one of two forms: either as a flat stand-alone horizontal box (it is then said to be *flat bed*) or rack-mounted.

Most of the input and output sockets are to be found at the back of the unit, except perhaps for a headphones socket at the front. Typically a mixer will have three types of socket for connecting different types of equipment: *jack*, *phono*, and *XLR* connections.

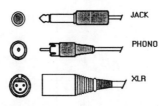

Figure 9.1: Types of audio connections

Jack connections are used for domestic and semi-professional musical applications, usually found equipment such as synthesisers, microphones, electric guitars, effects units and headphones.

Phono connections are mostly used in domestic audio equipment, such as tape recorders, amplifiers and CD players.

XLR (also known as *balanced XLR*) connections are used in professional audio applications, and they give the best results. They use three wires instead of the two used by the other two types of connection. More importantly, XLR inputs and outputs are balanced, that is to say that all their electrical characteristics match each other, thus avoiding unwanted electro-magnetic interference (noise). Balanced XLR connection is usually provided only on more expensive equipment, and in most cases is not essential, but it is desirable that all microphone connections on the mixer are of this type.

Each input into the mixer is channelised, that is to say that it follows a separate path where it is manipulated independently and shaped up, then mixed with the rest of the inputs to give a combined output.

The number of channels on a mixer is an important factor to consider. As a practical rule of thumb, the number of channels required on a mixer for a particular studio is the number of acoustic instruments or vocal lines, plus the total number of audio outputs from MIDI instruments needing separate equalisation (tone control) and effects. Factors like volume and stereo panning (see below) can normally be dealt with from the sequencer.

9.1.1 Individual Channel Controls ⁄ *for notes*

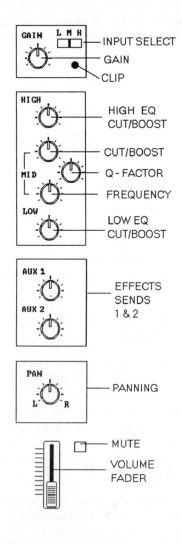

Figure 9.2: A typical set of channel controls on a sound mixer

For each separate channel, a sound mixer may offer some or all of the following:

Input Select

There are three categories of electrical audio signal levels which can be sent from electronic instruments and sound devices:

❑ Low level: output by microphones (and some electric guitars)

❑ Mid level: output by electric guitars (and some synthesisers)

❑ High level: output by keyboards, sound modules, most sound effects units, and tape recorders (this level is commonly called *line level*).

In order to understand the differences between these signals, a little elementary knowledge of electrical current, and a little more of the physics of sound, are required. We shall certainly not scratch beyond the merest outer skin of physics, but three concepts are apposite here: *watts*, *volts* and *decibels*.

Watts need some explanation because the power of amplifiers and loudspeakers is measured in them.

The term *horsepower* was originally the amount of work an average horse could do in one day, and it was used as a measurement of steam engines when they replaced horses as the main source of power. A watt is 1/746 of a horsepower. Car engines are rated in horsepower, and electrical appliances in the home in watts and kilowatts (a kilowatt is 1,000 watts, or roughly 1.3 horsepower).

In measuring sound, however, we must distinguish between the amount of energy radiated, and the amount required to produce that radiation, and there is a big difference between the two, since the vast majority of the energy expended is lost. It may take a 10-kilowatt engine to drive a theatre organ, but the sound which comes out of it will be no more than about 20 watts. A full symphony orchestra may generate about 70 watts, but the combined efforts of the players will run into many kilowatts.

In sound, watts are related to loudness, which is measured in *decibels*, usually abbreviated to *dB*. A decibel is one tenth of a *bel*, so called after the inventor who changed all our lives, Alexander Graham Bell. The human ear is so extremely broad in its range of sensitivity, that decibels work on a logarithmic rather than a linear scale, otherwise the range of decibels which we can hear would have far too many divisions. Consider a very sensitive set of post-office scales capable of measuring the weight of a single postage stamp. If those scales had the same sensitivity range as the human ear has for sound, they would also be able to measure the weight of several jumbo jets.

Yet, for reasons which we shall not go into here, it so happens that one decibel is about equal to the smallest change in loudness which the average person can distinguish. The loudness of a sound of 0 dB is on the threshold of hearing, and 120 dB is on the threshold of pain. An ordinary conversation between two people takes place at about 60 dB. A violin played softly heard by an audience a few feet way is heard at about 20 dB, and the sound of a full orchestra heard by someone sitting in the front row can top 100 dB.

Volts are used to define a difference in electrical energy, and one way of thinking about voltage is to use the analogy of a waterfall. The higher the waterfall the greater the potential energy as the water leaves the top – a high voltage is a high waterfall. Of course, the *amount* of water falling is of critical importance if you are standing underneath, but if you were in a helicopter above Niagara Falls and poured a bottle of water into it, the potential energy of the poured water would be greater than that of the Falls because it was starting from a greater height. The *amount* of water, in this analogy, is equivalent to the electrical *current*.

The matter is complicated, however, by the fact that it is usual practice not to denote the power of audio signals in volts, but in dB (or -dB when nothing could actually be heard if sound was emitted at that level), because there is a direct relationship between the two.

Now, since within the range of musical equipment which can be connected to a sound mixer there are varying levels of output, the mixer should be able to cope with these differences and to match its input to them, otherwise the signal will be distorted, weak, hissy or barely heard.

Most mixers have a switch for specifying the required input level, though some models, called *line mixers* accept only line-level (high-level) signals and can therefore not be used directly for microphones and electric guitars. Line-level mixers are intended for use with keyboards and sound modules only.

The dB ratings for each level are:

❑ Microphone or low level: about -50 dB or less

❑ Guitar or mid level: about -35 dB

❑ Line or high level: -10 dB, though some professional equipment works at a balanced level of +4 dB.

Gain

This is usually a knob, and it is used for increasing or decreasing the amplification of the audio signal.

Clip level

This is usually a red light (an LED – Light Emitting Diode) which illuminates when the input signal is too strong, therefore creating distortion.

Insert point /

This is an input/output socket which will take an effects unit. With such a device connected, the signal leaves the mixer, is treated by the effects unit, and returns via the same socket. This is very useful for compressing the signal (see below Section 9.2.2).

High and Low Equalisation (High/Low EQ) /

Typically, this is a set of two control knobs which increase or decrease the level (amplitude) of high and low frequencies, and is therefore similar to the treble and bass controls on a domestic audio system. The High EQ usually acts above 10 KHz, and the low EQ below 100 Hz. They can add or subtract about 10 to 12 dB from the high and low frequencies of the signal.

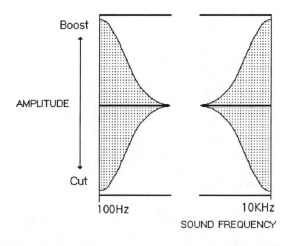

Figure 9.3: High and Low EQ

Mid Equalisation (Mid EQ) /

Again, this is usually a set of two control knobs, in this case for finer EQ control, generally found on professional and semi-professional mixers and known as *sweep* equalisation. The knobs are there to allow adjustment of the middle frequencies, which is done by varying two parameters: one for the range of frequency to be boosted or cut (typically centred anywhere between 500 Hz and 6 KHz, at the discretion of the user) and the other for the strength of the boost or cut (again, plus or minus about 10 to 12 dB). On high-range professional mixers there may be two sets of Mid EQ controls, allowing two separate frequencies to be boosted or cut independently.

When a frequency is boosted or cut, adjacent frequencies are also affected. On professional-level mixers, a third parameter (called a *Q* (Quality) factor) adjusts the sharpness of the *peak* – in other words, it allows adjacent frequencies to be widened or narrowed. The process is known as *parametric* equalisation. Take a simple example: a microphone connection is giving an annoying buzz at, say, 200 Hz. This frequency could be cut to reduce the loudness of the buzz, perhaps even to cut it out altogether, but the surrounding frequencies will also be affected unless the knob controlling the Q factor is set to make the range of frequencies around 200 Hz as narrow as possible.

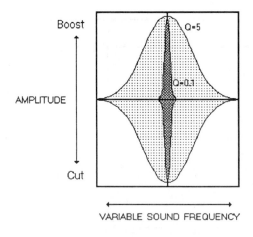

Figure 9.4: Parametric EQ

Effects Send

This is a control for how much of a given signal will be affected by an effects unit for adding reverb, echo and so forth. So, if two channels (for instance, piano and strings) each simultaneously send part of their signal to an effects unit to be treated for echo, the Effects Send knob for each channel can be adjusted to allow more or less echo for each instrument. Many modern mixers offer a number of Effects Sends, typically between two and six. In this way, all channels can be treated collectively for echo, say, instead of having an echo machine for each separate channel.

Pan /

Again usually a knob, which allows control over the position of the signal in the stereo spectrum.

Channel Volume (slide

The volume of each channel is typically controlled by a sliding fader. In this way, it is possible to determine how loud each channel will be in the mixdown. Some mixers have an LED (Light Emitting Diode) display to indicate the level of the signal as the music plays, so that the faders can be adjusted to get a strong but distortion-free signal.

Mute /

This is a switch to turn the signal on and off, and is often used as an adjunct to the Channel Volume faders. Say, for instance, that all the faders have been set to precise levels. It is usually quite difficult to get the perfect mix, that is to say just the right balance of instruments, and it would be irritating to have to turn one of the faders to zero to cut a channel out. The Mute switch allows it to be cut out temporarily without altering its fader setting. So, to hear a channel on its own after the mix has been set, all other channels could be muted.

9.1.2 Overall Signal Controls

So far we looked at how the signal within each individual channel is controlled. But mixers also have controls for handling all channels at once.

Overall Effects Send /

All the signals from the Channel Effects Send are collected into one, and this single signal is routed into an effects unit. The overall level can be controlled using this knob or fader. So, if for example the total signal going into an effects unit is too strong, the Overall Effects Send knob can be adjusted, instead of having to adjust each individual Channel Effects Send.

Effects Return /

Again, this can be a knob or a fader. When the signal returns from an effects unit, it controls the volume of the returned effect, in other words how much of it will be mixed with the rest of the input signals.

Note that although each channel has its own Effects Send control, it does not have its own Effects Return, which is only ever a collective return. In addition, in some mixers, collective Effects Sends and Returns can be treated for Equalisation and Panning.

Overall Volume

There are commonly two of these controls (usually faders), one for the left stereo channel and the other for the right. There is also a display (usually LEDs) indicating the level of the output signal.

9.1.3 The Range of Available Mixers

MIDI Control

Some mixers are capable of being controlled via MIDI.

At the bottom end of the range, snapshots of different settings can be stored in memory in the mixer, and recalled via MIDI Program Change numbers, with a cross-fade function giving control over how gradual the change is to be between one setting and the next.

At the higher end, real-time control for each parameter is available, with the mixer being treated like any other MIDI device. As a knob or a fader is moved, MIDI messages are sent to a sequencer to be recorded along with the musical score. On playback, data comes back from the sequencer and controls the mixer functions.

Motorised faders are to be found at the very top end of the range. Here, MIDI not only controls the signals flowing through the mixer, but also moves the faders accordingly so that their positions can be seen and further adjustments made. Note, however, that, real-time automation is necessary only with acoustic sounds, which MIDI cannot control. MIDI instruments can of course have their loudness and panning controlled via a sequencer, but this is not possible with recorded vocals or other natural sounds.

Analogue versus Digital

Most of today's mixers are still analogue, and modern digital technology is only just beginning to make inroads. The advantages of a digital mixer are a clearer signal (less distortion, though not less noise), and a higher dynamic range. Future added benefits could include built-in effects and a degree of automation. However, much depends on the quality of the equipment, and a cheap digital mixer may give poorer results than an high-specification analogue mixer.

9.1.4 General Advice on Choosing Mixers

Buying second-hand is a good option with mixers, since unlike tape recorders for example, the only moving parts are the knobs and faders. Many people sell their mixers because they want to upgrade to models with more channels, and second-hand bargains are there for the taking, often advertised in specialist magazines. We would suggest that a minimum requirement is an 8-channel mixer, although 12, 16 and even 24 channels will probably be a good investment for the future.

It may be advisable to pay some attention to the *signal-to-noise ratio* of a mixer, a specification denoting the amount of background noise (hiss) relative to the sound of the signal itself. Figures are often given in dB as *EIN* (Equivalent Input Noise). Professional mixers will have a value of -130 dB and above, and for this reason they are expensive. Anything less that about -120 dB is likely to prove too noisy. It is worth mentioning, however, that specifications such as these can sometimes be difficult to compare, since manufacturers can have different ways of expressing them. The only sound advice (so to speak) is to trust one's ears rather than a manufacturer's list of specifications, and this of course goes for any audio equipment.

A final feature of some mixers is built-in *phantom power* so that *condenser* microphones can be connected to them. Phantom power and condenser microphones are discussed in Chapter 10 Section 10.1.1.

Very cheap mixers start at about £150, but we would not recommend them. For reasonable quality you can expect to pay prices around £250 for eight tracks, £600 for 16 tracks, and £1,000 or more for 24 tracks.

9.1.5 Choice Checklist for Mixers

The following are questions to consider when selecting a sound mixer:

❑ How many channels are required?

❑ How many Effects Sends and Returns are likely to be used?

❑ Do the instruments in the studio require sophisticated EQ, or do they already give the right sounds at source?

❑ Are microphone or guitar inputs required, or will a line mixer suffice?

❑ Is automation required, and if so, is real-time automation a necessity?

❑ What is the mixer's signal-to-noise ratio (though see the caveat above in Section 9.1.4)?

❑ Is a multi-track tape recorder required as well as a mixer? (see Chapter 10 Section 10.2)

❑ If the use of a condenser microphone is envisaged, does the mixer have phantom powering? (see Chapter 10 Section 10.1.1)

9.2 Effects – the Spices of Sound

Fresh food is often rich enough to interest the taste buds without the need for extra seasoning, while processed food needs seasoning agents to make it more interesting. In modern sound production, the situation is identical. First-hand sounds, like those of a flute or a guitar being played live, are naturally rich and normally require no further processing. Canned sounds, like the ones emptied out of sound modules and synthesiser keyboards, and especially the ones packed in samplers, can be dull and thin. But the final sound of canned music can be enriched by passing it through through a sound-effects unit.

Adding sound effects means using devices which take an audio signal and alter it in some way, and they can act on individual sounds or on the whole composition. The effects can be used for various purposes:

❏ to change a sound's dynamic range in order to make it recordable without distortion

❏ to change its harmonic content, for example to make it brighter and stand out from other sounds

❏ to boost and/or cut some of its frequencies so that it does not clash with other sounds and fits better within the overall arrangement

❏ to change it completely and create a new sound

❏ to simulate different acoustics – a cathedral, a concert hall, a disco, a small room, and so on – by using echo, reverb and so on

❏ to cut out unwanted noise.

A sound-effects unit has at least one input and one output socket. It also has some knobs for controlling the amount of effect to be added, which can vary between two extremes: a *dry* signal and a *wet* signal. A dry signal means that the sound is not affected at all, and a wet signal is the effect alone without the original sound.

Some effects units work in stereo, but they all come in one of three forms: as a foot pedal, in a rack-mounted box of full, half or a third width (rack adaptors allow half-size or third-size units to be put into a rack), or in non-standard boxes.

9.2.1 Analogue and Digital Effects Units

Early effects units were all analogue, but about half of them are now digital. All analogue devices have controls on the front panel for setting effect parameters, or altering them in real time – a reverb, for instance, can be made longer. With digital effects units, parameters are mostly programmed before the effect is activated.

Some digital units are pre-set at the factory, some allow the user to program effects, but most offer a combination of both.

With digital units, control is also possible via MIDI. In its simplest form this entails using MIDI Program Change messages to switch from one effect to another. In more complex devices, some effects parameters are assigned to MIDI Controller messages and can be altered in real time. In this way, a reverb can be made longer just as on an analogue unit.

Some effects units provide only one type of effect, and most early analogue devices were of this variety – they came as reverb machines, echo machines, and so on. In modern digital devices the effects are programs stored in their microchips rather than being in dedicated circuitry. By applying these programs to digitised incoming sound, different effects can be achieved within the same device. Indeed, the latest units cover most types of known sound-processing effects.

Even though many digital effects units may offer 100 or more different programs, most can still handle only one signal, and therefore only one effect, at a time. However, multi-effects units are becoming increasingly available, which can handle up to five or six effects simultaneously. They work in basically the same way as single-effects units, but a single program simulates the result of a number of effects.

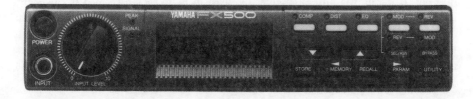

Figure 9.5: The Yamaha FX500 multi-effects unit

9.2.2 Available Effects

It is impossible to describe satisfactorily in words the sound which can be achieved by using effects units. Our aim here, therefore, is limited to explaining how the effects are produced and giving some practical advice on using them. In the right hands they are powerful tools which can give life and movement to music in a way which is not easily achieved in a purely acoustic performance.

The major effects available on effects units are as follows:

Reverb /

Reverberation is the result of thousands, or even millions, of sound-wave reflections within a confined space like a concert hall – it is as if the sound continues of its own accord. It differs from echo (see below) in the same way that singing into a hollow pipe differs from singing in a high-sided valley: in the case of reverb, there is no repetition of the sound. Reverb can thus give depth to a dry and uninteresting sound, and is probably the most important of all effects.

The latest programmable digital reverb units allow the reverberation characteristics of rooms and halls to be simulated. It is possible to specify parameters related to room acoustics such as the dimensions of the room, the sound-absorbing qualities of the walls, and so on.

Echo (

For an echo effect, the signal going into the sound-effects unit is sent back to the mixer at specified repeated intervals with a decrease in amplitude until the sound dies out. If the unit is programmable, the least to be expected from it is to specify the rate of decay (how long it takes for the echo to die away completely) and the *delay time* (the time between each repeat), which is the same as saying that it is possible to set the number and duration of the repeats. A stereo echo effect can also be achieved by setting different values between the left and right channels, giving two different echoes.

A small amount of echo works well with sounds which would otherwise die away too quickly, and echo is generally most effective when the delay time is related to the tempo of a piece of music. With snare drums, say, the delay time might be set to match the beat.

It is worth noting that the terms *echo* and *delay* are sometimes used to mean the same thing – a *digital delay*, for instance, is a sound-effects unit for producing echoes. But occasionally a distinction is made between delays and echoes, because an echo is merely one type of delay.

Chorus /

Chorus, can multiply a single sound, thus creating a *pseudo many* effect. It can simulate, for example, a number of people singing or playing instruments in unison. In real life it is virtually impossible for people to sing or play precisely in time with each other, and at precisely the same loudness. Some will lag slightly behind others and/or sound slightly louder, and at other times they may be slightly ahead and/or sound slightly softer. These are the imperfections (when they do not obtrude) which make ensemble work sound so perfect. The aim of each first-violin player in an orchestra is to sound as much like the other first-violin players as possible, but since the players do not actually achieve this aim (it would be impossible, for example, perfectly to synchronise vibrato) the result is the sound of strings, a distinctly different sound from that of a single violin, not just a louder sound.

The chorus effect is achieved electronically by splitting an incoming signal into two parts (or three for stereo). One part is left unaffected. The other one, or two, are delayed for a very small amount of time, less than about four milliseconds (4 msec, or 4/1000 of a second). In addition the delay time as well as the amplitude of the affected signals are oscillated, thus simulating the real-life random effect of players moving ahead or behind each other, and varying in loudness relative to each other.

By changing the depth and speed of these variations in timing and amplitude, it is possible to simulate a chorus of more than two, indeed the number is theoretically limitless, though it reaches a point at which the ear is unable to distinguish any difference.

It is also possible to create chorus effects by oscillating pitch, just as in a real choir or orchestra, where the singers or players are unable continuously to produce sounds in perfect tuning. This is a very useful feature for thickening sounds, especially strings and vocals.

Flanging /

Flanging is a process used extensively in film and broadcasting to create a futuristic atmosphere. The voices of creatures from outer space are often plain earthly voices which have been flanged. The effect is created in a way similar to that of chorus. The differences are (a) the amplitude of the signal is not varied, and (b) part of the signal (the amount can be defined) is continually fed back and re-processed.

Phasing /

A phasing effect gives the impression that a sound is travelling backwards and forwards between the source and the listener. As with chorus and flanging, the signal is split, but then there is a time-oscillation centred around a delay of about 8 msec. This creates a false impression of a Doppler effect (like the the change in pitch heard when the siren of an ambulance approaches and recedes).

It is worth noting that flanging and phasing can be produced by altering the delay time in chorus. This is sometimes the method adopted in less expensive effects units.

Pitch shifting /

Here the signal is split into two parts (or three for stereo). One part remains unchanged, while the other(s) are shifted up or down in pitch. The change in pitch can be small (less than a semitone) which will thicken the sound, or it can be in semitone steps so that harmonies are created. For this reason pitch-shifting devices are sometimes called *harmonisers*, and some smart harmonisers can be programmed to cope with key changes, the defined intervals changing to stay within the required key. Harmonisers, despite their name, can of course also create discords.

Psycho-acoustic enhancement

Enhancers (sometimes called *aural exciters*) brighten sounds. Their purpose is to put back into sound what has been lost by processing it. The effect is not as evident as, say, that of echo or reverb – in fact, the difference between an enhanced and an unenhanced sound is often noticeable only when the effect is turned off.

An enhancer works by adding harmonics to the signal. As is explained in Chapter 8 Section 8.6, when a live voice or live acoustic instrument produces (say) the note A at 440 Hz, it is also producing other frequencies, the simplest being 880 Hz, that of the octave above. These other frequencies are the harmonics of the main frequency. They have an enormous effect on the timbre of the sound, but they are subtle because they are weak, and are very easily lost while a sound is being processed. A voice recorded on analogue tape, then transferred to another, then another and so on, is affected not only by an increased noise level but by a loss of presence. The job of an enhancer is to re-create the harmonics and put them back into the signal (or add new ones) thus bringing back the presence.

It is possible to define the intensity of the enhancement (the number of harmonics to be added), and to enhance only a particular range of frequencies.

Equalisation

Graphic equalisers are more elaborate versions of those found on domestic audio equipment (they are called *graphic* because the sliders appear to make a visible graph). Ten or more controllable frequency bands are common on equalisers used in MIDI studios, as opposed to the half dozen or so found on most domestic hi-fi systems. A graphic equaliser with ten frequency bands will give a resolution of about one band per octave. Professional graphic equalisers can have as many as 30 bands or more, which zoom into one third of an octave or less.

Graphic equalisers can be used to shape up an important single signal in the mix such as a vocal line, or – and this is a more common use – they can be connected to the overall mix for making final adjustments. They come as mono or stereo, analogue or digital, and manual or programmable. Programmable units can remember different settings and switch from one to another via MIDI.

Parametric equalisers (see above Section 9.1 Mid Equalisation) can also be used for effects.

Compression, limiting, expansion, gating

These four effects can often be found on a single unit, and are all concerned with altering the dynamic range (amplitude levels) of a signal.

For a signal to be recorded properly, it has to be recorded at a reasonably high level, that is to say loudly enough, so that it is clear from tape hiss. But it should not exceed a given threshold beyond which it becomes distorted because the recording capacity of the tape has been overshot. Most audio signals coming out of electronic musical instruments are well-behaved in this respect, but acoustic signals picked up via a microphone are very hard to control. For example, singers can create recording problems by moving too close to, or too far away from microphones.

A *compressor* is an electronic signal-level guard. It listens closely to the signal, and when the limit begins to be exceeded (this limit, known as the *compression threshold*, can be defined as required), it pulls the signal back, allowing only a given fraction of it to pass through. The amount which would have passed through relative to that which actually does pass through is known as the *compression ratio*. Thus, if the compression ratio is 2:1, half the signal above the compression threshold will pass through. If the compression ratio is Infinity:1, none of the signal above the compression threshold will pass through. This effect is known as *limiting*.

It should be mentioned that compression and limiting can be hard to implement successfully, and the result can easily sound unnatural. And a further difficulty with compression is that when the effect is released, there is a consequent increase in perceived noise. This can be remedied, however, by an opposite process: *expansion*. An *expander* effect can also be used with drums to increase dynamic contrast (note that the word *expander* here is used in an entirely different sense from that of expander sound modules, as treated in Chapter 7 Section 7.2.1).

A *noise gate* mutes the signal completely if this falls below a definable level, cutting off unwanted background noise and hiss. It can be used with vocals and instrumental parts where there are rests, during which the signal can be gated off completely and any noise eliminated.

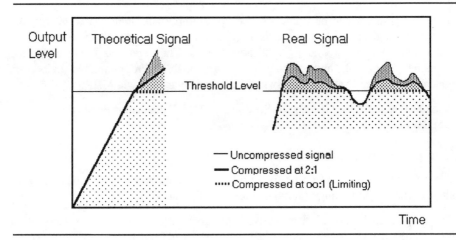

Figure 9.6: Compression and limiting

De-essing

Certain sounds in human speech and singing contain high frequencies, especially sounds such as *S*, *SH* and *T*. When recorded, speech and singing can sound unnatural because these frequencies stand out more than when they are heard live (they can be over 10 dB louder than the surrounding recorded sounds). Equalisation is not used to filter them out because they are *phonemic*, that is to say that meaning depends on them. A de-esser (so-called because it removes part of the S sounds) compresses the signal when a sound with S-type frequencies occur in it, thus making the overall effect more natural.

The same effect can actually be achieved by the combined use of a graphic equaliser and a compressor. The compressor is triggered by the output of the equaliser which is set to boost the S-type frequencies.

Pan

Panning in the world of film means moving a camera to give a panoramic view, or in its more general sense to move the camera slowly from left to right or vice versa. The same is true of the world of stereo sound, where a *pan* means that the sound appears to pass perceptibly from one speaker to another, or any range in between.

As an effect, panning continually shifts the signal in one direction (left to right or right to left) or alternates between left and right movement.

9.2.3 Choice Checklist for Effects Units

The following questions are pertinent when considering almost any effects unit:

❏ If the effect is be used on a MIDI instrument, can it be produced by the instrument internally?

❏ Is the unit stereo or mono?

❏ In a stereo unit, how good is the separation between channels (how little *crosstalk* is there)?

❏ How high is the signal-to-noise ratio? (see above Section 9.1.4)

❏ Is the unit controlled via MIDI?

❏ Is the unit programmable?

❏ Can the unit produce more than one effect at the same time?

9.3 Products

Sound mixers

Manual mixers

A circle (o) indicates that the feature is implemented. In the *Phantom power* column, it indicates that phantom power is provided for condenser microphones. Microphone sockets on all these models are XLR. Prices are guides, not necessarily those recommended by the producer.

Producer/model	Mix	Effects Sends	Rack mounted	EQ controls	Microphone sockets	Phantom power	Price	Comments
Alesis 1622	16:2	6	o	2	8		F	Bulky. Low noise.
Roland M16E	16:2	4	o	3	8	o	F/G	High specifications.
- M24E	24:2	4		3	12	o	G	High specifications.
Tascam M216	16:4	2		3	16		F	Low noise.
- M224	24:4	2		3	24		F/G	Low noise.
Yamaha MV1602	16:2	4	o	3	8		F	18 inputs because two channels are stereo.
Studiomaster Session 16	16:2	4		3	16	o	F	Low noise.
Session 12	12:2	4	o	3	12	o	F	Low noise.

MIDI-controlled mixers

Producer/model	Mix	Dig/An	Price	Special features
Akai MPX-820	8:2	Analogue	F	
Simmons SPM 8:2	8:2	Analogue	C	New version expected next year
Yamaha DMP7	8:2	Digital	H	Motorised faders.
- DMP11	8:2	Digital	F/G	Rack-mounted. Best buy.
- DMP7D	8:2	Digital	H+	Motorised faders.

The Yamaha DMP11 and DMP7D are sonically better than DMP7. The DMP7D does not include the A/D and D/A converters, which have to be bought separately and cost about £3,000. With all three, more than one unit can be cascaded to provide 16, 24 or more channels.

Effects units

Separate effects units

MIDI on its own here indicates that the unit can be controlled from a MIDI device or a sequencer. All units are rack-mounted unless otherwise specified.

Producer/model	Price	Comments
Akai EX80E	B	Mono enhancer.
Alesis ME230	C	30-band stereo graphic equaliser.
- Microverb	B	16 pre-set reverb settings. Everyone loves it.
Aphex Aural Exciter Type C	C	Stereo. Widely used.
Aria EQ515	C/D	15-band stereo graphic equaliser.
Ashly PQ63	D	3-band parametric equaliser.
- PQ66A	F	4-band stereo parametric equaliser.
Boss RCL10	B	Mono compressor/limiter/expander.
Court GE60	F/G	30-band stereo graphic equaliser.
DBX 263X	B	Mono de-esser.
Digitech IPS-33B	F	Harmoniser. 256 programs. MIDI. Intelligent 1- or 2-note harmonising.
Drawmer LX20	C	Stereo compressor/expander.
Lexicon PCM70	G/H	Famous early professional digital reverb. Too expensive.
- LXP1	E	Recent cut-down version of PCM70 with MIDI enhancements.
Marantz EQ551	B/C	10-band stereo graphic equaliser with spectrum analyser and pink noise generator (see Chapter 10 Section 10.5.1). Domestic audio machine.

Producer/model	Price	Comments
Peavey Autograph	E	Mono graphic equaliser. MIDI. Constant Q factor, real-time analyser, pink noise generator, auto-equalisation function analyses frequency response of a sound system and provides suitable EQ.
- CDS 2	C	Stereo compressor/limiter/de-esser.
Roland DEP-3	E	Programmable digital reverb. MIDI.
- GE-131	B	31-band mono graphic equaliser.
- RE-3 Space Echo	D	MIDI-controlled echoes.
Yamaha DEQ7	F	Digital programmable equaliser with 90 memories. Graphic, parametric etc. MIDI.
- R100	C	Budget digital reverb, with some echoes. MIDI.

Multi-effects units

All products here are MIDI-controllable unless otherwise stated.

Producer/model	Price	Comments
Alesis Midiverb III	D	Simultaneous effects: EQ, delay, chorus, reverb. 100 pre-set and 100 programmable settings.
- Quadraverb	D	Simultaneous effects: reverb, delay, EQ, pitch shifting. 100 settings.
Digitech	DS	P128P D 128 effects.
- DSP256	E	256 effects.
Korg A3	F	Up to six simultaneous effects.
Symetrix 528 Voice Processor	E	Broadcast-quality voice processing. Includes phantom power, microphone amplifier, compressor, de-esser, parametric EQ. Recommended.
Yamaha SPX90	C	Historically (1986) the first multi-effects digital processor. 30 pre-set and 60 programmable settings.
- REV5	G	Top-of-the-range stereo programmable digital effects.
- REX50	C	Budget version of SPX90. Includes distortion effects. Geared towards guitarists.
- SPX1000	F/G	Latest grandchild of SPX90 with stereo processing, enhanced sound quality, five simultaneous effects, and digital Input/Output.
- FX500	C/D	Budget version of SPX1000. Six simultaneous effects, and real-time control of effect parameters. Recommended.

10

Adding Acoustic Sounds

The equipment and software mentioned so far, if used with care, are more than sufficient for producing excellent sound: it is simply a matter of connecting the output of the sound mixer to a domestic amplifier and speakers. But technology has not reached the point at which synthesised and sample sounds can be a total substitute for the natural sounds of acoustic instruments and the human voice. Although at the IRCAM music research centre in Paris there are computers which can produce surprisingly good simulations of human singing and natural instruments, no computer has yet equalled the subtlety of the voice of Janet Baker or Geraint Evans (the IRCAM computers merely produce *aaahs*), or the special tone and articulation of a clarinet played by Jack Brymer or Benny Goodman.

In all, although synthesisers can produce sounds which are in some ways more complex than natural sounds, and be made to do things which no human being could do, they cannot yet offer the same range of performance possibilities as acoustic instruments and the human voice. Think of all the different ways in which a saxophone can be blown. A MIDI wind controller can produce saxophone sounds, but it has no reed, and in any case a computer is simply not powerful enough a piece of equipment to handle all the minute tonal adjustments made by the player's lips, teeth, jaw and tongue. MIDI works very well in its simulation of instruments with a limited range of performance characteristics, such church organs, but it cannot yet perfectly simulate all the nuances possible on a viola.

The only way accurately to capture these and many other natural sounds is to record them directly. But they can then be merged with the sounds produced by electronic devices, resulting in a marriage between the two which draws on the best of both worlds. Alan Parsons once said that he never uses synthesised natural-instrument sounds, however accurate they may be – he employs musicians to play natural instruments if the music requires them. This comes as something of a surprise from someone who dares to admit on the covers of his albums that his music is programmed rather than played, and who has made his name because of his ability to use technology in music. The truth is that he and similar musicians do not compromise their sound. Technology and its new sounds are not an easy way out, but a new world which enriches what is already available.

To record natural sounds on tape, two pieces of equipment are required: a microphone and a tape recorder. A microphone converts sound waves picked up from the air into electrical signals which are then sent to the tape recorder.

10.1 Microphones

A microphone is the one piece of musical equipment whose price is nearly always directly related to quality, and the one for which economy should always be low on the list of selection criteria. Microphones cost between £2 and £3,000.

10.1.1 Types of Microphones

There are many categories of microphones, the main ones being *dynamic*, *condenser*, *ribbon*, and *pressure-zone* (usually referred to as *PZM*). They use different mechanisms to pick up sound and convert it to electrical signals, and although any microphone can be used for any application, each category includes types of microphones designed to give the best results with specific applications. For example, there are dynamic microphones oriented towards vocals, others towards acoustic instruments, and so on. Dynamic and condenser microphones are by far the commonest categories. Ribbon microphones are particularly suitable for speech, but do well with low strings such as 'cellos. PZMs are especially suitable for recording orchestral performances.

Dynamic microphones

These are based on a moving diaphragm and coil. On average they are the cheapest variety, though some professional models cost a great deal of money. They are of rugged construction and therefore ideal for stage work, particularly since they require no external powering. As a general rule, they are especially suitable for recording vocals and percussive sounds.

Condenser microphones

These use a system of measuring variations between a diaphragm and a fixed plate. They are generally expensive, of delicate construction, and normally limited to studio work. They give a clear, crisp sound, but they tend to emphasise *S* sounds and other sounds containing very high frequencies, which may have to be removed with a de-esser (described in Chapter 9 Section 9.2.2). They are suitable for vocals and acoustic instruments, but because they are so sensitive they are not normally used for sounds which involve high-pressure waves such as those made by drums (more than 25 per cent of the power produced by a full symphony orchestra playing *double forte* comes form the timpani alone). It is also generally advisable not to cough directly into a condenser microphone – this, and dropping one, are the most common causes of damage.

Condenser microphones require electrical power, which they can get either from an internal battery (not all can take one) or a special electrical transformer called a *phantom power supply*, which provides a very steady (usually) 24 or 48 volts DC (other values down to 9 volts are occasionally seen). This is built into many professional mixers, but a dedicated unit can also be bought separately (price range: categories A to E). Phantom power uses the same socket as the audio signal, and condenser microphones are usually built to receive it at any of its voltages.

There are also microphones of the condenser variety known as *electret* microphones, which do not require external power but will run on a small battery. They were originally a cheap form of condenser microphone, though modern ones are capable of excellent results.

Condenser microphones are sometimes called *capacitor* microphones.

10.1.2 Microphone Characteristics

The following characteristics apply to all types of microphones:

Directivity

This is the catchment area of the microphone, and it is important that the right type is used for the required application.

Uni-directional microphones are more sensitive to signals arriving at the front, though all other signals are picked up to a lesser extent. The directivity pattern in this case is known as *cardioid* because it is shaped like a heart. There are also *super-directional* or *shotgun* microphones which narrow the catchment area down even further. They can be used to cut out most of any unwanted sound, such as that of a car passing outside the cardioid area, or people talking in a room behind or to the right or left of the microphone.

Bi-directional microphones work with a figure-of-eight directivity and are therefore sensitive to signals coming from opposing directions, for example two singers facing each other and using the same microphone.

Omni-directional microphones pick up sounds from all directions equally. The have their uses (background noise is sometimes required) but they can easily produce feedback from speakers. They are often used for recording orchestral music in the UK, partly because they pick up the natural reverberation of a concert hall and the *ambience* (reverberation, and background noises such as those made by an audience). In the USA, the practice tends to be that of *close-miking*, that is to say the use of a number of microphones placed close to the instruments.

PZMs (pressure-zone microphones) are characterised by their directivity. They have a unique hemispherical pick-up pattern which allows them to pick up sounds accurately and evenly in a 180 degree area in front of them. They are therefore good for recording orchestras and ensembles sitting in a semi-circle.

Frequency response /

This is the range of frequencies (pitches) to which a microphone is sensitive. As a general rule, the wider the better, with the average range being between 60 Hz and 16 KHz. Be wary, however, of manufacturers' raw specifications, since the frequencies at the outer fringes of the stated range may not be picked up as well as in the middle.

The better the response across the entire range of frequencies, the *flatter* it is said to be – a completely flat response would mean that a microphone is equally sensitive to all frequencies. The idea of flatness comes from the graph which can be drawn of frequency and loudness – see Figure 10.1.

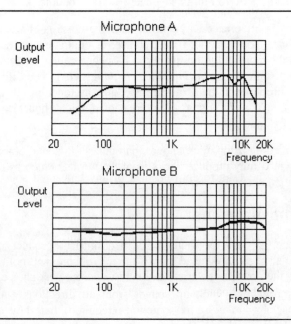

Figure 10.1: Frequency response graphs of two microphones, showing the difference between a relatively flat response (B), and a less flat one on a cheaper model (A)

Proximity effect

The closer a microphone is to a sound source, the higher its sensitivity to sounds of low frequency – experienced singers know that the closer they get to the microphone, the more bass will be produced. Some microphones have a switch which reduces the proximity effect.

Foam Windscreen Filter

This is a shield which can reduce *pop* and feedback from speakers. Pop is an unwanted sound resulting from plosive consonants such as *P* and *B*, especially when they are pronounced very close to the microphone. Prices range from £2 to £40.

Acoustic booths and stands

An acoustic booth (vocal booth) is a sound-insulating box in which a singer or instrumental player can stand or sit so that a recording is relatively free of extraneous noise. It is quite usual to construct a home-made one, lined with sound-absorbing material. Professional acoustic tiles in various thicknesses are available from specialised shops (one such being Studio Spares in London – see Appendix B). A thickness of 75 mm is adequate for vocal booths.

A microphone stand is often necessary so that handling-noise is eliminated. It can also help to eliminate possible radio interference: if equipment is not properly wired, even relatively short and good-quality microphone cables can act as aerials which pick up radio stations (*and a bad earth is dangerous*). The effect is made far worse if the microphone is held in the hand, just as touching an aerial on a radio set can improve a weak signal. The price of a microphone stand can be anywhere between £15 and £150.

A final word on recording using microphones, particularly in a studio at home: any electrical sources which may produce clicks from thermostats (such as fridges and central-heating pumps) should be turned off.

10.1.3 Recommendations

A good microphone is vital for a good finished musical product if acoustic instruments or vocals are to play a lead part. If the microphone will not be used for stage work, one of the condenser variety is likely to be the best choice. Much of course depends on available finances.

For products, see below Section 10.6.

10.2 Multi-track Tape Recorders

A domestic recorder usually works in stereo. In other words it has two tracks, one for each speaker. And it records or plays back both tracks simultaneously. A multi-track tape recorder used in a studio allows for recording and playback on more than two tracks, and for independent playback and recording. For instance, on a 4-track tape recorder it is possible to record and play back on all four tracks, or play tracks 1 and 2 while recording on 3 and 4, or play on 1, 2 and 3 and record on 4, and so on.

Multi-track tape recorders come in a variety of designs, making use of ordinary compact cassettes, reel tape, and media such as computer hard disks which can be used as logical multi-track tape recorders. Indeed, fewer tracks are required today than just a few years ago because computers with MIDI are able to simulate multi-track recorders.

The recording quality of a multi-track tape recorder generally depends on the width of the tape and the speed of recording and playback.

10.2.1 Types of Multi-track Tape Recorders

Cassette-based recorders

These generally use either four, six or eight tracks, and are intended for serious-amateur or semi-professional use. They cost anything between £200 and £2,000. With almost all makes, manufacturers specify the use of Chromium Dioxide (CrO_2) or equivalent cassettes. The recorders are fine-tuned for this kind of tape to give their highest performance.

At the bottom end of the range, cassette multi-track recorders use the same speed as normal cassette recorders, that is to say 4.75 centimetres per second (cm/sec). However, a double speed of 9.5 cm/sec is used by many high-end machines, giving an increased performance both in frequency response (more high frequencies are recorded) and a better signal-to-noise ratio. Recently, there has been a trend for middle-range and even cheap machines to use this higher speed. Some machines can be switched between the two, some cannot.

With multi-track recorders only one side of the tape can be used, and with models using the double speed this means that a cassette will last a quarter of its specified sale value (for instance, a C60 will give only 15 minutes of multi-tracked music).

Some cassette models use even higher speeds, and specially made non-standard cassettes, to achieve a better performance and to offer more tracks. Such non-standard cassettes use a wider tape, and can give results similar to reel-to-reel recorders (which are generally better) but without the inconvenience of open tape.

Reel-to-reel recorders

Reel-to-reel multi-track tape recorders use either 4, 6, 16, or 24 tracks with tape widths of 0.25 inch, 0.5 inch, 1 inch or even 2 inches (48 tracks can even be achieved by synchronising two 24-track recorders). The normal speed on professional models is 30 inches per second (in/sec), and some offer speeds of up to 60 in/sec, but on semi-professional models the speed is limited to 15 in/sec. Note that speed on reel-to-reel machines is usually given in inches rather than centimetres per second because they have been in existence for longer, and old habits die hard.

In terms of sound quality, reel-to-reel machines are superior to cassette machines, and are for semi-professional and professional use. Prices start at about £1,200 and can rise to six-figure sums.

Porta-Studios

Multi-track cassette recorders sold on their own used to be a rarity. They usually came as part of a package: a single unit containing a cassette recorder and a budget sound mixer. This kind of package is often referred to as a *Porta-Studio* (see Chapter 9 Section 9.1 on sound mixers).

10.2.2 Sound Signals and Noise Reduction

Most multi-track tape recorders incorporate some method of noise reduction. The audio signal is encoded before it is recorded on the tape in order to accommodate the fact that not all frequencies are recorded evenly, and therefore to increase the signal-to-noise ratio. The audio signal is then decoded on playback, which is why high levels of hiss are heard on a tape recorded with noise reduction but played back on a machine which does not have it. The best known methods of noise reduction for tape recorders are dbx™, and Dolby™ Types B, C, and HX Pro (domestic) and SR (professional).

Noise reduction is essential when *bouncing* from one track to another to create a second-generation recording. The bouncing process (also known as *ping-pong* recording) is best described by example:

Suppose ten instruments are to be recorded on a 4-track recorder (the maximum which can be achieved with four tracks). Three are recorded separately on (say) tracks 1, 2 and 3, then these three recorded tracks are *bounced* to track 4 together with a fourth instrument, leaving the original three vacant. A further two instruments are then recorded on (say) tracks 1 and 2, which are bounced to track 3 with the seventh instrument. Track 1 is then used to record the eighth instrument, which is bounced to track 2 with the ninth, and the tenth is recorded on track 1.

Bouncing creates hiss and noise, as any re-recording does, and a noise reduction facility can be used as an antidote. However, better results are often obtained by simply running a tape at a higher speed, if the facility is available. If a decision has to be made between spending extra on a tape machine which offers a higher tape speed, and one offering a more sophisticated noise reduction system, the choice should be the higher speed. Having both is best of all.

But in any case, noise reduction – especially with the cheap methods associated with Porta-Studios – can mean some loss of presence, and for best results it should be used in conjunction with an enhancer (see Chapter 9 Section 9.2.2) *during the recording*. In many enhancer manuals (and in much other material written on this topic) it is suggested that since enhancers put back the presence lost during the recording process, they should be used on playback. We suggest the reverse approach for the following reason, proven in practice: if a signal contains noise, enhancing it will increase the noise, whereas if a signal is enhanced before it goes to tape it will be all the richer for it though with increased hiss. However, some of the hiss added by the enhancer will be lost during the recording because tapes do not record high frequencies particularly well. It then becomes a matter of making sure that the signal is not over-enhanced before before being recorded. True, this is a less flexible method because little can be done to change a signal once it has been recorded, but it does give superior results.

While on the subject of noise reduction, it is worth mentioning that tape recorder heads should be de-magnetised and gently cleaned regularly using cotton-wool buds and a pure spirit such as acetone. The wet method should be used in preference to a head-cleaning tape, which is likely to scratch the heads.

For products, see below Section 10.6.

10.3 Synchronising with an Acoustic Performance

In order to mix MIDI and recorded acoustic performances, the two have to be synchronised. There are several ways of achieving synchronisation which we described in Chapter 4 Section 4.1.1 (MIDI to FSK and back, SMPTE, and so on). Before reading on, it might be necessary to refer to that section, since here we are concerned with putting some of the methods into practice.

Whichever method is used, there are three pre-requisites:

❑ a multi-track facility to record the acoustic sounds

❑ a MIDI sequencing facility (computer software or a dedicated sequencer), to record and play the MIDI performance

❏ a synchronisation facility which keeps the two running together.

Some synchronisation facilities may be found on the MIDI interface, or they can be bought within a separate device.

10.3.1 General Considerations

The synchronisation code needs to be recorded on a separate track on the multi-track recorder (whether a physical recorder or a logical one on a computer hard disk). Some multi-track recorders provide a special track for synchronisation. Others do not, which means one track less for the music. In any case, it is wise to finish as much of the composition as possible using the sequencer alone before synchronisation, to get an idea of tempo and the overall length of the piece.

Once a draft copy of the composition has been completed, it is a matter of following the steps set out in one of the following example sync sessions (depending on the synchronisation method which is to be used). The steps are not sacrosanct, and there can be variations with different pieces of equipment, but the principles still apply.

10.3.2 A Sync Session using FSK Tape-Sync

For FSK (Frequency Shift Keying), the tape-sync port on the MIDI interface is connected to an input port of the multi-track recorder, say track 1.

Using a sound mixer, the audio outputs from all the MIDI instruments are mixed, preferably in mono, then sent to a second input on the multi-track recorder for recording, say, on track 2. This is used as a guide track.

The correct tempo for the composition is then adjusted on the sequencer, which is also set to Internal Clock (that is, it is instructed to output tape-sync code if needed). Recording on the multi-track recorder is turned on, and after about 15 to 20 seconds, the sequencer is started. When the piece finishes, the multi-track recorder is stopped.

This process will have put a tape-sync code on track 1 of the multi-track recorder, which means that the sequencer is no longer required for the moment. For the moment, too, the sync code on track 1 is ignored, and the draft mono copy of the music on track 2 is listened to as a guide while acoustic parts are recorded on tracks 3, 4 (and so on, if there are more than four and if they are required).

When the acoustic parts have been recorded, the sequencer is brought back into the system. The output of track 1 on the multi-track recorder is connected to the sync input of the MIDI interface. The sequencer is set to External Clock (this can have different names on different sequencers but will be something like *FSK*, *External* or *Tape Sync*).

At this point, Play mode on the sequencer is activated. It will not start but will generate a message on the screen, of the variety: *Waiting for external sync*. The tape is then re-wound to a position preceding the beginning of the tape-sync signal, and Play is pressed on the multi-track recorder. The sequencer should then get its start and tempo from the tape-sync code, and begin to play.

With ordinary FSK, synchronisation will be possible only if the tape starts at the beginning of the signal. But with a sequencer capable of recognising MIDI Song Position Pointers, or with some form of enhanced tape-sync method such as Chase Lock, it may be possible synchronise at any point in a piece of music, as can be done with the SMPTE method described in the next section.

Once synchronisation has been achieved, more tracks can be added to the MIDI performance, or the existing ones polished so that they blend with the acoustic parts on the tape. The whole thing (MIDI performance from the electronic instruments run by the sequencer, and acoustic sounds from the multi-track recorder) can be mixed and recorded in stereo.

10.3.3 A Sync Session using Time Code

Time-code (SMPTE) synchronisation is far more flexible than ordinary tape-sync. With this method, an SMPTE Reader/Generator sits between the sequencer and the multi-track recorder. It can be an external device or a facility offered on a MIDI interface.

The first step is to *stripe* a tape with time code (record the code on a track of the recorder). Since SMPTE time code is a measure of real time (hours, minutes, seconds and frames), and has no relationship with the tempo of a composition, it can be put on a tape independently; in other words, the music does not have to be played at the same time as the striping is carried out. It is possible to stripe an entire tape, or just the section of it intended for the music.

Once the tape is striped, the output from the multi-track recorder containing the SMPTE code is connected to the time-code In socket of the MIDI interface, or that of the dedicated Reader/Generator. On this device (or on the sequencer if the MIDI interface has a built-in SMPTE facility) the time signature and tempo of the composition are set, as well as an *offset time*, which tells the multi-track recorder at which point after the SMPTE code begins, it should start sending Song Position Pointer messages to the sequencer.

The sequencer is then set to Chase mode, and it will wait for a command from the SMPTE device to start playing at a specific Song Position Pointer – measured as the number of semiquavers (16th notes) which have elapsed from the beginning of the performance.

On playing the multi-track recorder, SMPTE code from the tape is fed into the MIDI interface or Reader/Generator. There, it is converted from hours, minutes, seconds and frames into Song Position Pointers, and is transmitted to the sequencer together with a MIDI Continue message. In this way, the multi-track recorder can actually drive the sequencer from any position within a composition.

From here on, the steps are the same as for tape-sync using FSK described above: a mono mix of the music is recorded on a second track of the recorder to be used as a guide for adding the acoustic parts of the composition, and so on.

10.3.4 Synchronisation Hints

❏ Record the sync code on an outside track, either track 1 or the last track

❏ Note that it is becoming normal practice to use the last track on a multi-track recorder for the synchronisation code (the examples above which use track 1 were chosen for the sake of clarity).

❏ Try to avoid recording anything on the track adjacent to the sync code – it is better left blank in order to ensure that the code does not become corrupted

❏ If leaving a blank track is not a practicable possibility, record something on the adjacent track which has a constant level, does not require a high amplitude setting, and contains as few high-pitched sounds as possible

❏ Do not process the sync code using noise reduction systems, except with multi-track recorders which specify a track to be used for sync code (which can also be used for music), since when it is used for sync code, noise reduction does not affect it

For synchronisation products, see Chapter 4 Section 4.10.

10.4 Analogue and Digital Recorders

Nowadays, in the professional world most multi-track recorders tend to be digital, but many amateurs are still waiting for digital recording technology to get cheaper. Domestic tape recorders, such as cassette recorders found in hi-fi systems, are analogue and do not play as crisply or as cleanly as CD players, which are digital. Why?

10.4.1 Analogue Recording

The method used by an ordinary tape recorder to record sounds is an analogue method. Tape is coated with fine-grained magnetic material, and the electro-magnetic head of the tape recorder produces magnetic waves which act on the random coating of particles on the tape, changing their pattern to represent a a kind of sound photograph. On playback the process is reversed. It is an analogue method because the magnetic waves sent from the tape head are analogous to the original sound waves, and the resulting pattern of particles are representations of them.

This method should be expected to work well, and it does. But it has some disadvantages which affect the sound quality.

First, an optimum signal is required to force the particles on the tape to move from their unrecorded position to a new position representing a picture of the sound signal. Particles left in their random position create background hiss. A musical signal has soft and loud components, and quiet signals may not be powerful enough to move all particles. It is worth mentioning in this context that previously used tape can often give better results than tape which has never been used before, because it is smoother and has shed excess particles.

Secondly, the alignment of the tape as it passes over the tape head is critical. If the tape does not pass over precisely the same path on playback as it took when recording, the reproduction will not be 100 per cent accurate. In practice, it is impossible to achieve complete accuracy.

Thirdly, friction created by the tape moving over the magnetic head creates further background noise.

Lastly, both the head and the tape become worn with use, and the head gets dirty and magnetised, all of which can cause a further loss in sonic quality.

10.4.2 Digital Recording

Digital recordings are not snapshots of the sound but numeric descriptions of it. This might not appear a very promising approach because photographs say more, and are therefore more accurate, than descriptions. Imagine, however, a computer which can visually analyse an object in very fine detail, perhaps beyond what the human eye can register. If these details are then recorded as co-ordinates, the computer can reproduce an accurate image of the object at any time, and with no deterioration in quality. A photograph, on the other hand, can fade, and its quality in any case depends on the printing method and type of photographic paper used, and so on.

The same idea applies to digital sound recording. In digital recording, an A/D converter changes an electric sound signal into a stream of numbers. Each number is a measure of the amplitude of the signal at a specific point in time, with time intervals set to very small amounts, beyond the perception of the human ear. Once the signal is converted into numbers, they are recorded as pulses. And since digital recording uses a binary system, the quality of the recording is unimportant as long as the 0 pulses and 1 pulses are clearly distinguishable. On playback, a D/A converter produces a signal whose amplitude at specified times is represented by the recorded stream of numbers.

Thus, all the problems of quality associated with analogue recordings appear to be solved. But the solution is unfortunately an expensive one, because of the technology required to achieve it. The quality of digital recordings depends on the amount of detail recorded, and in order for such detail to go even just beyond the capabilities of the human ear, many numbers are required, which means large amounts of memory and/or fast processing. Multi-track digital recording remains a luxury for the amateur.

There is a range of digital multi-track recorders intended for professionals. They use reel-to-reel tapes, use 24, 32, or even 48 tracks, and cost in the region of £70,000. The only two cassette-based digital multi-track recorders available at the moment, both aimed at the semi-professional world, are the Akai DR1200 and the Yamaha DMR8, though calling this kind of equipment semi-professional is a debatable point: their price tags are about the same as those of professional analogue multi-track recorders, and their sound quality as good as the professional digital variety, if not better.

Digital tape recorders can use one of two types of tape heads: stationary or rotary. Stationary heads work like those on an ordinary domestic cassette recorder (though their construction is different): the tape moves along a fixed non-moving recording head. Rotary heads work like those found on domestic video recorders, on which the head spins at high speed as the tape passes round it. This is also the method used on DAT (Digital Audio Tape) recorders – see below Section 10.5.2.

The Akai DR1200

The DR1200 (£14,000 for the basic unit) uses the rotary-head method. It has 12 available digital tracks, and one analogue track used for synchronisation to other tape recorders or computers. It also has a built-in A/D converter.

It records at 44.1 or 48 KHz, using 16-bit quantisation and a format unique to Akai called ADAM (Akai Digital Audio Multi-track), though it uses ordinary Video 8 camcorder cassette tapes which are widely available and relatively cheap. However, the DR1200 runs at about four times the speed of camcorders. A 60-minute tape (a P5-60) lasts only 16 minutes for recording at 44.1 KHz, or 14.5 minutes at 48 KHz.

The Yamaha DMR8

Whereas the Akai DR1200 has been on the market for a couple of years or so, the Yamaha DMR8 (about £18,000) is a brand new design. It uses a stationary head (which is easier to maintain than the rotary variety), has eight digital recording tracks, plus another four analogue tracks for time codes and other analogue signals. It also incorporates a 24-channel mixer with motorised faders and built-in digital effects.

The DMR8 uses an 8 mm tape cassette housed in a special box made by Yamaha (not the Video 8 cassette format used by Akai.) It gives 20 minutes of recording at 48 KHz, 22 minutes at 44.1 KHz, and 30 minutes at 32 KHz. Its resolution is 20 bits, therefore higher than that of the Akai. But unlike the Akai, the Yamaha does not include an A/D converter. This comes as a separate unit: the AD8X with eight channels (price category H) or the AD2X with two channels (price category F/G).

10.5 Monitoring and Mastering

The beauty of a computerised MIDI studio is that once all the parameters of a performance have been programmed, it can be reproduced identically as many times as required. And unlike an acoustic performance, a MIDI performance can include parameters which define not only the sounds used, including effects such as reverb and delays, but also other performance characteristics such as sound-mixer settings and fader movements. All can be incorporated in the same MIDI performance file.

Yet it is still convenient to record the final version of a piece of music on tape so that it can be played any time, anywhere outside the MIDI studio, on any tape recorder. The process of making a good final recording, one which can be used to make copies, is called *mastering*. Normally, the audio signals from all MIDI devices and from a multi-track tape recorder, are mixed using a sound mixer, then sent to a stereo tape recorder. The output from this mastering tape recorder goes to an amplifier, and finally to the loudspeakers so that the sound can be *monitored* before the final master recording is made.

10.5.1 Monitoring

A composer may spend a great deal of time getting a performance just right, yet when it is played outside the studio, the sound may be different. There are two basic reasons for this state of affairs: the acoustics of the room in which the studio is housed, and the characteristics of the playback equipment (amplifier and speakers).

Acoustics are an entire field in themselves, and it is not possible to deal here with such a complex topic, but it is clear that a performance given in an empty church sounds different from the same performance given in a living room. Similarly, listening to a recording on a hand-held radio hardly compares with the same recording played back on good hi-fi system. On the small radio, many sounds will not be heard because the small speaker and poor amplifier are unable to reproduce them.

The fact is that sound is very susceptible to being altered by the acoustic characteristics of rooms and loudspeakers, and the electrical characteristics of amplifiers, tape recorders and other media through which it has to pass during processing and reproduction. And this fact is sometimes overlooked, until a recording is taken out of the studio in which it was created and played in different surroundings on someone else's hi-fi equipment, where it sounds quite distinct from the 'original'. For example, speakers which give a so-called West Coast sound (a warm sound typified by JBL and Altec Lansing products) will reproduce the music differently from those which give a clearer but somewhat colder sound (speakers from Tannoy, Spendor, Rogers, KEF, and so on). There is no complete answer to this problem – monitoring is the weakest link in the audio chain – but it is possible to ensure that the recording stands at least a chance of sounding as it did in the studio by analysing the factors which cause it to change.

Range of frequencies

An amplifier and speakers together form a window on the music passing through them. If the window is not large enough, there are sounds which will not be processed. If a speaker's lower frequency response goes down, say, to only 100 Hz, it will be impossible to monitor sounds below that level because they will not be heard. The tendency is then to boost the bass on the EQ of the sound mixer, which ends up on the recording, so that when the tape is played back through better speakers, the bass frequencies drown the rest of the music. The same applies to high frequencies, though to a lesser extent.

Speakers should be able to reproduce as wide a range of frequencies as possible. In practice, they should have a frequency response of between 60 Hz (preferably lower) and 18 KHz (preferably higher). The bottom end is what usually means more money. This is partly why headphones are not normally used for studio recording – they cannot reproduce the bass frequencies well enough. They are really only for used for recording in locations where it would not be practicable to use loudspeakers.

The problem of frequency response is not as great when it comes to amplifiers, which can usually reproduce a wide range of frequencies. Problems with amplifiers tend to arise from background noise (hiss), though modern amplifiers are less susceptible to this than they used to be.

The combination of amplifier and speakers is a significant consideration, and they should always be listened to together: one amplifier may drive speakers differently from another. The only real way to decide on the best combination is to listen, since specifications may not take into account the myriad factors affecting the way speakers react to particular amplifiers. Listening is best done at a hi-fi dealer's showroom, and the dealer should preferably be a member of BADA (British Audio Dealers Association). BADA members will usually offer proper demonstrations and sensible advice.

Loudspeaker products can be found in Section 10.6 below. We do not list amplifiers because any good domestic model is sufficient.

Flatness of the response

The flatness of a frequency response as it applies to microphones (see above Section 10.1.2) applies equally to amplifiers, speakers and rooms. A flat recording room does not add to or subtract anything from the sound, such as bass, treble, or any other frequency. An amplifier and speakers should also give as flat a response as possible. The amplifier, speakers and the room can thus be considered as one system as far as frequency response is concerned.

Not everybody can afford (financially and/or space-wise) the perfect recording room and the perfect amplifier and speakers, but much can be done to counteract the colouring effects produced by less than perfect conditions and equipment, by using a good graphic or parametric equaliser, which sits between the mastering tape recorder and the amplifier. If the room acoustics and playback equipment are adding or subtracting specific frequencies, the equaliser can be set up in such a way so as to counteract any irregularities by boosting or cutting the amplitude of different frequencies as necessary.

In order to be able to set the equaliser correctly, and therefore to fish out the unwanted frequencies, a number methods are available.

The first involves the use of a *spectrum analyser*. This can be a separate device, but more often comes as part of a graphic equaliser, and it displays a real-time graph of the amplitudes of the different frequencies in the sound spectrum. These are shown in frequency bands, and the more bands, the finer the analysis (the 27 or more bands, found on high-level equalisers, give a very fine analysis). When the graph is more or less horizontal, all the frequencies are at the same amplitude, and this is the flat response required.

But a reference guide is needed too, a specific sound which has flat frequency characteristics. This is a particular type of sound called *pink noise*, and it is used in the following way:

All the controls on the graphic equaliser are set to their central positions. The pink noise created by the spectrum analyser is passed through the amplifier and speakers (it is also affected by the acoustics of the room) and is picked up by a microphone placed where the listener will be sitting while monitoring the music. The signal picked up by the microphone is sent to the spectrum analyser, and the display shows the frequency-response characteristics of the amplifier, speakers and room combined. The controls on the graphic equaliser are then adjusted, one channel at a time, to balance out all the peaks and troughs until a reasonably flat shape is achieved.

Once the graphic equaliser has been set in this way, it can be left as it is for all subsequent recordings. It will balance out many frequency-response inadequacies of the room and playback equipment, but of course only when the listener's ears are at the position where the microphone was placed during the adjustment. Different positions are affected differently by the acoustics of the room and require a different setting on the graphic equaliser.

The second method involves the use of a sound-level meter, and a variable pure tone (such as a sine wave) spanning the sound frequency spectrum.

A sound-level meter is a piece of equipment with a built-in microphone and a display showing the overall sound pressure in dB. Pure tones can be obtained from a special pure-tone generator (found in stores which specialise in electronic components) or from a suitable test recording (LP, CD or cassette, available from some top hi-fi shops). They can even be generated on a synthesiser by someone who knows enough about editing synthesiser sounds.

By generating a pure tone, one frequency at a time, and measuring the sound level, the whole sound spectrum can be examined. Initially this is done in large frequency steps, and an outline is drawn. In areas where the irregularities are more than plus or minus 3 dB, further measurements at finer intervals can be taken, until the maximum deviation point is obtained. In this way, a fairly accurate representation of the room's frequency response can be mapped. Of course, if a test recording used, the frequencies will be at fixed points.

If the analysis produced by the spectrum analyser, or the sound level meter, shows that only two or three frequencies are outstanding, more control can be had with a parametric equaliser (see Chapter 9 Section 9.1.1) than with a graphic equaliser. If the number of outstanding frequencies is greater, or if a 4-band parametric equaliser cannot be justified cost-wise, a graphic equaliser will do.

A third method, providing a very rough guide (but better than nothing) is to connect up a CD player and play a recent recording containing a wide range of frequencies, and which you consider well produced. The equaliser can then be set so that all the instruments can be heard clearly.

It is worth remembering that any equalisation carried out as we have described should be for the purpose of monitoring only, and should not be applied to the recording.

Some people doubt the capabilities of cheaper measuring instruments, and prefer to invest in a very good pair of speakers with a flat response. They then monitor by sitting relatively close to the speakers (about two or three feet away) without carrying out any corrections to the room acoustics at all. This method can be satisfactory, since the closer one gets to the speakers, the less the effect of the room.

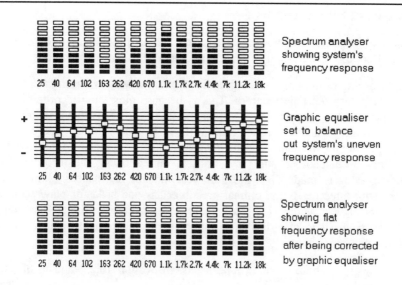

Spectrum analyser showing system's frequency response

25 40 64 102 163 262 420 670 1.1k 1.7k 2.7k 4.4k 7k 11.2k 18k

Graphic equaliser set to balance out system's uneven frequency response

25 40 64 102 163 262 420 670 1.1k 1.7k 2.7k 4.4k 7k 11.2k 18k

Spectrum analyser showing flat frequency response after being corrected by graphic equaliser

25 40 64 102 163 262 420 670 1.1k 1.7k 2.7k 4.4k 7k 11.2k 18k

Figure 10.2: Graphic equaliser showing a flat response

For graphic equaliser products see Chapter 9 Section 9.3.

Room reflections

In the same way that there are problems with the frequency characteristics of rooms, there are also problems with sound reflections. A room can create reverberation and echo, both of which should be eliminated. This can be done by using sound absorbing materials to cover the walls, floors and ceiling: carpets, curtains, foam, or acoustic tiles specifically made for studios and auditoriums (110 mm thickness are good for absorbing low frequencies – see above Section 10.1.2, Acoustic booths). A non-reflective room shape can help, such as an angled ceiling, and objects in the room which break straight uninterrupted lines, one of the main causes of audio reflection. A special room which is (more or less) completely free of reflections is known as an *anechoic chamber*.

Speaker manufacturers often give specific instructions about how their speakers should be positioned in a room, but generally speaking they should be kept away from corners, not placed right next to a wall, isolated from the floor with sound-insulated stands, positioned at the same level as each other, and directed towards the listener's ears. An approximate guide to positioning is to make the listener and the two speakers form an equilateral triangle with imaginary sides of about six feet.

Three-head tape recorders

Tapes have frequency-response characteristics, and as might be expected these are not flat. Here too, therefore, it is important to be able to make corrections.

When recording or dubbing (making copies of) tapes, what is usually heard is the signal going into the tape recorder. This is because most tape recorders use the same tape head both for recording and playback, which means that it is impossible to listen to the actual recording until after it is made. Some tape recorders, however, have an extra tape head for playback only. This picks up the signal just after it has been recorded and plays it back, thus allowing the recording to be monitored as it is made. We therefore recommend, if finances allow, a tape recorder with three heads (an ordinary recorder has one head for play/record and one for erase). We would also recommend a tape recorder with a Bias control, which can be used to alter the equalisation of the recording to match different types of tape.

The advice given about cleaning tape heads, in Section 10.2.2 above, of course applies equally here.

Tired ears

As human beings get older, so hearing degenerates. But it can also be affected at any age by fatigue of the auditory nerves: listening to music continuously over long periods of time, particularly at high volume, can affect our perception of the sound. As a result, there may be a tendency during the monitoring process to boost certain de-sensitised frequencies, and to increase effects such as reverb and echo to make the sound more interesting. Consequently, it is wise to work on mixing a composition so that everything is balanced and equalised, then turn the equipment off and come back early the next morning to listen to it, when fine adjustments can be made before recording while the ears are fresh. It is our experience that tiredness produces unbalanced recordings (just as much as unbalanced writing).

For monitoring products, see below Section 10.6.

10.5.2 Mastering

Cassette recorders

This is the cheapest method of making master recordings, but also the one which gives the least satisfactory results because of the comparatively poor reproduction of the cassette medium itself. If nothing better can be afforded, then at least a 3-head cassette recorder should be used (separate heads for playback and record).

A second cassette recorder is also usually required for making copies of the master cassette. We do not recommend a twin-deck cassette recorder for dubbing (duplication). Although these dub at higher speeds, they usually have two heads which give an inferior quality. Nor do we recommend that more than about £300 is spent on a cassette recorder for mastering, since beyond that price, other recording methods and formats begin to be attractive.

Reel-to-reel analogue recorders

Until recently, the majority of mastering machines used in the professional world were stereo reel-to-reel tape recorders. These days they are being increasingly replaced by DAT recorders (see below). Domestic models of reel-to-reel analogue machines exist, and they give almost incomparably better results than domestic cassette recorders. But they are more expensive, and some DAT recorders cost no more.

Video recorders

A relatively cheap method of mastering, which used skillfully gives results approaching those of reel-to-reel analogue recorders, is to use a domestic video tape recorder incorporating stereo hi-fi sound.

Video-8 deck recorders use the Video-8 cassette format found in camcorders, and they can be used to record digital sound sampled at 32 KHz – not as good as CD quality but quite acceptable. A single tape can give 18 hours of digital sound. The only model still in production is the EVS1000 from Sony (price category F/G), but other models can be found second-hand.

Taking the idea further, a device called a *digital encoder* can be used in conjunction with a domestic video recorder to give professional results (though Beta and U-matic recorders are the most widely used in this case, as opposed to the dominance of VHS in the domestic video market). With these encoders, CD-quality digital sound can be achieved by taking an ordinary stereo audio signal, sampling it at 44.05 KHz, and encoding it into a video signal. The method has been widely used in professional studios over the last few years, and is only now beginning to be replaced by DAT recording (see below). Sony models are the most common (PCM701, PCM501, PCMF1 – ranging in price category from D to G.

DAT

DAT stands for Digital Audio Tape, and it is increasingly found in domestic and professional stereo recording. It was developed some years ago, but its arrival was delayed as a result of arguments between the music industry and manufacturers about formats, and the fear of CD piracy.

DAT is the tape equivalent of the CD. It records digitally, and in principle can sample, record and play back at 44.1 and 48 KHz. But in order to prevent piracy, ordinary domestic DAT recorders cannot record through their digital inputs at 44.1

KHz, the rate at which CDs are sampled. If the facility were not disabled, it would be possible to take signals from the digital outputs of CD players and record to tape with no loss of quality, which means that a pirate could copy and re-master a CD. However, modified domestic models as well as professional machines are available which can record at CD frequency, as well as professional machines.

DAT recorders come with either a Sony and Philips Digital Interface (SPDIF) or an interface which conforms to the American and European digital interface standard (AES/EBU – Audio Engineering Society/European Broadcasting Union). The former is used on domestic models.

At the time of writing, Panasonic, Philips, and other companies are on the point of releasing a new domestic recorder (DCC - Digital Compact Cassete) based on the DASH (Digital Audio Stationary Head) system used in some professional digital multitrack recorders. This new tape recorder will use traditional compact cassettes, and will also be able to play back ordinary analogue recordings.

Recording direct to disk

There is an increasing tendency to record directly on hard disks. This method offers something which cannot be achieved using tape. With analogue recorders, a tape can be edited by splicing it and sticking it together again; with digital tape-based recorders, this form of editing is far too crude. Recording to disk gives instant access to any part of the music, precise flawless editing, time compression and expansion without a change of pitch, and much more. Such systems can be multi-track or stereo. Ordinary audio signals are fed in, sampled at a specified rate (usually, but not necessarily at 44.1 KHz), and the result is stored as a computer file. Computer expansion boards for this purpose are beginning to appear on the market.

Software, usually with graphical editing screens showing waveforms and envelopes of the sound, is used for Cut and Paste operations, and other manipulations as required. It works out that one minute of stereo sound, recorded at 44.1 KHz and 16-bit resolution takes about 10 Mb of disk space, but some recent devices use data compression methods and can achieve a minute of music with only 2 Mb.

The finished copy can if necessary be sent back to tape or to a *WORM* (Write Once Read Many) – an optical disk which, as its name suggests, can be used just once for recording data, but which requires an expensive drive.

There are also units dedicated to recording direct to disk, such as the New England Digital PostPro, but they can cost huge amounts of money (see Figure 10.3).

For mastering products, see Section 10.6 immediately below.

Finally, a mention should be made of re-writable optical disks, which are read by lasers, and which have very high storage capacities, but for which the drives are

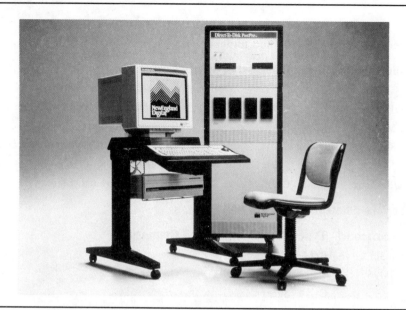

Figure 10.3: The New England Digital PostPro direct-to-disk recorder, starting at £80,000

again expensive. The AKAI DD1000 (about £9,000) is the first mass-produced dedicated stereo optical disk digital recorder. It uses 650 Mb standard Sony magneto-optical disks, and offers 50 minutes of recording time sampled at 48 KHz with 16-bit resolution (or up to 80 minutes at 32 KHz). It has four tracks (two stereo pairs) and it is possible to record and play at the same time, so that tracks can be over-dubbed and merged. It also incorporates SMPTE time code.

10.6 Products

Microphones

Key

Microphone types
C: Condenser
E: Electret
D: Dynamic
R: Ribbon
PZM: Pressure-zone

Directivity
Bi: Bi-directional
Ca: Cardioid
Om: Omni-directional

Power supply (unless mains or phantom power)
Ba: Can be powered by a battery

Starter microphones (£200 and under)

Producer/model	Type	Directivity	Power	Comments
AKG C1000S	C	Ca	Ba	Designed for hand-held vocals.
- C535EB	E	Ca	Ba	Specially suitable for female vocals.
Beyer M130	R	Bi		For ensembles, flat response.
Shure SM58	D	Ca		The world's most popular stage mike.
- Beta 58	D	Super Ca		Update of SM58.
Tandy/Realistic	PZM	Ba		Good for pianos and ensembles.

For serious amateurs (£200 to £400)

Producer/model	Type	Directivity	Power	Comments
Amcron 30FS	PZM			
Shure SM96	C	Ca	Ba	Good for vocals.
- SM87	C	Super Ca		

For professionals and semi-professionals (£400 to £1,000)

Producer/model	Type	Directivity	Power	Comments
AKG C414	C	Bi, Ca, Om		
Bruel & Kjaer 4003X, 4004X, 4006X, 4007X	C	Om		High specifications. Uncoloured sound.
Neumann U87Ai	C	Bi, Ca, Om		Industry standard for lead vocals.
Sennheiser				Flat response.
- MKH20	C	Om		
- MKH40	C	Ca		

Loudpseakers

The following is a small selection. Prices are per pair.

Producer/model	Price	Comments
ATC SCM20s	G	Used in professional studios .
Tannoy DC200	D	
Rogers LS range	C/D upwards	Used by the BBC.
Realistic S100	B/C	Just about adequate and a cheaper alternative to famous names.
JBL 44 range	C/D to H	American sound, hard top end.
Yamaha NS10S	C	Widely used.
- NS40M	C/D	Latest model in NS range.

Multi-track tape recorders

We do not list any multi-track cassette tape recorders or Porta-Studios which do not use the double speed of 9.5 cm/sec. Those which record at half this speed are widely available and much cheaper (price category C), but we recommend double speed as a minimum. In a MIDI studio all the electronic instruments are recorded live (as so-called *first generation*). If vocals and acoustic instruments are not recorded at this quality, the difference between the two becomes all too apparent.

This is a small selection of what is available:

Cassette

Producer/model	Tracks	Noise reduction	Price	Comments
Sansui MR6	6	Dolby	E/F	
Tascam 234	4	dbx	D/E	Old model.
- 238	8	dbx	G	
TOA MR-8T	8	dbx	G	With basic mixer.
Vestax MR66	6	dbx	G	With basic mixer.

Porta-Studios

Producer/model	Tracks	Mixer channels	Noise reduction	Price	Comments
Akai MG614	5	6	dbx	G	The fifth track is used for sync code. Expensive but good sound.
Fostex 160	4	4	Dolby	C E	Good sound quality for the price.
Tascam 644	4	8	dbx	F/G	MTC sync. Automated routeing, muting, and Punch In/Out. Good value.
Yamaha MT100II	4	4	dbx	D	5-band stereo graphic EQ. Almost the cheapest 4-track which records at 9.5 cm/sec.
- MT3X	4	6	dbx	E/F	Automated Punch In/Out. Can be found discounted.

Reel-to-reel

We list here only semi-professional models, the very expensive professional variety being mostly limited to commercial recording studios.

Producer/model	Tape width (inches)	Tracks	Speed (in/sec)	Noise reduction	Price
Fostex R8	0.25	8	15	Dolby C	G
- G16	0.5	16	15	Dolby C	£5,000
ReVox C278	0.5	8	15/7.5/3.75	(none)	£5,000
Tascam 38	0.5	8	15	(none)	G/H
- MSR16	0.5	16	15/7.5	dbx	£4,500
- MSR24	1	24	15/7.5	dbx	£7,000

Alternative cassette format

The Akai MG1214 (about £5,000) is a 12-channel mixer and 14-track recorder combined. It uses a special cassette with 0.5 inch wide tape running at 15 or 7.5 in/sec, and lasting 10 or 20 minutes. It has dbx noise reduction, and offers a controllable tape transport mechanism to slave the machine to external synchronisation. The MG14 (price category H) is a tape-only rack version.

DAT recorders

All products listed here, except for the Casio DA-2, will record and play back at sampling rates of 41.4 and 48 KHz. The Casio DA-2 will record at 48 KHz and play back at both rates. It has no digital interface.

Key

SPDIF: Sony and Philips Digital Interface
AES/EBU: American and European digital interface standard

Producer/model	Digital interface	Min. Signal to Noise ratio (dB)	Price	Comments
Aiwa HD-X1	SPDIF	85	E/F	Portable.
Casio DA-2		85	E/F	Portable.
Denon DTR-2000	SPDIF	90	F	Good value.
Fostex D20	AES/EBU	92	£5,000	XLR sockets, SMPTE.
Sony DTC1000ES	SPDIF	92	G	Popular domestic model adapted.
- PCM 2500	SPDIF AES/EBU	92	H	XLR sockets. Top model.
Tascam DA30	AES/EBU	94	G	XLR sockets.
Technics SV360	SPDIF	96	G	XLR sockets.

Recording to disk

Note that a computer and a hard disk are required with these products. Typical storage times are 10 Mb per minute stereo, sampling at 44.1 KHz and 16-bit resolution. In the case of the PC, an AT (286 or 386) is assumed unless an XT is specified as being powerful enough.

Producer	Product	Computer(s)	Price	Comments
Akai	DD1000	(dedicated)	9,000	Optical disk. Four tracks. 50 minutes at 48 KHz. SMPTE.
Audio & Design	Sound Maestro	Atari Mega ST	4,500	Two tracks. Includes 380 Mb hard disk.
Audio View	PC Replay	PC XT	150	Single track (mono). 3 Mb per minute at 40 KHz. 8-bit, sampling at 10, 20, 40 KHz.
Digidesign	Sound Tools	Mac II Atari Mega ST	3,100 2,000	Four tracks. A well-known system.
Digigram	PCX3	PC	3,000	Two tracks. 32, 48 KHz. Uses data compression to achieve a staggering 2 Mb per minute.
Digital Audio Labs	Desktop Recording Board	PC	1,000	Two tracks. 6 Mb per minute at 48 KHz.
New England Digital	PostPro	(dedicated)	80,000+	16 tracks. 6 Mb per minute. Samples at up to 100 KHz.
Studer-Editech	Dyaxis	Mac II	(not fixed)	Two tracks.
Waveframe	Audioframe	(dedicated)	65,000	Eight tracks. Price includes PC.

Recorders for duplication

All our recommended cassette models have three heads, and Bias control.

Producer/model	Noise reduction	Price
Aiwa ADF640	Dolby B, C	C
Denon DRM700	Dolby B, C, HX Pro	C
Technics RSB705	Dolby B, C	D

The above represents a personal choice of recorders for duplication, and there are many others.

11

Aids to Composition

Few people would be happy with a visit to the doctor's surgery which entailed sitting at a computer typing the answers to questions about the symptoms of their illness, and seeing a diagnosis and consequent treatment appear on the screen. Yet medical diagnosis, prognosis and recommended treatment are moving in that direction, the direction of *expert systems*.

Expert systems are a branch of Artificial Intelligence. In an expert system, the computer is provided with a *knowledge base* (a database of facts and judgements) using which it is able to make decisions. The knowledge base is built from information provided by human experts, but the computer uses it to search what can become a very complex branching arrangement, in fact too complex for the human mind to manage. In the case of medical diagnosis, the knowledge base is made up of current knowledge and expertise about the meaning of various symptoms. The patient is therefore relying not on the diagnosis of a single doctor but on the pooled expertise of many. We are not yet at the stage where a visit to a doctor's surgery does not involve seeing a doctor, but some forward-looking doctors are already using expert systems.

One important point here is that the computer analyses and suggests, but does not impose. A doctor is at liberty to accept or reject the computer's suggestions, and so it is with many fields in which expert systems are being applied. For translation to and from foreign languages, for instance, there are computer programs which take some of the drudgery out of a first throw, so that human translators can tidy things up to their satisfaction. Nobody has yet produced a translation program which can handle more than a small percentage of the complexity of natural languages, but suggested translations made by computer can at least provide a starting point.

So it is with expert systems when applied to music. A level of artificial intelligence has been built into certain computer programs and pieces of hardware, which are capable of making decisions by accessing the facts and rules contained in their knowledge bases, thus allowing the composer to milk the expertise of other musicians. Basic musical ideas are turned into a complete composition, either ready for performance if the composer is prepared to accept it as it stands, or more usually for editing in a sequencer. Two types of musical expert system can be distinguished, though they overlap in their functions: *composers* and *arrangers*. Composers create variations on musical themes, and arrangers arrange melodies and chords to fit musical styles.

Such tools are of course aimed principally at people whose musical knowledge does not extend much beyond a few chords and single-line melodies. But experienced musicians sometimes have to work under time pressure, such as when producing a film score, and a composing program can at least supply a basic score to work on. Furthermore, even professional musicians are not familiar with every musical style, and music produced by a sophisticated arranger can even be a more or less finished product if the musician is not too fussy about originality, though again it is normal to edit the computerised output.

Tools designed to work in this way can be divided into two types: algorithmic composers, and arrangers.

11.1 Algorithmic Composers

Algorithms have already been mentioned in the context of FM synthesis (Chapter 7 Section 7.3.1). An algorithm sets out the steps which must be followed in order to complete a task or solve a problem, and it is often based on algebraic and trigonometric equations. Algorithmic composers access a stored database of algorithms and transform them into sequences in order to generate melodies and variations of musical passages. Such software often works by allowing the user to enter ideas such as chords and rhythms, and to set a wide range of variables to different positions. By switching between these variables, he or she is able to alter the music, in some cases while it is being played back, as subtly or as dramatically as desired.

Algorithmic composers are, then, kinds of super sequencers - instead of merely playing back what has already been composed, as sequencers do, they become part of the actual process of composition, often using an element of randomness (they are occasionally listed in catalogues as *random composers*). Some programs generate melodies, others expect musical patterns to be entered by the user, sometimes literally in that these patterns are drawn as shapes. Some instruct the computer to work on automatic pilot with each playback, others allow the human composer to take some of the controls. The results can in any case usually be loaded into an ordinary sequencer for further manipulation.

Typically, each voice is recorded individually from a MIDI keyboard, the tempo and time signatures set, MIDI channels assigned, and so on, just as would be done on an ordinary sequencer. For playback, however, there can be variations in parameters like accents, note order, note lengths (to create legato and staccato effects) and MIDI Program Changes (to alter the sound of each voice).

Most programs of this variety work with collections of melodic notes and chords, and variables can be changed while patterns are being repeated. For example, notes may pass through a filter which can be varied to a percentage level, the percentage being the chance of a note passing through or not. Thus setting the filter to 1 in 2 would give a 50/50 chance that the note will be played. If it is not played, either the previous note will be held or a rest will be inserted.

The same kind of flexibility can be applied to many other musical parameters which would normally be rigid. Notes can be re-ordered according to limits set by the user, and therefore new melodies created. A range for dynamic accents can be set, with the program subsequently creating dynamic light and shade according to the rules in its knowledge base and the steps defined in its algorithms. The program can alter orchestration by changing instruments on playback. It can determine the amount of legato and staccato, again depending on the setting of a variable to determine the acceptable range, or make subtle changes to rhythms by altering the amount of time between the beginning of one note and the next.

This last feature demonstrates the kind of practical use to which algorithmic composers can be put. It allows different musical parts to be speeded up or slowed down within defined time ranges, the result being that the parts are slightly offset. Swing and shuffle are standard examples of such time manipulations, since their rhythms require almost imperceptible (though characteristic) offsets, and speeding up and slowing down, within the space of a couple of crotchets. This is difficult to achieve manually, but an algorithmic composer handles it automatically.

Once the variables have been set, the music is played back. In this way, many different variations can be tried, and when a satisfactory one is achieved it can be stored. It is also often possible to store sound snapshots of particular settings, and to recall them as necessary, in some cases as the music is being played, to see what effect they have on the piece. The number of variations which can be produced and listened to is limited only by the patience (and indecision) of the user.

The best-known program in this category is *M*, which offers a large number of variables of different kinds, and has many sophisticated features. Originally written for the Apple Macintosh, it is now available in versions for the PC, the Atari ST, and the Commodore Amiga.

In some types of algorithmic composer, a mouse is either used to draw pictures from which music is created by the program, or used to turn the computer into a genuine musical instrument. Music Mouse, for the Macintosh, Atari ST and Amiga, belongs to the latter category and is very impressive. It is the brainchild of

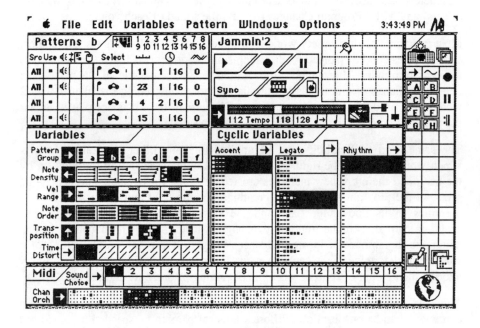

Figure 11.1: A screen from M

New York composer, Laurie Spiegel, and it is perfect for those who have few keyboard skills. Laurie Spiegel calls it her intelligent instrument, and there are good reasons for thinking of it in that way. Two sets of a total of four voices are presented on the screen, and the mouse is used to alter the pitch of the voices - up and down for one set, left and right for the other. Typically, one voice would be a melody, with the remaining three forming the accompaniment set. It is possible to choose between parallel motion (notes rise or fall in pitch together) or contrary motion (rise or fall in opposite directions). Harmonisation, tempo, dynamics, articulation, aftertouch and so on are controlled with the left hand from the computer keyboard, while the right hand rolls the mouse around to create the notes. In a very real sense, therefore, the computer is played like a musical instrument, except that it also continuously makes decisions, for example about the best harmonies to choose, and will produce its own sequences if it is asked to do so.

For other products, see below Section 11.4.

11.2 Arrangers

Software arrangers are the equivalent of a backing band. Chord progressions are entered into the computer in step-time, a style is chosen, and the program creates a standard accompaniment by accessing its knowledge base. The time gained by being able to enter a chord progression and instruct the computer to produce, say, a ballad accompaniment without further intervention, can be invaluable.

There are very few pieces of software in this category, but an inexpensive though quite powerful one is Band in a Box, which runs on the PC, Macintosh and Atari ST, and which produces a backing consisting of drums, bass and piano chords. Chords are entered into a grid of cells on the screen (using their names rather than notation) and a selection is made from 24 different musical styles from Country to Latin American. Each style has two variations and a drum fill. It is possible to transpose to any key, to set sections to be repeated, and to split a composition into Intro, Verse and Chorus. Songs can be saved as chord progressions, or as standard MIDI files to be loaded into a sequencer. A library of about 500 songs is available on disk.

Expert systems can be hard-wired into a piece of equipment. The equipment then becomes a brain like a computer, but one used solely for arranging raw compositions, which it does by accessing its dedicated knowledge base. Such equipment is sometimes incorporated into synthesiser keyboards, and low-level versions of the feature (which some see as a gimmick) have been available for some time on home electronic organs, called *auto-accompaniment* or some similar designation. There are now MIDI keyboard models, however, which will create draft arrangements intended for use with a sequencer so that they can be expanded. There is also a stand-alone keyboard-less model made by Roland - the CA-30 Intelligent Arranger - which goes well beyond the capabilities of software arrangers and most keyboard-based versions.

The CA-30 comes in its own box which is connected to a computer. To use it, as with a software arranger, a selection is made from a variety of musical styles and rhythms - Waltz, Disco, Samba, Rock and so on. Real-time chord and melody data coming from the computer or a MIDI instrument is then fed into the arranger. It recognises the input chord, and depending on which style has been selected, generates an arrangement consisting, say, of bass, drums and three accompaniment parts.

To do this, it makes decisions by accessing the musical knowledge embedded in its chips, together with data contained on ROM cards (ROM cards are available separately, and each contains four musical styles) and it produces results which are not simply musical clichés. Basic variations within each musical style are limited, but complex arrangements are achieved because the CA-30 causes differences to occur between the patterns for various types of chord.

All the functions of the machine are controllable via MIDI, so it is possible to change style or tempo, to change from original to variation, to break for a bar, or to put in an ending, all by sending down the appropriate Program Change number from the computer. After the arrangement has been generated, the CA-30 sends the data through its MIDI Out port either to a sound module or back into a computer for recording by a sequencer. A melody part coming in is harmonised according to the chord sequence which has been received, then re-transmitted out. And a typical introduction and ending can be supplied for each musical style, as well as fill-in patterns.

The CA-30 has been designed to work with the Roland MT-32, CM-32L, CM-32P and CM-64 sound modules, and there can be no guarantee that it will perform properly with others. The reason is that when it sends out the arrangement information, it also sends Program Change messages to set the various instruments, for instance the appropriate bass guitar for the bass part. However, in theory it is perfectly possible to make it work with other sound modules by changing their sound configurations to match the positions of the sounds in the MT-32 (1 to 8 for pianos, 9 to 15 for organs, 65 to 72 for bass guitars, and so on).

For other products, including auto-accompaniment keyboards, see below Section 11.4.

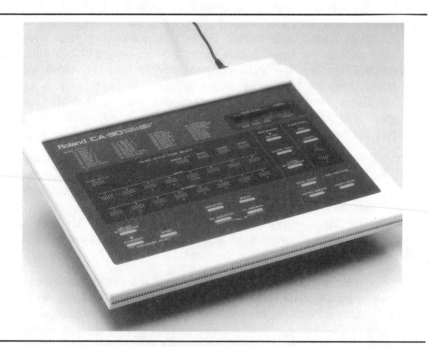

Figure 11.2: The Roland CA-30 Intelligent Arranger

11.3 A Plea for Artificial Intelligence

Ravel, one of the greatest orchestrators of all time, said that music is choice. Quite what he meant by that is open to debate, but we suspect he was saying that there are many ways in which a melody can be developed, varied and orchestrated, and that the musician's job is to experiment with possibilities, then choose the most appropriate result. Arranging machines and smart composition software will generate ideas, but in the end it is the job of the human musician to decide what to accept. Just as in medical diagnosis or natural-language translation, such aids to musical creativity are just that: aids not substitutes.

If that fails to satisfy the sense of outrage some may feel at the erosion of human originality by electronic tools of the kind described here, there is little hope of convincing them otherwise. But those who do not feel threatened by what can be achieved with an imaginative piece of programming, may find within musical expert systems a gold mine of ideas, and very useful musical assistants.

11.4 Products

Product	Producer	Computer(s)	Price	Comments
Band in a Box	PG Music	Mac, PC, ST	A	Arranger. See above Section 11.2.
Fingers	Dr T	Am, ST	B	
Jam Factory	Intelligent Music	Mac	B/C	
Ludwig	Hybrid Arts	ST	B	
M	Intelligent Music	Am, Mac, ST	B/C	See above Section 11.1.
M/pc	Voyetra	PC	C	
MidiDraw	Intelligent Music	ST	A/B	Pictures drawn with a mouse are turned into music.
Midigrid	Composers Desktop Project	Archimedes, ST	B	Concept similar to Music Mouse (see above Section 11.1)
Music Mouse	Dr T	Am, Mac, ST	A/B	See above Section 11.1.
RealTime	Intelligent Music	ST	C	
Sound Globs	Twelve Tone Systems	PC	C	
Tunesmith	Dr T	Am, ST	B	6-part compositions.
UpBeat	Intelligent Music	Mac	C	

Key

Software
Am: Commodore Amiga
C1: Yamaha C1
Mac: Apple Macintosh
PC: IBM PC and compatibles
ST: Atari ST

Hardware arrangers and auto-accompaniment keyboards

Producer	Product	Price	Features/Comments
Casio	CT-670	D	5-octave keyboard. 12-note polyphonic, 110 styles each having a 5-part accompaniment.
	MT-750	C	As CT-670 but mini keys.
Farfisa	DK250	F	5-octave velocity-sensitive keyboard, 16 definable accompaniment patterns, 4-track sequencer, 24 pre-set styles, extra Arabian scale (see Chapter 8 Section 8.6).
Korg	PSS60	F	Arranger and sound module combined (no keyboard). Works like a glorified drum machine with extra bass and chord accompaniment. 70 styles, 50 pre-set sounds, 20 sounds selectable from an accompanying library of ROM cards.
Roland	RA-50	E	CA-30 Intelligent Arranger (see above Section 11.2) plus a CM-32L sound module. No internal sound amplification.
	PRO-E	F/G	CA-30 in a 37-key velocity-sensitive keyboard, 6-track sequencer. No internal sound amplification. Can be found heavily discounted.
Yamaha	E series	F to G	CA-30 in a 5-octave keyboard.
	PSS series	B to C	Auto-accompaniment keyboard with mini keys.
	PSR series	B/C to F	Top of the range is the PSR4500, with 5-octave velocity-sensitive keyboard, 8-note polyphony, 100 sounds, 100 pre-set accompaniment styles (five definable), a 4-song memory sequencer, built-in reverb.

12

Music Notation Software

Some MIDI musicians will never need to produce musical scores in traditional notation on paper, but for those who expect their scores to be played or sung by other musicians, it is essential to do so. No musician will accept a sequencer printout of bar charts and lists of MIDI events, and traditional notation is still the only universal form of musical communication, even if the twentieth century has seen many variations of it. But writing out a score and – worse – the individual instrument parts of a score, is a tedious business except for those who love doing it, and those who consider their scores to be works of art in themselves. The answer can be score-editing software.

Score editors are specialised versions of generic desktop-publishing programs. Notation can be entered via computer keyboard or a mouse, and in some cases via a musical keyboard in real- or step-time. And just as desktop publishing packages allow files from other programs to be imported, so some score editors allow a similar process to take place with files produced by sequencers, transcribing them into notation once they have been read in.

In addition, certain score editors are able to play a score by sending notes to a MIDI instrument. However, generally speaking, score editors will not check a composition for musical sense. Some will not even add up the values of the notes in each bar to verify that they fit the time signature. But the principal aim of score editors lies in form not content: they are there to take some of the drudgery out of copying parts with a pen, to produce neatness, and they give a professional image, quite apart from the fact that unclear parts waste time and therefore cost money.

Score editors are without doubt, then, a boon to many musicians, and the natural extension of computerised music. For years, as computers became ever more powerful and ever more available to the general public, musicians dreamed of a time when they could play their instruments into one and see a score come out at the printer. To a certain extent, that dream has come true, but we should not give the impression that currently available software is capable of handling huge amounts of complex information such as that produced by a musical instrument, and intelligently producing a perfect printed score of it without any further intervention on the part of the musician.

In reality, many factors slow down and complicate the process. However smart the score editor, each track will almost certainly have to be quantised for both start time and duration of notes, and other editing functions performed too, before the data is read in. And once the music is in the score editor, a considerable amount of further editing is normally required before printing. Score editors can save the musician hours of work, but may also involve hours of tweaking and fine-tuning to make *them* work as they should. Word processors are far better at processing text than score editors at processing musical notation. Nevertheless, once their quirks have been learned and their limitations accepted, they can be useful tools.

Score editors are often found within integrated packages containing a sequencer and perhaps other modules. While some of the more expensive ones offer a realistic alternative to buying a separate score editor, for professional results a stand-alone program is usually needed. The great advantage of integrated packages is that there is normally no constraint on transferring data between their various modules. Their disadvantage is that the modules are not often of equal power, flexibility or quality, and since score editing has a limited market, notation-printing tends not to be the best served.

12.1 Methods of Input

Input of the score into a score editor can take place in one or more of the following ways:

12.1.1 Input from the Computer Keyboard

With this method, the keys on the computer keyboard are re-assigned from their normal alphabetic state to one in which they generate note shapes and other musical symbols. The cursor keys are used to indicate the position of the symbol on the stave, or above or below it, the appropriate key is pressed, and the symbol is placed on the screen.

It sometimes comes as a surprise to computer-novices to learn that keys can be re-assigned in this way, but on a computer as opposed to a typewriter, pressing a key generates a code representing a series of dots which normally correspond (though not, of course, precisely) to the textual symbols on the keytops. There is no reason why they should not generate other codes representing other patterns of dots, and indeed font editors are available on many computers to change the shape of letters and numbers as they appear on the screen. Musical symbols are merely patterns of dots to a computer, and it handles them just as it does alphabetic characters. Some score editors come with plastic or paper key-strips showing musical symbols which are placed over the existing keytops.

12.1.2 Mouse Input

In this case, notes and musical symbols are picked up by clicking with a mouse on pull-down menus, or from palettes as in a computer Paint program, and put in the appropriate place in the score. This kind of selection can also be accomplished with the cursor and Return keys on a computer keyboard, but the mouse is a far better tool for pointing to a given place on the screen.

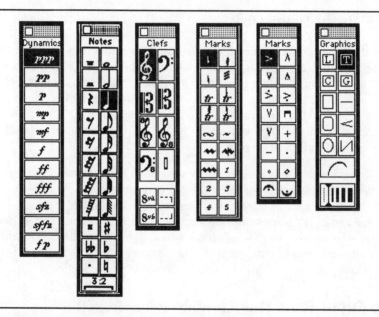

Figure 12.1: Palettes of musical symbols (from Passport's Encore for the Atari ST, Apple Macintosh and PC)

12.1.3 Input with a MIDI Instrument in Step Time

Typically for this method, note durations are set on the computer keyboard or by using a mouse, and a musical keyboard is used for entering pitches. In some cases, however, note durations too can be entered via the musical keyboard, the duration depending on the length of time for which the key is held down. While it is being held down, a highlight bar or other highlighting indicator moves across the values of notes shown in a menu on the screen, usually in standard notation. When the key is released, the value reached by the highlight bar is the one displayed as a note of that duration in the score.

12.1.4 Input with a MIDI Instrument in Real Time

With this method, a MIDI keyboard is played as normal, and the score editor records the performance and converts it into notation.

Such programs fall into two types: those which use a buffer and those which do not. With buffered programs, the music is played, the program gathers the data invisibly, and displays it at a command from the player issued on the computer keyboard or using a mouse. Programs which do not use a buffer display the music on screen as it is played. The choice between the two types is often a matter of taste – some people like to see the notation appear as they play, others do not.

12.1.5 Input from Disk

One of the most useful features found in many score editors is the ability to read from disk not only their own special files (all can do this) but also files containing MIDI data produced by other programs. So, a file created with a sequencer can be fed into a score editor and standard notation produced from it. The file in question can be a standard MIDI file, or a file peculiar to the sequencer. Some score editors will read standard MIDI files, some will read files created by well-known sequencers, and some will do both.

It would seem best to buy a score editor which can read external files, but certain programs are superb except for their inability to do so. Equally, it would seem best always to choose a score editor which can handle standard MIDI files, since an increasing amount of sequencing software can save files in this format. However, for those who already own a sequencer which does not produce standard MIDI files, it may make more sense when choosing a score editor to give other features a higher priority. As with all MIDI products, choice is never simple.

12.2 Output of the Score

12.2.1 Printing

Printing is the principal aim of a score editor, and it is generally carried out on either a dot-matrix or a laser printer.

Dot matrix

Professionals might use a dot-matrix printer for drafts, and a laser printer for top copies, though a 24-pin dot-matrix output produces perfectly acceptable if not quite publishing-quality results. Dot-matrix printers vary in the quality of their output, a measure of which is the resolution of the dots (dots per inch or dpi). Anything above 140 dpi will give adequate results. The choice between 9-pin and 24-pin is of course related to the kind of quality required.

Unless a computer has its own range of printers (as is the case with Apple) it is best to select a dot-matrix printer which is either made by Epson or which is Epson-compatible (there are many compatible models on the market). Although some score editors offer a choice of output to different types of dot-matrix printer, all can send their output in Epson format.

Because they are mostly used for printing text, the speed of dot-matrix printers is measured in characters per second (cps), with draft mode (maximum speed) often being used as the benchmark. Fast printers work at over 200 cps and, obviously, the faster the better, though speed has to be set against quality and price. Generally speaking, it is not worth paying a great deal extra for increased speed unless large (or urgent) outputs are envisaged, though it should be noted that some score editors are very slow when printing, especially in high-quality mode, and it can take up to 20 minutes for a single page to be printed on a slow dot-matrix printer.

If finance allows, it is useful to have a dot-matrix printer which will take wide sheets of paper.

Laser

Laser printers have resolutions of between 200 and about 400 dpi, and the results are virtually indistinguishable from professional printing. Certain top-of-the-range score editing programs will output their data to Postscript files (standard desktop publishing files for laser printers which support it) which are essential for sending camera-ready copy on disk to go to the printers.

The files created by score editors can be very large, and in most cases require 1 Mb or more of memory within the laser printer. This may have to be bought as an extra. And with the exception of Apple printers used with Apple computers, it is quite important to choose a Hewlett-Packard (HP) Laserjet or one which is compatible with this standard (many are), since most score editors expect it and some will not handle anything else.

Other

Ink-jet printers have a resolution of about 350 dpi, and most of them will take wide paper. They give excellent results, but have been little used since the price of laser printers started to fall two or three years ago.

A plotter can be used instead of a printer. Plotters use lines drawn with pens as opposed to dots or tones, and are mainly used for plotting graphs and making line-drawings. They are very accurate and can give impressive results, but would not normally be chosen specifically for score printing.

If either an ink-jet printer or a plotter is to be used, it is obviously important to check that the score editor supports it.

Figure 12.2: Dot-matrix (9-pin) and laser printouts of two lines of music (not continuous)

12.2.2 Output to Standard MIDI Files

Some score editors will save their data as standard MIDI files so that they can be loaded by other music software (such as sequencers) for playing, being transmitted over the telephone using a modem, or read by someone else's score editor of a different make but which also handles standard MIDI files.

12.2.3 Output to MIDI Instruments

Certain score editors have the ability to output a score directly to an instrument in the form of a musical performance contained in a MIDI performance file, or they include built-in sequencer modes. Notes and musical symbols are translated into MIDI messages, and it is possible to assign staves to MIDI channels.

Of course, with some musical symbols, the meaning is plain – a repeat is a repeat. But how is the score editor to interpret the note velocity for marks such as *pp*, *pf* or *ff*? The interpretation of dynamics can take various forms, and they are implemented using a mathematical function which the programmers of the software have chosen to include. However, some score editors allow the values to be altered, or alternative sets of values are provided.

12.2.4 Monitoring Output

Internal computer sound

Some computers have reasonably good internal sound chips, and score editors make use of them. Even the (normally) monophonic IBM PC sound chip and its tinny speaker are used, and by programs at the top the range. The result may be poor-quality sound, but if all that is required is a broad idea of how a line sounds, the facility can be useful.

PC MIDI interface cards incorporating sound modules

It is possible to monitor output using normal MIDI studio equipment. However, certain people may wish to use MIDI only for score editing, in which case they do not need external sound modules, but may nevertheless wish to hear a quality and complexity of sound superior to that produced by a computer's internal sound chip and speaker. The solution is either IBM's Music Feature Card or Roland's LAPC-1 (see Chapter 4 Section 4.2.5), both of which are MIDI interfaces and sound modules combined.

12.3 Editing

12.3.1 Editing Screens

Usually, but not always, the screen of a score editor is divided into a grid of (unseen) cells around which a cursor can be moved using the computer keyboard or a mouse, and on which notes and musical symbols can be placed. In most cases, there is also a status line showing information such as the current coordinates of the cursor, the amount of memory left, the filename, the editing mode (musical notation or text), and single-note or chord input.

Some score editors work on a menu-tree system – menus with options which lead to sub-menus or other windows from which further options can be selected – and modules allowing keys to be re-defined for different input modes. It may often be necessary to jump to a Help screen as a reminder of the various key assignments. For example, the F key in three different editing modes might mean *fortissimo*, the note F, or the letter *f* as a textual character.

12.3.2 Editing Facilities

Score editors differ quite considerably in the range of editing facilities they offer. Most have the basic desktop-publishing functions, such as Insert, Cut, Copy, Move and Delete, and allow these operations to work at the level of notes and symbols, and as blocks of information at the level of the stave, or even of the whole page. In some score editors, however, such editing functions are quite severely limited. Certain programs, for instance, will not even allow a marked block to be moved anywhere on the page, or one file to be incorporated into another.

Any score editor worth its salt, however, will be able to handle quantisation of note start times and durations before input from a source other than the computer keyboard or mouse. A score read into a notation program from a sequencer or sent in directly from a live performance will almost certainly contain too fine a range of durations (and probably also pitch adjustments) to be handled, and thresholds have to be set up beforehand. If this is not done, the score editor – which is far more sensitive to matters like timing than any musician – will score exactly what is played, which will not be the intended result. For instance, it may put rests after staccato notes, and notes will start slightly earlier or later than really intended. Quantisation takes care of this to a great extent, and the timing can be left as is despite any stretching which may have been part of the original playing. A score can sometimes look unnecessarily complicated if a composer has tried to put every nuance of timing into it, where a textual instruction to anticipate the beat or play across it will keep the notation simple, and actually be better understood by instrumentalists.

12.3.3 Musical Symbols

All proper score editors offer the fundamental music-notation symbols, that is to say the sticks, ellipses and blobs of notes, and basic marks such as rests, treble and bass clef signs, accidentals, triplet indicators, ties and slurs, staccato dots, repeat signs, and the elongated arrows used for dynamics. They nearly all also offer a text facility for handling lyrics and any descriptive musical terms.

Not all, however, offer the full possible range of marks, and the less common marks are often missing from the sign libraries of low-end score editors, marks such as those for fermata (pause), double staccato, tenuto, segno, upper and inverted mordents, turn, appoggiatura, acciaccatura, and even trill. In addition, some score editors cannot handle alto and tenor clef signs, let alone percussion staves, or mix sharps and flats in a key signature as is required in some twentieth-century music, or allow a beam to cross from one stave to another because the two staves of a piano part are treated independently. Others can cope with every known mark, or at least will allow the user to draw them and store them on disk. But *complete* flexibility is not offered by any available score editor.

One of the biggest problems in printing music is spacing. In polyphonic music, notes, rests and other marks which fall on the same beat normally have to be aligned, but this involves a good deal of computer processing because one voice may contain many more notes and/or marks than another. A typical result on a low-end score editor may be that accidentals are pushed too close to notes, making them unreadable. The question of page-turns is a related problem which is a far more complex one in music than it is with text. A word processor need only be programmed not to leave the first line of a paragraph at the bottom of a page, or the last line at the top of a page. In music, the end of a page should fall at a logical break, which is more difficult to achieve because it can often only be done by spacing.

In assessing score editors, the range of available marks, and the flexibility with which they can be manipulated, is plainly of the greatest importance, but individual requirements are paramount.

For professional printed output, the full range will be required unless only one type of music will ever be printed (in pop music many of the less common signs are never seen). For less-than-professional printed scores, it may not be vital to have the full range even for music which normally requires it, since the occasional rare mark can always be inserted by hand, or fudged in some way.

Some score editors have a limited range of available slopes for beaming, and whereas for a professional score a large number of slope steps (or even an infinitely variable slope pattern) will be required, for semi-professional purposes a range of four angles up or down may be quite sufficient. If a professional composer uses very unusual rhythms, the full range of time signatures will be crucial if the look of a score is not to be spoiled by writing them in by hand, while for many people the standard time signatures which most score editors will handle will be sufficient. For anyone who needs to produce parts for musicians plus a conductor's part, major considerations will be the ease or otherwise of extracting them from the complete score, and the number of staves which can be accommodated on a single page. These will be insignificant considerations for some people. It may be important to some people to have at their disposal a range of character fonts and sizes for lyrics, titles and so on, in order to produce a really professional result, whereas many will consider it merely a bonus if such a facility is available.

It should be added that some score editors produce files which can be read into Paint programs. This means that a rough draft can be produced, then the Paint program used to draw anything which the score editor has been unable to cater for. However, this can be a long process, and of course once a score has been edited and enhanced in this way, it will change format and contain marks which the score editor cannot understand, so it will be useless as a performance file.

12.4 Computer Hardware Requirements

Score editors need graphics, and graphics need memory and processing power. Many of the limitations of score editors are therefore imposed by the machines they are meant to run on, and the market dictates that programs tend to be written either for the lowest configuration of any particular machine, or the lowest configuration which is generally used. Nevertheless, pride in their work and a desire to get as close as possible to perfection is (happily) a trait common in professional programmers, and these virtues constitute a powerful force which Financial Directors of software houses cannot always resist. Writing graphics-intensive programs is always a trade-off between the ideal solution and maximising the size of the potential market.

What this means for the user is that the choice of score editor is a function not only of features desired, but of the machine on which it is meant to run. It is therefore vital that before buying a score editor, a check is made to ensure that the configuration of the system intended for running it is up to doing so to an adequate level. The only way of being sure is to see the software working on the machine in question, but the following general points should be born in mind:

❏ Score editors generally require large amounts of memory, especially during compilation of pages ready for printing

❏ A hard disk will be often be required because of the large files generated

❏ A mouse is usually an important input device, without which the score editor may be very difficult to use

❑ High-resolution monitors can display more staves on the screen, and give better clarity when displaying chords and small musical symbols. A resolution of above 640 x 480 (and preferably higher, though this will be costly) will mean clarity and a minimum of eye strain.

12.5 Score Editor Checklist

Input, editing and processing

Musicians who read printed scores are concerned not only with the accuracy of the note information – the position of notes on the stave, their duration, and so on – but also with certain musical conventions to which they are trained to react. Indeed, if such conventions are not followed, many musicians will have considerable difficulty in interpreting a score. There are many such conventions, and many score editors can take care of the basic ones, but in selecting a program, the following questions should be considered:

❑ Does the program allow quantisation at input?

❑ Does it allow you to set the way in which accidentals will be processed before the music is entered (enharmonic changes)? Trained musicians expect to see a flat or a sharp (even a double flat or double sharp) depending on the key signature, and can be momentarily put off by the wrong accidental even though the pitch of the note is the correct one. This is not a crucial point, but for certain people it may be significant.

❑ Is there a facility for determining the vertical direction of the note-stems in any one line of the music? The conventions for stem direction are part of the unconscious process of reading standard musical notation, and wrong directions will be seen as curious, even though the musician reading the part may not actually understand the conventions themselves

❑ Can the grouping of notes in a bar be defined, and does the program then automatically supply the correct beaming?

❑ Is there an appropriate range of built-in musical symbols?

❑ Are cross-stave beaming and cross-stave stems allowed?

❑ Is the spacing adjustable?

❑ How extensive are the editing functions?

❑ Is the input of chords from a MIDI instrument processed in real time?

❑ Does the program allow musical lines already entered to be played back while another line is being played? MIDI musicians who enter music line by line need this facility if they are not to be paralysed by the score editor

❏ How easy is it to extract a part from a full score?

Output

❏ What quality of print is required? In other words, for whom is the printed output intended?

❏ How long does it take to print one page?

❏ Is the maximum size of the score created by the score editor sufficient for all likely requirements? Some programs have restrictions on the number of pages they can handle because they are designed for budget computer systems with (by today's standards) severe memory restrictions

❏ What type of score is required – lead sheet music (parts for lead instruments) or conductor scores with multiple staves?

12.6 Products

All score programs support dot-matrix output. Laser printer output is indicated in the Comments column.

Key

Am: Commodore Amiga
Mac: Apple Macintosh
PC: IBM PC and compatibles
ST: Atari ST

Product	Producer	Cmptr	Price	Comments
Basic Composer	Education Software Consultants	PC	A/B	Budget package. Double stave.
Composer	Mark of the Unicorn	Mac	D/E	Laser, Postscript. Full professional specifications.
Copyist series	Dr T	Am, PC,	ST	
– Apprentice			B	Budget package. Five pages.
– Professional			C	In fact, semi-professional. Laser, 50 pages.
– DTP			D	Laser, Postscript, 100 pages.
DynaDuet	Dynaware	PC	C/D	Includes 16-track sequencer, drum pattern editor.
Encore	Passport	Mac, PC, ST	D/E	Professional. Laser, Postscript. Up to 16 files of 64 staves each, open simultaneously. Easy to use.

Product	Producer	Cmptr	Price	Comments
EZ Score Plus	Hybrid Arts	ST	B	Up to three staves.
Finale	Coda Systems	Mac, PC	Mac: F PC: E/F	Professional. Laser, Postscript. 128 staves, able to make a piano transcription out of an orchestral score, or vice versa. PC version requires Microsoft Windows.
Laser Music Processor	Teach Services	PC	B/C	Laser. Single page only.
Masterscore II	Steinberg Research	ST	D	For Pro-24 sequencer (see Chapter 5 Section 5.11). Checks notational grammar.
MESA	Roland	PC	E	Laser. Includes 8-track sequencer. Successor to MPS, one of the first sequencer/scoring packages for PC.
Music Printer Plus	Temporal Acuity Products	PC	E	High-level. Laser, real-time scoring.
MusicProse	Coda Systems	Mac	C/D	Laser, Postscript, eight staves.
Music DTP	Take Control	ST	D	Laser, Postscript with add-on. Mono monitor required. 99 pages. Full-specification professional program.
Notator	C-Lab	ST	E	Laser. Very versatile scoring package for the Creator sequencer (see Chapter 5 Section 5.11).
- Notator Alpha			C	Cut-down version of Notator.
Notewriter II	Passport	Mac	D	Laser, Postscript. Very flexible, capable of a wide range of score styles.
Personal Composer System/2	Jim Miller	PC	D/E	Laser, Postscript. Includes 32-track sequencer and librarian for Yamaha DX, TX series. Compatible with LISP (Artificial Intelligence language).
Score	Passport	PC	E	Professional. Laser, Postscript. Handles 64 staves.
Scorewriter	ElectroMusic Research	BBC	B	Two ROMs and utility disk.
Scorewriter PMS	ElectroMusic Research	Archi-medes	E	Laser, Postscript. Uses a text-based language.
Showtune	Computer Music Supply	PC	B	Laser. Works under Microsoft Windows.

13

Musical Education

13.1 The Theory of Music – A Crash Course for the Absolute Beginner

It is assumed that those who are reading this book wish to make music, but some readers may know little or nothing about the principles on which music is based, and it is impossible to get very far in music-making without some theoretical understanding of the subject. Indeed, the need for theoretical knowledge does not diminish as a musician achieves ever higher levels of practical skill, and even in taught courses oriented heavily towards performance, some theory is nearly always obligatory. A computer can help here, since there are programs which aim to teach music theory (see below Section 13.6) and some of them are excellent. But much can be learned in an hour or so spent reading about the subject, and in any case the computer programs which deal with absolute basics tend to be aimed specifically at small children, and for use with a human teacher.

The following crash course in music theory is therefore intended as a digestible snack for the musically starved. It covers some of the fundamentals of music, assuming no knowledge whatsoever of the subject, and gives the basic musical vocabulary necessary for getting to grips with electronic music beyond merely fumbling in the dark, which is possible but not desirable. It therefore leaves more questions unanswered than it answers, and for the sake of simplicity has to make do with compromises, omissions, and half-truths. We nevertheless believe that it is adequate for its modest purpose, as well as forming a starting point for novices who may wish to take the subject further.

13.2 What is Music?

Music is *pitch* (how high or low a note is) and *rhythm*.

There is no need to define rhythm because it is instinctive. Tap out the rhythm of *God Save the Queen*, and most people will immediately recognise the tune. Play the notes of the tune on a piano with the right pitch but the wrong rhythm, and you can fool most people. So let us begin with what everybody already knows – rhythm – but may not be able to describe in musical terms.

13.2.1 Rhythm

Although some contemporary composers use eccentric ways of writing down rhythms, most divide their music into *bars*, which has been the tradition for centuries.

A bar contains a given number of rhythm units, called *beats*, and the most common beat is the *crotchet*. In the USA, a bar is called a *measure*, and a crotchet a *quarter note*. These, and some other differences between UK and US English mentioned below, are points worth remembering when it comes to MIDI because a fair proportion of available music software is American or American-influenced.

A crotchet is a quarter note because the most common type of bar contains four crotchet beats (the rhythm is then called *common time*) which together make up a whole note. There are also half notes, 8th notes, 16th notes and so on. The following is a summary of the fundamental units of musical rhythm, with their English and American names:

Half a crotchet is a *quaver* or *8th note*.

A quarter of a crotchet is a *semiquaver* or *16th note*.

Two crotchets make up a *minim* or *half note* (that is to say that a minim has the duration of two crotchets).

Four crotchets make up a *whole note*, which in the UK is traditionally called (as if deliberately to confuse) a *semibreve*, while a *breve* is two whole notes, not one.

If a bar is meant to contain (say) four beats, it can be made up of any combination of the above. For example, it could contain one minim (= two beats), two quavers (= one beat), and a crotchet (= one beat), making a total of four.

Sometimes, it is necessary to play three notes in one beat. In this case the three notes are bracketed with a little figure 3 above or below them when printed in a musical score, and the combination is known as a *triplet*.

A period of silence is called a *rest*, and it is measured in beats as an ordinary unit of rhythm. A minim rest, for example, is a period of silence lasting two beats, and a semiquaver rest is a period of silence lasting 1/16 of a beat.

The *time signature* (which may look something like $\frac{3}{4}$) indicates how many beats and of which kind there are in each bar. The lower figure is the unit, the upper figure how many of them. The number 4 represents a crotchet because four crotchets make up a semibreve (a whole note). So, $\frac{3}{4}$ means three crotchets to a bar, $\frac{6}{8}$ means six quavers to a bar, and so on.

It is unusual to find time signatures like $\frac{13}{16}$ meaning 13 semiquavers to the bar, though such rhythms are by no means unheard of in contemporary music, particularly in so-called serious music (Radio 3 variety).

The speed at which beats are played (as opposed to the number of beats in a bar) is called the *tempo*. This is measured in beats per minute. It is sometimes difficult for beginners to understand the difference between the kind of beats in a bar and the tempo at which they are played. What needs to be understood is that a basic beat of a crotchet, say three to a bar (waltz time), can be played at any tempo. Put another way, waltzes always contain three beats to a bar, but there are fast and slow waltzes.

13.2.2 Pitch

The standard way of naming the pitch of notes in Western music is to use the letters of the alphabet from A to G, then to start again at A – in other words, eight notes including the two ends, making up an *octave*. A *scale* is an alphabetical list of notes going up or down from a starting note.

The division of notes into octaves is not arbitrary – a note which is one octave higher than another is sounded by producing double the frequency of the lower note (see Chapter 7 Section 7.1.3), something of which our ancestors were unaware because they did not have the equipment to measure note frequency, but which their ears told them was the case, as do ours. Play a white note on a piano keyboard, then play its equivalent eight white notes further on (where it fits into the same pattern of black and white notes). The pitch is higher, but the note sounds much more like the lower one than a note from anywhere else in that octave range.

Notes go up or down in steps, called *intervals*. The interval between a note and the one immediately above or below it is called a *tone*, except between B and C, and E and F, where the interval is a *semitone* (half a tone). There are good reasons for these anomalies, but this is not the place to explore them. All tones, however, can be divided into two semitones. Highering a note by a semitone *sharpens* it. Lowering it by a semitone *flattens* it.

So, the note F sharp (written F#) is a semitone below the note G. G flat (written G♭) is a semitone above F. They are the same note with different names, and the term *enharmonic* is used to describe a note which changes its name but not its pitch. The choice of how such notes are written is something of a complex issue in musical theory, and need not concern us here.

Sharps and flats can be switched off by *naturals*, the symbol for which is ♮ . So G♮ means plain G: it was sharpened or flattened, and it has been returned to its original natural state.

Sharps, flats and naturals are called *accidentals*. There are other accidentals, such as double sharps and double flats, but they are of less significance as far as many MIDI applications are concerned.

Now, suppose you wish all Fs to be sharp, or all Bs and Es to be flat. Clearly, it makes sense to indicate this just once, at the beginning of a passage of music.

A *key signature* (sharp or flat signs usually found at the beginning of each line of music as a reminder) indicates which notes are sharpened or flattened throughout, that is to say what *key* the music is in. It also indicates the 'home' note or *key-note*. For instance, the key in which Fs are sharpened throughout but all other notes are natural (unless sharpened or flattened individually) is the key of G. G is therefore the key-note of the key of G.

Some other common keys are C (all notes natural), D (F and G sharpened), F (B flattened) and B♭ (B and E flattened).

Transposition means moving from one key to another and therefore altering the pitch of all the notes by a given number of semitones. The pitch of the notes relative to each other does not change, but their absolute pitch does. If a tape is played at a faster speed than its manufacturers intended, the overall pitch rises. Play it fast enough and the music is deformed because the tempo has changed. Within MIDI, however, transposition can take place without a change in tempo.

When a number of notes are played simultaneously, they are said to form a *chord*. If a chord is split into it constituent parts, so that each is sounded one after the other, the result is an *arpeggio*.

Chords are the best way of explaining the last points which needs to be made about general musical theory: that of the difference between *major* and *minor* keys. It has nothing to do with the words *major* and *minor* in their everyday sense of being more or less important.

Play the notes C and E together on a piano and you have a major chord, that is to say a chord built of notes from a major scale. Play C and E♭ instead of E♮ and you have a minor chord. Few people are unable to hear the difference between the two, and many people associate the minor sound with sadness.

Minor chords are constructed by taking the key-note of the key in question, taking two steps forward alphabetically, and flattening the third note in the sequence. For instance, we have seen that the key of D major has two notes sharpened (F and G). To construct a two-note chord of D minor, the third note in the sequence D, E, F (in this case F#) is flattened to become F♮ The construction of minor scales, and chords of more than two notes, is complicated, and we shall avoid the subject for that reason. However, the fact that to produce a two-note minor chord, the third note of a major scale is flattened, is a basic one, and therefore worth noting.

13.3 Musical Notation

Every now and then, someone invents a new and better system of writing down music. But standard notation, for all its quirks, is deeply rooted, and there is little chance of it ever being dislodged. Some music programs avoid it, either because the programmers have felt that it is not intuitive or because traditional notation on a computer screen eats up large amounts of memory; but even in these cases it is often used in the documentation. It is therefore important for the MIDI musician, even one who does not want to print out scores in traditional notation, to have some basic information about the way it works.

Here, in essence, is that information:

A *stave* (sometimes written *staff*) consists of five lines, and therefore four spaces (see Figure 13.1 Stave A). Notes, represented by a filled or unfilled blob, are placed either on a line or in a space, (see Stave B). The higher up the note on the stave, the higher the pitch.

A semibreve (whole note) represented as ○. A minim is written as ♩, a crotchet as ♩ , a quaver as ♪, and a semiquaver as ♬ (see Stave C).

Notice that a stick added to the semibreve note halves its value; that filling in the blob of a minim does the same; and that thereafter the halving of values is done by adding tails to the stick. Whether the sticks go up or down has no bearing on the meaning of the notation.

In normal notation, groups of quavers and semiquavers often have their tails joined, but the joins are straightened out and become a line, as shown in Stave D. The line is called a *beam*, and beaming is something which score editing programs (programs intended specifically for printing out music) should be able to handle, or they are not worth considering. However, certain MIDI packages which show traditional notation on screen do not use beams, and only the fussiest of musicians would worry about this.

A dot after a note means that it is extended by one half of its length. So, a dotted crotchet (♩.) is one and a half crotchet beats, a dotted minim (♩.) is three crotchet beats, and a dotted quaver (♪.) is 6/32 (1/8 + 1/16) of a crotchet beat.

Figure 13.1: (notation)

Everything which applies to the duration of notes, also applies to rests, which are written as follows:

Semibreve rest: ≡

Minim rest: ≡

Crotchet rest: ⅄

Quaver rest: ⅄

Semiquaver rest: ⅄

The end of each bar is indicated by a *bar line* cutting the stave (see Stave E).

One last basic concept to learn about staves is that of *clefs*. The simplest way of understanding clefs is to imagine that the five lines of a stave, which are not enough to fit the full range of possible notes, are a window on a larger number of lines. As notes go beyond the window, so there is a move to another. The clef sign at the beginning of a stave indicates which window is being used.

The two most common clefs are the *treble* clef, written 𝄞 , and the *bass* clef, written 𝄢 (see Stave F). The treble clef normally corresponds to the upper notes (right hand) of a piano keyboard, and the bass clef to the lower notes (left hand). A stave with a treble clef at the beginning of it is known as a treble stave, and one with a bass clef as a bass stave.

On a treble stave, the bottom line is the note E, the space above it is F, and so on. On a bass stave, the bottom line is the note G, the space above it is A, and so on.

Since it is not practicable constantly to be changing clefs, *leger lines* are used instead. These are short lines drawn above or below the stave to indicate that the music has temporarily entered another window or is midway between two windows (see Stave G).

A handy way of indicating the position of a note on a stave without actually using the stave itself, or traditional music notation at all, is to put an octave number with the note in question, such as C3 or C_3, with the number denoting the octave, and therefore the stave position. So, if Middle C (on the first leger line under the treble stave) is C4, C2 is two octaves below.

Unfortunately, two different standards have been established for using such numbers in MIDI. Yamaha prefers to use C3 to indicate Middle C while Roland uses C4, though some Yamaha instruments conform to the Roland standard. Although this difference is not of crucial importance, it represents precisely the kind of potential confusion which MIDI should by rights forestall and if necessary abolish. Of course MIDI has its own invariable standard, that of the MIDI note number (Middle C is Note 60). However, it is important to be aware of the alternative system and its anomaly, since it does tend to be used, particularly in MIDI instrument documentation.

13.3.2 Qualifiers and Other Signs

A musical score does not just contain notes. It also contains numerous marks and symbols to indicate *how* the notes are to be played: loud, soft, and so on. Before computers entered the musical arena, such marks were (and still are in the vast majority of musical scores) rough and ready guides, often overlapping in meaning, sometimes to such an extent that two or more of them can mean virtually the same thing.

It is easy enough to indicate a tempo in beats per minute, so that a composer could write $\bm{\downarrow}$ = 60, and know that a conductor would beat at approximately one beat per second. It is less easy to indicate how loud a piece is to be played, or how precisely to interpret an instruction such as *sotto voce* (in a whisper or undertone) when applied to a violin.

MIDI has changed all that: the MIDI composer has complete control over his or her instructions about how the music is to be played, because measurements are available for every nicety of musical phrasing. But as with all aspects of traditional notation, knocking the tradition of vague musical markings off its perch is easier said than done, and the MIDI user should at least to be able to recognise the most common marks and instructions. These are included at the end of this course (section 13.5 below), together with a short glossary of related musical terms, most of them coming from Italian.

You will often see, in printed musical scores, curved lines over and under two or more notes. These can be either *ties* or *slurs*.

Ties are used to tie together two notes, one at the end of one bar, the other at the beginning of the next. They are necessary because of the strict rule that a bar can contain only a given number of notes. It is therefore impossible to have, say, a minim at the end of bar of $\frac{4}{4}$ if there is only a crotchet value left. In that case, the bar would end in a crotchet, the next bar would begin with one, and the two would be linked by a tie indicating that the first crotchet is to be played together with the second to form a minim.

Slurs are used for phrasing, often to indicate that the grouped notes are to be played smoothly together, with no 'air' between them. On a piano, this means pressing a key as soon as the previous key has been released, or even slightly before. On a wind instrument it means not stopping the passage of air from the mouth while the notes concerned are being played. On a bowed string instrument it means moving the fingers but keeping the bow moving smoothly, normally in the same direction.

The opposite of a slur is a dot above or below a note, indicating that it is to be played detached or *staccato* (see the Glossary in Section 13.5 below).

Other signs commonly seen in scores are:

⌢ which means pause at this point, then resume.

‖: :‖ meaning repeat the music between these two signs.

> indicating an accent (stronger beat) on the note above or below it.

See also *al* in the Glossary below.

13.4 Putting it into Practice

The bit of musical score shown on Stave H in Figure 13.1 represents the first part of *God Save the Queen* in the key of G (just the melody, without any accompaniment). The sharp sign on the F line indicates that all Fs are sharp.

Having taken this course, you have all the information necessary to work out what the notation means (though in order to keep things simple, not all possible marks have been included). Hum the tune to yourself and tap out the rhythm while following the score. This can be an eye-opening experience for those who have spent their lives baffled by all those lines, sticks and blobs.

The next step would be to study the score of other familiar tunes (a book of Christmas carols would be a good start), referring when necessary to a book on musical theory. We recommend *Rudiments and Theory of Music* (the 'little red book' used by generations of schoolchildren), published by the Associated Board of the Royal Schools of Music and available in most music shops. The title sounds daunting, but the book is actually quite straightforward. Music education software, as described earlier in this chapter, can also be very useful.

13.5 Glossary of Musical Terms

The following list is very far from complete, but the terms it contains are those commonly found in scores, and which significantly affect the intentions of the composer or arranger. Using Italian terms gives an impression of having been classically trained, though they are accepted as an international musical vocabulary.

Accelerando or **Accel.** – getting faster

Adagio – Very slow

al – to the, as in *Da Capo al Segno*: from the beginning to the 𝄋 sign

Allargando – broadening out in tempo and tone

Allegro – fast

Allegretto – not as fast as *allegro*

Andante – slow

A tempo – back to normal tempo after having slowed down or speeded up

Coda – tail-end passage of a piece of music

Crescendo or **Cresc.** or ———— – getting louder

D.C. or **Da Capo** – repeat from the beginning

D.S. or **Dal Segno** – repeat from the 𝄋 sign

Diminuendo or **Dim.** – getting softer

Decrescendo or **Decresc.** or ———— – getting softer

f – forte: loud. *ff* means double forte, or very loud, and up to four (*ffff*) or even five and beyond are occasionally seen

fp – forte piano: loud then immediately soft

Fine – the end

Fortissimo – very loud

glide – *portamento*

glissando – playing a series of notes in one movement, such as drawing a finger across a piano keyboard. See *portamento*. The convention within MIDI is to distinguish between glissando on the one hand, and portamento and glide on the other. In a glissando effect, the individual notes are heard, whereas portamento produces a smooth transition from the start note to the finish note. Thus a portamento effect can be produced with only a semitone interval

Largo – very slow

Legato – smoothly

Lento – slow

Maestoso – majestically

Meno mosso – slow down

mf – mezzo forte: moderately loud

mp – mezzo piano: moderately soft

p – piano: soft. *pp* means double piano, or very soft, and up to four (*pppp*) or even five and beyond are occasionally seen

Pianissimo – very quietly

Pizzicato or **Pizz.** – plucked, of a string instrument which is normally bowed

portamento – gliding smoothly across a series of notes. Usually used of stringed instruments or the human voice, but with particular significance in MIDI. See *glissando*. Portamento Time is the amount of time taken to complete a glide from the start note to the finish note

Presto – very fast

Prestissimo – as fast as possible

Rallentando or **Rall.** – getting slower

Ritardando or **Ritard.** – getting slower

Ritenuto or **Rit.** – held back (often synonymous with *Ritardando*)

Rubato – playing the notes of a musical phrase without strict timing for each of them

Scherzando – playfully, jokingly

sf or *sfz* or *fz* – sforzando or forzando: with a sudden accent, forcefully

Sotto voce – in an undertone

Staccato or **Stacc.** (or a dot above or below a note) – spiky, detached notes

Tacet – indicates that an instrument does not play at all for this part of the music

Tempo Primo or **Tempo I** – back to the original speed for this section

tr or *tr* ⁓⁓ – rapid moving between two notes of adjacent pitch

Tenuto or **Ten.** or ♩ – fractional lengthening of the note

transposition – moving from one musical key to another

Tremolo or **Trem.** – rapid alternation of two notes or the rapid repetition of the same note

Tutti – all the instruments are to play

vibrato – moving away from the true pitch and back again. Often used on wind and string instruments to produce a more pleasing sound than a note of a single pure pitch

Vivace – fast

13.6 Educational Software

There was a time when it was thought that personal computers would revolutionise teaching because children were so interested in them as game-playing machines: all that was needed, it seemed, was to give the games some educational value and the problem of teaching was solved. To a certain degree, computers have fulfilled their initial promise, but infinitely less so than early writers of educational software imagined. Nevertheless, since music can be intimately bound with computers, educational software which takes advantages of the computer's capabilities is in pole position. And since such software is intended not only as a means of teaching children but also of training adults, it is not surprising that developers have taken the market seriously.

Music education software is available for all type of activities: ear training (learning to recognise intervals, harmonies and rhythm patterns), reading scores at sight, instrument practice in a variety of styles from pop to classical, theory, even improvisation.

The range of available programs caters for people of different ages and different levels of ability and experience, some for use with teachers and others for self-edification. Some are designed to free the teacher from routine work by providing drills and exercises for pupils, others are aimed at increasing enthusiasm in the learner by making the educational process as much like fun as it can be. Some offer fixed exercises, others have *authoring* modules which allow a teacher to devise tailor-made exercises. Some cost hundreds of pounds, and are intended for serious continuous use, others are little more than toys.

The majority are at beginners' level, and are meant to supplement a human teacher. What is more, the higher the level of the program, the more important a teacher tends to become. There are exceptions, but this is particularly true, for example, of programs intended as aids to musical appreciation, or to the analysis and assessment of harmonic structures, in other words where personal taste can play a part. This is not to say, however, that such programs cannot benefit the lone student, provided that a sensible attitude is adopted.

Some programs are intended for use on the computer alone, without any MIDI hardware, often using the computer's internal sound-producing facilities. However, many developers of educational music software assume a basic MIDI studio, and some of the most interesting products are those which allow input and/or output via MIDI, since being able to interact with the computer using a musical instrument is enjoyable and therefore of educational value, and hearing high-quality sound as a result of one's efforts is obviously more satisfying than hearing the tinny sound of a computer's internal speaker. This is less important when it comes to theory – and there are good theory programs which do not depend on MIDI – though even pure theory programs benefit from examples heard in high-fidelity sound.

13.6.1 Examples

The following examples are intended to give a broad idea of the kind of educational software available.

Ear training

Here, the student might sing into a microphone, with a Pitch-to-MIDI converter used for analysing the sound. The program may start by asking for the voice range (bass, tenor, alto or soprano), or even establish the range for itself by asking the student to sing a few notes. The exercises are then transposed to fit the determined range, and they might consist of singing tunes by imitation, identifying harmonic intervals, and so on. In a clever program, if after a number of errors it appears that there may be some theoretical deficiency, the student will be asked to refer to a relevant theory module also contained in the program.

Singing or playing at sight

Programs of this kind for beginners tend to start with absolute basics such as the visual and aural recognition of notes on the stave presented randomly but at a speed which can be set by the student. For more advanced players, a complete piece might be displayed one screenful at a time to be played or sung at sight, perhaps with a bouncing ball or moving highlighted square whose speed is adjusted in real time to the speed at which the student is playing. The input will in any case be analysed, compared with a model response contained within the program, and a score given.

Keyboard Skills

At the lowest level, this kind of program might use graphics to establish fundamental musical ideas such as note names, rests, white and black keys, the stave, rhythm, time signatures, musical key structure, and intervals. For instance, the idea of pitch can be introduced by asking the student to play any key on a MIDI keyboard. This can be presented as a note in traditional notation on the screen, and a second note played can also be presented in order to show the difference in pitch, while also teaching notation by implication.

Standard left- and right-hand fingerings for scales can be displayed graphically on the screen by highlighting the correct finger to use at any point in the scale as it is played (though of course no computer can yet watch a player to check on fingering).

At a higher level, some programs can be used to develop an intuitive familiarity with the keyboard, or to learn a particular keyboard style, for instance the rhythms, accents and syncopation associated with Rock music, Rhythm and Blues, Jazz-Rock Fusion, and so on. The program might play a sample piece and ask the student to repeat it, as well as presenting some of the theory associated with the style. Finally, a student's performance can be checked against the original piece presented by the program, and a score given taking into consideration the student's level of keyboard proficiency.

At the highest level, this idea is taken much further, and there are programs which can give a very accurate account of performance problems. A score might be presented on screen, or a step-time editor might allow an exercise to be entered note by note by the student. The student then plays the piece in real time, perhaps to the beat of a metronome produced by the program, and mistakes are highlighted on the screen as the performance takes place.

Programs of this kind can watch out not only for note mistakes, but also for the clarity of dynamic contrast (both overall and between left and right hands), errors of staccato and legato phrasing, the correct placement of accents, rhythmic precision and so on. The degree of accuracy can be as fine as is required, even for example distinguishing between a Mozart, a Beethoven and a Tchaikovsky *sforzando*, with an error being marked if a piece by Mozart receives accents more suited to Beethoven.

The performance can be played back as it has been recorded, and compared with a model performance which may well have been recorded into the program by a famous professional player.

Chord sequences

Chord structures can be taught by asking the student to play particular sequences as an accompaniment to a melody played by the program and displayed on screen as notation. The input can be checked for accuracy, and mistakes highlighted, though here is an example of a case where there is a danger of the computer at best looking stupid and at worst killing creativity. It could well mark an inventive jazz chord as incorrect because the program has been written to accept only a straight Blues chord. Much depends here, of course, on the musical awareness and programming ability of the software developer, but no program is yet capable of infallibly distinguishing between genuine creativity and error.

Some programs, however, do offer a well thought-out teaching approach. So, the computer might play its series of jazz phrases, with the student being required first to select from an on-screen menu the appropriate chord name at each chord change, then to play the chord on the synthesiser keyboard, and finally to accompany the melody in real time.

Jazz improvisation

This is the most contentious area of music education software, since many would maintain that improvisation simply cannot be taught – as Louis Armstrong is said to have replied to someone who asked him in the early 1920s what jazz was: "If you can't hear it, I can't explain it."

But those who for the first time have suddenly come up against 24 bars of chord names marked *Solo ad lib* while sight-reading a big band score, will know that it is necessary for all but natural geniuses both to have a theoretical knowledge of melodic phrasing and to have practised again and again improvising to chord sequences. A computer can provide the chords instead of a play-along tape, teach something about what great players have made of the sequence, and suggest phrases tailored to the proficiency of the player.

Theory

Theory programs range from quizzes about musical terminology to exercises such as entering a bass line for a melody displayed on screen, or filling in a missing viola part in a string-quartet score.

Of course, music theory is not quite like theory in many other subjects. We are aware that deaf musicians may take issue with us, but we would maintain that the majority of people cannot meaningfully study music theory beyond the absolute basics without actually hearing sounds. A discord can be explained in theoretical terms, but it cannot be exemplified unless it can be heard. Furthermore, learning music theory is intimately bound up with responding on an instrument or by singing. The best theory programs, therefore, have an element of active musical participation on the part of the student, and MIDI is the perfect medium for this.

Nevertheless, many theory programs do not require MIDI, and some rely solely on presenting musical facts on screen without even using a computer's internal sound capabilities. They are simply electronic books, though they may have an interactive element in the form of evaluating responses and counting a student's score. In our view, while such programs can serve a purpose for people who simply enjoy using a computer, or for teachers with large beginners' classes, a book is just as good, if not in many respects better.

Musical history

Musical history programs do not require any MIDI equipment, and apart from notation shown on screen, are no different in essence from the many other pieces of educational software aimed at presenting facts. Often, a system of searching is possible, as opposed to sequential tutorial screens. For instance, it might be possible to specify a period and see what musical styles were in vogue. Quizzes are common in such programs.

A new generation of musical history programs – and perhaps music education programs generally – is about to emerge in the form of multimedia software (that is, software which mixes images, text, and sound). Multimedia is heavily oriented towards education and training, and some impressive musical 'titles' are currently being developed, such as those which allow analyses of musical scores while selectively playing individual orchestral parts. Multimedia databases are perfect for illustrated musical histories.

13.6.2 Choice Checklist for Educational Software

The following are questions which should be asked, where appropriate, before choosing musical education software:

❏ Is the software primarily written for use with a teacher, or for self-study?

❏ Is any previous knowledge of music theory required?

❏ What level of playing skills are expected?

❏ Is the software written mainly for children or adults?

13.6.3 Products

A wide range of music education software is available for every home and business computer. Since the BBC micro was for many years the official schools computer, the range is particularly extensive, but the other families of computers are all very well served. Prices vary from price categories A to E for individual pices of software.

For information about music education software for the Amiga, the Atari ST, the PC and the Macintosh, contact any of the major software suppliers as they appear in Products lists elsewhere in this book. For the BBC micro, there is a veritable host of producers and suppliers – a first port of call is Acornsoft. See Appendix B for addresses.

14

Selling Music

It is a commonplace in the literary world to hear best-selling authors remembering their humble beginnings when they pinned rejection slips on their study walls. It is far less common to hear any of the much larger number of unsuccessful writers talking of the way they too have pinned up their numerous rejection slips and have finally given up trying. What makes the eventually successful author keep going is usually the satisfaction of writing for its own sake, and the Devil take the publishers who send the rejection slips. But that attitude has to be very firmly entrenched to be of any value.

Needless to say, it is the same in the world of music. If the activity is not enjoyable, it is not worth composing in the hope of retiring on the proceeds of compositions, and therefore for anyone but an established composer, it is not worth buying electronic equipment as an investment.

Take pop music. The sobering truth is that each year UK record companies receive over 30,000 cassette tapes containing original compositions, of which about 300 are accepted, and of which perhaps a dozen or so make it to the charts.

To reach number 10 in the charts requires sales of about 23,000 singles. To reach the top 40 (in other words to be heard by the public) sales of 6,000 or so are needed. The royalty on each single sold is in the region of 11 pence, and that is assuming a reasonable deal has been struck with the record company. Thus, if the composition reaches number 40 for a week, gross income will be about £600. At number 1 for a week – the ultimate accolade – it will be about £8,000. And for the composer to reap all these rewards, the entire composition – music, lyrics and actual singing – will have to have been accomplished alone.

These are raw figures purely from the sale of records, and they do not take into account seasonal adjustments which can affect them enormously. Indeed, some composers ensure that they release new compositions at times when the competition is likely to be less, therefore certainly not just before Xmas! Nor do the figures take into account appearances on television, performing rights, sales in other countries, and so on. Nevertheless, when expenses are set against possible income, the picture is far from rosy.

Of course, there are many professional musicians who get on with things in a workman-like way, playing and composing all kinds of music during their careers, and perhaps dreaming of fame but not being too concerned if it never comes. On the other hand, only The Determined Few stand a chance of becoming The Happy Few. For them – the ones who are not content with the purely personal satisfaction of giving form to their musical inspiration – a fortune awaits, with someone else helping to cover their expenses to boot. When record companies sign up a new act, they tend these days to advance the money for a professional computer-based home-recording studio. Raper and Wayman, one of the largest suppliers of professional equipment, say that 60 per cent of their business is now oriented towards individual songwriters rather than professional studios. The professional equipment they supply does not differ fundamentally from the kind we have described in this book, though the sonic quality is of the very best, as might be expected from an advance on royalties of anything between £30,000 and six figures.

Even those who have a song accepted without hitting such heights will have made a move upwards, and that means learning to deal with people who may have little love for music. A nose for what will sell and an appreciation of good music are not necessarily the same thing, nor even related to each other. This is the point at which some people who are true believers in the Muse, and who for years have lived contentedly as amateurs with their MIDI studio, are suddenly stopped in their tracks (as it were). As with any other activity, becoming a professional, particularly in the world of pop music, means being punched in the face by the real world.

Outside the pop industry, life can be a little less tough. Musicians involved with big bands, brass bands, concert bands, folk music and so on, can use MIDI for orchestrations (especially for printing them out using score editors). They may then wish to record and distribute their compositions themselves, or even try to get them released on a major record label. But determination will still be the order of the day, even if the cynicism and hard-headedness demanded by the pop business are likely to be required in smaller dollops.

14.1 Practical Advice in Specific Areas

For those who are ready to face the difficulties and frustrations awaiting the new composer, the following practical hints are born of our own experience and that of many others who have shared theirs with us.

14.1.1 Popular-Song Writing

Above all else, it is important when composing to put oneself in the position of the record companies, in other words to compose something which they are likely to think of as a saleable product – it is a sad fact that the market is never ready for wildly original ideas. True, if all composers had thought like that, music would not have advanced beyond Plain Song. But it is worth remembering that most successful composers, including Beethoven and the Beatles, began by producing material which was firmly rooted in the traditions of their time. The real experiments came once they were established.

The men and women who sign up songwriters are the A & R (Artist & Repertoire) people, and they are by and large conservative. Once the Beatles had become immensely famous, these people went in their droves to Liverpool to sign up anyone off the street who could vaguely sing in tune. Basically they always search for variations of what is currently marketable. This is why it is important for a new composer mentally to ask a vital question: assuming that £250,000 were at his or her disposal, would he or she have enough faith in a song to risk it on producing a first CD? This is what A & R people have to decide, and a couple of mistakes might well mean the end of their career.

Having said all that, a composition has to have something different in order to make an impression, and achieving the right balance between originality and marketability is the hardest job of all. It is a matter of judgement, and your judgement is as good as ours.

There are nevertheless more concrete matters which can be addressed, the result in our case of (usually bitter) experience:

In making a tape, it is obviously important to ensure that the recording is of a reasonable quality, but it is not worth over-spending on the production. The ideas are more important than the polish. Many A & R people pride themselves on being able to distinguish a good song whatever the production quality, though the truth is that busy people do not have the patience to labour through a bad recording.

It is also vital to think about the physical appearance of a tape. It will sit on a desk among hundreds of others, and plainly stands a better chance if it says "Listen to me!". We should add, however, that composers have tried many imaginative ways of getting attention, from delivering a tape in person to having it delivered with a Kissogram. A & R people are long in the tooth.

What is more, they listen to dozens of tapes every week, and are likely to hear only the first few seconds of a tape unless what they are hearing rapidly hooks them. It is therefore important that the opening few bars of a composition are the best that can be achieved.

It is equally important to be prepared for not having a tape returned even if it is sent with a self-addressed stamped envelope. A small survey which we recently made shows that the time lag between sending in and receiving back a tape can be anything from a week to eight months, and that about 40 per cent of the tapes sent to record companies seem to disappear permanently. Those who are really cynical may even assume that a tape returned within a week from a major record company with a backlog to clear, has not been listened to at all, especially if it is still neatly re-wound to the beginning. Being prepared for this situation is more than half the battle in keeping determination alive.

It is best to make several copies of a tape (short tape lengths save money), then to do some market research in order to select a number of record companies specialising in the appropriate kind of music – Classical (frankly, there is little hope here unless you are already famous, and preferably dead), Rock, Rap, Dance, Heavy Metal, Light Pop ... whatever. There are companies specialising in particular musical styles, and they can be identified simply by browsing in a record shop and noting those which predominantly produce the target type of music, and by looking in the musical press for lists of specialised charts, and noting the companies involved.

The next step is to telephone the selected companies in an attempt to speak to the A & R person responsible for the kind of music in question so that the tape can then be sent personally to him or her. This is an essential step, but the initial telephone contact, even if it is achieved, might not help at all. The experience of one songwriter is salutary in this context. Telephone contact was made with an A & R person who was more than just polite – he was enthusiastic, and impatient to hear the demo tape. It later transpired that the company had a policy of not recruiting any new composers.

There are more than 250 record companies in the UK, of which about 50 could be considered major. Chances are probably better with a medium-sized company – there are many cases of composers having been signed up by a minor company, then later sold on to a larger one. But much also depends on one's personal faith in the composition, since if a composer has been signed up with a small company and is very successful, the company may not wish to sell, and the composer may lose out because a major company could do more in the way of promotion. Again, it is a matter of judgement, and nobody can give the right advice.

Rather than approaching a record company directly, many musicians have found success by approaching a music publishing company. Some of these companies do not make records, and do not necessarily expect a more or less finished product. Indeed, much of their business may be with songwriters who do not record their own music, but simply write it for artists to perform. But publishing companies will accept demo tapes and A & R people will certainly listen to a tape from a major publisher, if only because it has already passed a first assessment hurdle. There is nothing to prevent a composer sending a demo tape both to recording and to publishing companies (recording companies are also sometimes publishing companies), though of course once a contract has been signed, exclusivity is a legal obligation.

Many music publishing companies offer a compilation CD album service. For around £300, it is possible to get ten CDs pressed with the distribution and follow-up being taken care of by the company. Some composers maintain that demo CDs stand a better chance than tapes.

It is also worth thinking in DIY terms. While an A & R person might have to risk hundreds of thousands of pounds on a decision to accept a composition, a do-it-yourself job can cost a tiny fraction of that amount, and is worth serious consideration, particularly by musicians who do live gigs and who can sell tapes on the spot. It is an education in itself, and even if only a modicum of success in sales is achieved, it is the most likely thing to grab the attention of A & R people. Small owner-run studios can be contacted for parts of the operation which individuals may not be able to carry out for themselves.

A final point for songwriters:

Despite our pessimism, which we prefer to call realism, copies of tapes cost little more than £1, including a well-presented insert. Spending £50 can mean that 40 record companies hear the song, and it is always worth throwing seeds to the wind. The seventeenth-century French philosopher Pascal formulated what has become known as his un-losable bet: he maintained that one might as well pray to God, since if He exists one gains everything, and if He does not, one has lost at worst a little time in meditation. We do not need to cross the Ts.

14.1.2 Library Music (Production Music)

Library music is so-called by analogy with the long tradition of photographic libraries. When a magazine, for instance, needs a general photograph, perhaps to print in half-tone behind some text – anything from a view of the earth from space to a classroom of children standing round a computer – the most convenient (and sometimes the only) method is to use a photo library and pay the royalty. The same is true of the world of sound, except that the music or sound effect will probably be sold only once, that is to say that the buyer will also buy the rights to duplicate the music.

Library music is heard in the background while a television announcer reads out the evening's viewing, as opening musical sequences on radio and television programs, and so on. Writing jingles of this kind can provide a more than adequate living, and taken a step further can even become a lucrative source of income – the theme tune for *Coronation Street* has given its composer considerable wealth (though this further step means being commissioned to write a piece rather than offering an off-the-shelf selection to prospective clients).

Royalties for library music begin only when a piece is used, though it may be part of an entire LP or CD of jingles produced by a music-publishing company. The disc may contain the work of several composers, or just one, and will be distributed to film and television companies, advertising agencies and so forth, but the fact that a piece is published in this way brings in no revenue until it is actually bought.

Writing library music is not the most glamourous of musical professions – stardom is virtually unknown – but it can provide a steady income, and it is a way of breaking into the music business. It has to be said that this area, even more so than that of writing for the charts, has an air of exclusivity around it, probably because many writers of sound libraries have already been working as producers, directors or actors, or have been part of the pop scene in some way, before they started writing music, and therefore know the right people. But there is always room for new talent, and the way to start (for those who have no connections) is once again to send demonstration tapes to appropriate music publishing companies.

Library musicians are sometimes thought of as mass-producers of music churning out jingles as if on a conveyor belt. But library music need not necessarily lack creativity. Indeed, once again, originality is everything in getting work accepted, because finding standard material is easy enough. But a special kind of thinking is required, and the composer must always bear in mind that library music should be (a) unobtrusive (b) memorable. The music may be needed for backgrounds only, where it must not overshadow the message, or it may be needed to promote a product or to be associated with a show in the mind of the viewer or listener, in which case it must have a strong melody line which men will whistle in the street. Achieving just the right register in either case is a tricky matter, and takes a good deal of talent. In addition, library music should be editable, that is to say that those who buy it should be able to cut parts out, perhaps to use them but in any case without spoiling the overall composition.

14.1.3 Film

The MIDI composer is at an advantage over traditional composers when it comes to writing film scores. Many famous film scores have been recorded in real time while the film is being shown on a screen which the conductor can see. Using MIDI, the score can be made to fit more easily, if only because the tempo can be adjusted without any change in pitch.

Nevertheless, even the MIDI composer using SMPTE synchronisation has to work under enormous constraints, and is likely to expend as much effort making the music fit the timing of a scene as in the creative process, not to mention the matter of long discussions with those making the film about the kind of music required and the intended atmosphere. With title music, or music for end-credits, there is likely to be considerable freedom. Writing music to fit behind a dialogue or some action, for some composers feels like working in a metaphorical straight jacket.

But the field is perhaps the most exciting of all, because it is the one where musical has the most direct impact on those who hear it. André Previn once gave an astounding demonstration at the National Film Theatre in London of the manipulatory power of film music. The same banal scene – a woman entering a house – was played over and over again with different musical scores accompanying it. It became a terrifying scene from a horror movie, a scene of intense Hitchcock-like suspense, a comic scene, a tear-jerking scene, a scene of romantic expectancy, of mild sadness, of joyful relief, of despair, of triumph ... so it went on. If the right music is there, a shot showing a man and a woman running towards each other is enough to bring tears to many people's eyes, even if the rest of the film has not been seen.

In fact, film music is so powerful that it sometimes takes on a life of its own, to be borrowed by other films or other visual media. Vangelis's Oscar-winning theme music for the film *Chariots of Fire* has become the standard television background music to accompany scenes depicting running (shown always in slow motion, as in the film). The scary two-chord orchestral stabs as used in *Psycho*, the theme music from *Gone with the Wind*, the *Pink Panther* theme ... these are all examples – and there are many more – of film music which has come to represent particular situations. The curious thing is that few people actually listern to the music of a film unless it is given prominence (as in a musical), yet its effect is all-powerful.

Writing film scores (and this includes scores for television films and videos) is therefore an enormous responsibility for the composer. And it is an area where demo tapes are inappropriate. Film scores are like honorary degrees: they come by invitation as a result of a composer's reputation and/or film experience. The only advice to an unknown composer who desperately wants to write a film score (apart from becoming less unknown and/or making contacts in the film or television industry) is to write one for a home movie. That, at least, will demonstrate how tricky it is to do.

Products

There are a number of software scoring tools for use with film and video. Basically they take some of the donkey work out of synchronisation.

Product	Producer	Computer(s)	Price
Clicktracks	Passport	Macintosh	D
Cue	Opcode	Macintosh	E
Hitman	Dr T	Atari ST	C
Q-Sheet A/V	Digidesign	Macintosh	F

Hitman works with the KCS sequencer (see Chapter 5 Section 5.11).

14.2 Locating Companies and Using Organisations

Certain regular publications list the names and addresses of record companies, music publishers and other organisations relevant to the professional, as well as being a gold mine of other appropriate information.

The following is a selection (see Appendix B for details of the publishers):

The DML Directory of Record Companies (this can save you sending Rock cassettes, for example, to a Rap label)

International Music and Recording Industry Year Book

The Making Music Handbook

Music Business Directory

Music Week Directory

British Phonographic Industry Year Book

Organisations such as the International Songwriters Association (ISA) and the British Academy of Songwriters, Composers and Authors (BASCA) distribute newsletters to their members which are valuable sources of information. And *International Songplugger*, a monthly magazine for publishers and songwriters, not only lists A & R guidelines for the types of material required by specific companies, but also artists looking for songs.

14.3 Royalties and Copyright

Any music which is played in public (on television, on the radio, in hotel lounges, in clothes shops or wherever) or which has been used for commercial purposes (such as in a computer program) attracts a royalty. Publishers who have signed contracts with composers collect the royalties for them from one of the official bodies, that is to say the PRS (Performing Rights Society) and the MCPS (Mechanical Copyright Protection Society), and after deducting a percentage as defined in the contract, pay the money over.

Composers who have their music used for commercial purposes but who are not contracted to a publisher, may be able to claim royalties by contacting one of the official bodies directly. The PRS collects performance and broadcast royalties, and the MCPS licenses reproduction in so-called *lumpy* form, that is in the form of records, tapes, and so on.

As for copyright, the body to contact is Stationers' Hall Registry. Entries made here are for the purpose of assisting in the proof of the existence of a work on a given date in case of infringement. It used to be that the only acceptable material was musical notation on paper, but recently it has been agreed that works can also be accepted on audio tape, video tape, record, audio compact disc, and computer disk. A copy of the work registered has to be filed at the time of the registration.

Both lyrics and music can be registered, and either single songs or, to save expense (the fee is currently £23 for a period of seven years) a group of songs can be treated as an album, listing all the songs under one title.

The addresses of all these bodies, together with other institutions of interest to professional musicians, are given in Appendix B. The list also includes the MU (Musicians Union) which looks after the interests of musicians, offers legal advice, insurance, contract vetting, and the like. Membership currently costs £33 a year.

14.4 The PR Factor

Everyone realises that it is often not what but who you know, and this in nowhere more true than in the music profession, despite what you may hear to the contrary. It is important for the prospective professional composer to talk to and get to know the right people by attending relevant events, making phone calls and doing a self-PR job, and even drinking in the right bars! Once a good contact is made on the right side of the fence, climbing up it will be that much easier. And, of course, one contact leads to another.

One way of meeting top professionals is by joining an organisation such as the ISA or BASCA mentioned above in Section 14.2 above. It can mean all the difference in the world, as many professional composers will testify. BASCA also organises the London Songwriters Showcase, where professionals meet professionals (and others).

A Last Word

Notions of what is acceptable in music change with the generations. Beethoven was considered unmelodic by some of his contemporaries. Stravinsky's Le sacre du printemps *caused a riot when it was first performed. The new music of today is moving towards something which differs as fundamentally from its predecessors as the music of Beethoven did from that of Mozart, or the music of The Six from that of Debussy (not surprising, then, that the latest word from Ravel, transmitted through a medium, is that he is getting tired of turning in his grave).*

As we approach the end of this century, it is time to wonder what future historians will think of as its musical milestones. Will the 20th century be seen as the century of jazz? The century of the Beatles? The century when music the industry killed music the art? The century when the synthesiser replaced the piano? The century when the music studio began to recognised as a valid musical instrument?

One thing is certain. 20th-century technology has caused some irreversible changes. Historians of the future will not argue about how our music is to be performed - Stravinsky, Bernstein, Copland and the Beatles have left behind them sound as well as paper. Our technology has also transferred music from the concert hall to the living room, and has opened the door to musical creativity for many people who would previously have been thought of as musically incompetent.

Which brings us to a final question, and one to which we can put forward a tentative answer: will our century be thought of as the one when performers beat composers in the battle for fame? Well, it is true that few people remember the names of the composers who wrote songs made famous by Bing Crosby, Elvis or Michael Jackson, but these performers may just be passing fancies, while names like Jarre and Vangelis may endure as representatives of the generation of 'the composers who struck back'.

Appendix A

MIDI Messages

MIDI Message Specification

The information contained in this Appendix is the most up-to-date available at the time of writing. However, minor but sometimes important changes are occasionally made to the MIDI specification.

There are two classes and five types of MIDI message:

Channel   - Voice messages
              - Mode messages

System   - Exclusive
              - Common
              - Real-time

There are two types of MIDI bytes:

Type	Binary	Hex	Decimal	Comment
Status bytes	1nnnnnnn	80-FF	128-255	First bit is 1.
Data bytes	0nnnnnnn	00-7F	0-127	First bit is 0.

A MIDI message may consist of one status byte, or one status byte followed by one or two data bytes. A System-exclusive message may contain more than two data bytes, but must end with a status byte defining an EOX (End Of eXclusive).

A.1 Channel Messages

A.1.1 Channel Voice Messages

Status byte			Data byte 1		Data byte 2	
Binary	**Hex**		**Description**	**Value**	**Description**	**Value**
Description						
1000nnnn	8n	Note Off	0-127	Note number	0-127	Off velocity value
1001nnnn	9n	Note On[1]	0-127	Note number	0-127	On velocity value
1010nnnn	An	Polyphonic Aftertouch	0-127	Note number	0-127	Pressure value
1011nnnn	Bn	Control Change	0-120	Controller	0-127	Control value
			121-127 (see Channel Mode Messages)			
1100nnnn	Cn	Program Change	0-127	Program Number		
1101nnnn	Dn	Channel Aftertouch	0-127	Pressure value		
1110nnnn	En	Pitch Bend	0-127	Bend value LSB	0-127	Bend value MSB

Notes:

nnnn and n are MIDI Voice Channel 0-15 in binary and hex respectively.

1. Many manufacturers implement a Note On message with velocity 0 to denote a Note Off.

Controller Messages

Status byte is 1011nnnn (Bn hex), where nnnn (or n) is the channel number. This is followed by two data bytes. The first data byte is the Controller type and the second data byte is the value. Values can be in the range 0-127.

Controller number			Controller type
Binary	**Hex**	**Decimal**	
00000000	00	0	Program Bank Number MSB
00000001	01	1	Modulation
00000010	02	2	Breath Control
00000100	04	4	Foot Controller
00000101	05	5	Portamento Time
00000110	06	6	Data Entry MSB (sends whatever values are input on the instrument's panel during editing of parameters)
00000111	07	7	Channel Volume
00001000	08	8	Balance (stereo volume)
00001010	0A	10	Pan
00001011	0B	11	Expression Controller (accent above value of Controller 7)

Controller number			Controller type
Binary	**Hex**	**Decimal**	
00001100	0C	12	Effect Controller 1 MSB (control of parameters other than the depth – see below 91-95)
00001101	0D	13	Effect Controller 2 MSB (as 12)
00100000	20	32	Program Bank Number LSB
01000000	40	64	Damper Pedal (Sustain On/Off)
01000001	41	65	Portamento (On/Off)
01000010	42	66	Sostenuto (On/Off)
01000011	43	67	Soft Pedal (On/Off)
01000101	45	69	Hold 2 (Sustain 2) (On/Off)
01011011	5B	91	Effect 1[1]
01011100	5C	92	Effect 2
01011101	5D	93	Effect 3
01011110	5E	94	Effect 4
01011111	5F	95	Effect 5
01000000	60	96	Data Increment (pressing a + button on a synthesiser)
01000001	61	97	Data Increment (pressing a – button on a synthesiser)
01000010	62	98	Non-Registered Parameter Number LSB[2]
01000011	63	99	Non-Registered Parameter Number MSB
01000100	64	100	Registered Parameter Number 1 LSB
01000101	65	101	Registered Parameter Number 2 MSB

Notes:
Controllers 121-127 are reserved for Channel Mode messages (see below)
Controllers 33-63 are the LSB values for Controllers 1-31. They are used only if needed.
        The LSB for 0 (which is Controller 32) must be used even if its value is 0.
Controllers 16-19 and 80-83 are General Purpose Controllers (1-8)
Controllers 3, 9, 14, 15, 20-31, 68, 70-79, 84-90 and 102-120 are undefined.
1. Effects 1 to 5 denote the depth of an effect.

2. Registered and Non-Registered Parameters are extra data for various purposes. Registered Parameters are fixed, while Non-Registered Parameters can be used independently by manufacturers.

A.1.2 Channel Mode Messages

All these are a subset of Controller Messages, in other words they start with the status byte 1011nnnn (binary) or Bn (Hex) plus 176-191 (decimal), where nnnn and n are the number of the instrument's basic channel in binary or hex respectively. In decimal, if the basic channel is set to 1, the status byte will have a value of 176; if set to 2, the status byte will be 177, and so on.

| Data byte 1 | | Data byte 2 | |
Controller	Description	Value	Description
121	Reset all controllers	0	
122	Local Control	0	Local Off
127			Local On
123	All Notes Off[1]	0	
124	Omni Mode Off[2]	0	
125	Omni Mode On[3]	0	
126	Mono Mode On[4]	0	The number of channels is the number of voices in the receiving device
		1-16	The number of channels as set by the user
127	Poly Mode On	0	

Notes:
1. Sets all notes Off
2. Sets all notes Off
3. Sets all notes and Poly Mode Off
4. Sets all notes and Mono Mode Off

A.2 System Messages

A.2.1 System-exclusive Messages

A System-exclusive message starts with system-exclusive status byte and ends with an EOX (End Of eXclusive).

	Binary	Hex	Decimal
System-exclusive status byte	11110000	F0	240
Manufacturer's ID code	0mmmmmmm	00-7F	0-127
End of system-exclusive byte	11110111	F7	247

Notes:

When the manufacturer's ID number is 0 the next two bytes are used as an extension to that ID number.

Any number of bytes can follow between the manufacturer's ID code and the EOX, as long as they all range between 0-127, that is to say that they are data bytes (left-most bit is 0).

Any status bytes (except Real-time) sent during a System-exclusive message will cause it to terminate.

The following is a list of some common manufacturer's ID numbers:

Manufacturer	ID decimal			ID hex		
Akai	71			47		
AKG	10			0A		
Alesis	0	0	14	00	00 0E	
Apple	17			11		
Casio	68			44		
Elka	47			2F		
E-mu Systems	24			18		
Ensoniq	15			0F		
Fostex	81			51		
Hohner	36			24		
J.L. Cooper	21			15		
Kawai	64			40		
Korg	66			42		
Kurzweil	7			07		
Lexicon	6			06		
Moog	4			04		
Oberheim	16			10		
Opcode	0	0	22	00	00 16	
Passport	5			05		
Peavey	0	0	27	00	00 1B	
Roland	65			41		
Sony	76			4C		
Teac	78			4E		
Voyetra	3			03		
Waveframe	12			0C		
Yamaha	67			43		

IDs of other manufacturers can be obtained from the UKMA (see Appendix B).

A.2.2 System-common Messages

Status byte				Data bytes		
Binary	Hex	Dec	Description	Data byte 1	Data byte 2	Description
11110001	F1	241	MTC quarter frame[1]	0tttvvvv		ttt – message type. vvvv – value
11110010	F2	242	Song Position Pointer	0vvvvvvv (LSB)	0mmmmmmm (MSB)	
11110011	F3	243	Song Select	0nnnnnnn		nnnnnnn – song number
11110110	F6	246	Tune Request			
11110111	F7	247	EOX			

Notes:

Status Bytes 244 and 245 are undefined

1. MTC quarter-frame messages are transmitted when a system is running, and they come in groups of eight, that is to say 16 bytes in total. Each set of eight messages contains SMPTE time in hours, minutes, seconds and frames. The data byte is made of two *nibbles*: a 3-bit message type and four bits containing the actual value. The 3-bit message types are as follows:

0 – Frames count (Least Significant Nibble – LSN)
1 – Frames count (Most Significant Nibble – MSN)
2 – Seconds count (LSN)
3 – Seconds count (MSN)
4 – Minutes count (LSN)
5 – Minutes count (MSN)
6 – Hours count (LSN)
7 – Hours count (MSN and SMPTE type)

A.2.3 System Real-time Messages

Binary	Hex	Decimal	Description
	Status byte		
11111000	F8	248	Timing Clock[1]
11111010	FA	250	Start
11111011	FB	251	Continue
11111100	FC	253	Stop
11111110	FE	254	Active Sensing[2]
11111111	FF	255	System Reset

Notes:

There are no data bytes with these messages. Status bytes 249 and 252 are undefined.

1. Sent at intervals of 1/24 of a crotchet.

2. Sent every 300 msec, if there is no other data being transmitted. Not all makes and models of equipment implement this. If implemented, the device will expect to receive it, and if it is not received, the device will assume that the MIDI hardware connection has been broken.

Appendix B

Addresses and Publications

B.1 Assocations and Official Bodies

APC (Association of Professional
   Composers)
81A Priory Road
London
NW6 3NL

Tel: 071 624 7238

APRS (Association of Professional
   Recording Studios)
163A High Street
Rickmansworth
Herts
WD3 1A7

Tel: 071 624 7238

Arts Council
105 Picadilly
London
W1V 0AU

Tel: 071 629 9495

Associated Board of the Royal Schools of
   Music
14 Bedford Square
London
WC13B 3JG

Tel: 071 636 5400

BASCA (British Academy of Songwriters
   Composers and Authors)
34 Hanwell Street
London
W1P 9DE

Tel: 071 436 2261/2

BPI (British Phonographic Industry)
Roxburghe House
273-287 Regent Street
London
W1R 7PB

Tel: 071 629 8642

IMA (International MIDI Association)
5316 West 57th Street
Los Angeles
CA 90056   USA

Tel: (213) 649 6434

ISA (International Songwriters Association)
Limerick City
Eire

Tel: (353) 61 28837

MMA (MIDI Manufacturers Association) -
   see IMA

MPA (Music Publishers Association)
7th Floor, Kingsway House
103 Kingsway
London
WC2B 6QX

Tel: 071 831 7591

MCPS (Mechanical Copyright Protection
    Society)
Elgar House
41 Streatham High Road
London
SW16 1ER

Tel: 081 769 4400

MU (Musicians Union)
60-62 Clapham Road
London
SW9 OJJ

Tel: 071 582 5566

PRS (Performing Right Society)
29-33 Berners Street
London
W1P 4AA

Tel: 071 580 5544

SISC (Society of International Songwriters
    and Composers)
12 Trewartha Road
Praa Sands
Penzance
Cornwall
TR20 9ST

Tel: 0736 762826

UKMA (UK MIDI Association)
26 Brunswick Park Gardens,
New Southgate,
London
N11 1EJ

Tel: 081 368 3667

Copyright

BCC (British Copyright Council)
29/33 Berners Street
London
W1P 4AA

Tel: 071 359 9280

Stationers' Hall
Ave Maria Lane
Ludgate Hill
London
EC4M 7DD

Tel: 071 248 2934

Bulletin Board

TMS (The Music Network)
PO Box 5
Somerton
Somerset TA1 6SX

Tel: 0458 74281

B.2 Companies

*Addresses of foreign companies are given
only where no UK distributor is known.*

Acorn Computers
Fulbourn Road
Cherry Hinton
Cambridge
CB1 4JN

Tel: 0223 245200

Acornsoft
645 The Technopark
Newmarket Road
Cambridge

Tel: 0223 214411

Aiwa
Pen-y-Fan Industrial Estate
Croespenmaen
Crumlin
Newbridge

Tel: 0495 246462

Akai
Haslemere Heathrow Estate
Silver Jubilee Way
Parkway
Hounslow
Middx
TW4 6NF

Tel: 081 897 6388

AKG Acoustics
Vienna Court
Cateshall Lane
Godalming
Surrey
GU7 1JG

Tel: 04868 25702

Alesis - see Sound Technology

Amcron - see HHB Communications and
    Shuttlesound

Amstrad
Brentwood
Essex
CM14 4EF

Tel: 0277 228888

Aphex - see Sound Technology

Apple Computers
6, Roundwood Avenue
Stockley Park
Uxbridge
UB11 1BB

Tel: 081 569 1199

Arbiter Group
Wilberforce Road
West Hendon
London
NW9 6AX

Tel: 081 202 1199

Aria
Unit 12
Heston Industrial Mall
Church Road
Heston
Middx
TW5 0LD

Tel: 081 572 0033

Aries Gotam Electronics
Unit 3B
6-24 Southgate Road
London N1

Tel: 071 249 5306

Ashly - see Sound Technology

Atari
Atari House
Railway Terrace
Slough
Berks
SL2 5BZ

Tel: 0753 33344

ATC
Gypsy Lane
Aston Down
Stroud
Gloucs
GL6 8HR

Tel: 028576 561

Audio & Design
Unit 3
Horseshoe Park
Pangbourne
RG8 7JW

Tel: 0734 844545

Audio View
2A Russell St
Luton
Beds
LU1 5EA

Tel: 0582 457348

Audio Visual Research - see Audio View

Bacchus - see Computer Music Systems

Beyer Dynamic
Unit 14
Cliffe Industrial Estate
Lewes
Sussex
BN8 6JL

Tel: 0273 479411

Big Noise Software - see Digital Music

Blank Software - see MCM

Blue Ribbon Bakery - see Precision
Software

Boesendorfer London Piano Centre
68-72 Marylebone Road
London
W1M 5FF

Tel: 071 486 3111

Boss - see Roland

Bruel & Kjaer
Harrow Weald Lodge
92 Uxbridge Road
Harrow
Middx
HA3 6BZ

Tel: 081 954 2366

C-Lab - see Sound Technology

Casio
Unit 6
1,000 North Circular Road
London NW2 7JD

Tel: 081 450 9131

Cheetah Marketing
Norbury House
Norbury Road
Fairwater
Cardiff
CF5 3AS

Tel: 0222 555525

Coda Systems - see MCM

Commodore Business Machines
Commodore House
The Switchback
Gardner Road
Maidenhead
Berks
SL6 7XA

Tel: 0628 770088

Composers Desktop Project
11 Kilburn Road
York
YO1 4DF

Tel : 0904 623696

Computer Music Systems
5-7 Buck Street
London
NW1 8NJ

Tel: 071 482 5224

Court Acoustic Sales
29 Beethoven Street
London W10

Tel: 081 960 8178

Datel Electronics
Govan Road
Fenton Industrial Estate
Fenton
Stoke-on-Trent
ST4 2RS

Tel: 0782 744707

DBX - see Stirling Audio

Denon - see Hayden Labs

DHCP Electronics
32 Boyton Close
Haverhill
Suffolk
CB9 0DZ

Tel: 0440 61207

Digidesign - see Sound Technology

Digigram - see Soundbits Software

Digital Audio Labs - see SSE Marketing

The Digital Muse
44 Gloucester Avenue
London
NW1 8JD
Tel: 071 586 3445

Digital Music
27 Leven Close
Chandlers Ford
Hants
Tel: 0703 252131

Digitech - see Hohn Hornby Skewes

Dolby Laboratories
346 Clapham Road
London
SW9 9AP
Tel: 071 720 1111

Drawmer Distribution
Charlotte Street Business Centre
Charlotte Street
Wakefield
W. Yorkshire
WF1 1UH
Tel: 0924 378669

Dr T - see MCM (and Computer Music
        Systems for the PC)

Dynaware - see Computer Music Systems

Education Software Consultants - see
        Computer Music Systems
ElectroMusic Research
14 Mount Close
Wickford
Essex
SS11 8HG
Tel: 0702 335747

Elka
3-4 Fourth Avenue
Bluebridge Industrial Estate
Halstead
Essex
CO9 2SY
Tel: 0787 475325

E-mu Systems
PO Box 1
Prestonpans
East Lothian
Scotland
EH32 0TT

Tel: 0875 813330

Ensoniq
Ensoniq House
Mirage Estate
Hodgson Way
Wickford
Essex
SS11 8YL

Tel: 0268 561177

Evolution Synthesis
Maxet House
Liverpool Road
Luton
LU1 1RS

Tel: 0582 483711

Evenlode Soundworks
The Studio
Church Street
Stonesfield
Oxford
OX7 2PS

Tel: 0993 898484

Fabulous Audio Technology
Unit 7-8
Bonder Business Centre
London Road
Baldock
Herts

Tel: 0462 896262

Farfisa
Fraser Street
Burnley
Lancashire
BB10 1XJ

Tel: 0282 34531

Fostex
Unit 1
Jackson Way
Great Western Industrial Park
Southhall
Middx
UB2 4FA

Tel: 081 893 5111

FWO Bauch
49 Theobald St
Borehamwood
Herts
WD6 4RZ

Tel: 081 953 0091

Gajits Music Software
28 Dennison Ave
Withington
Manchester
M20 8AF

Tel: 061 434 2768

Geerdes - see Newtronic

Groove Electronics
Unit 22
Barnack Industrial Centre
Kingsway Trading Estate
Wilton
Wiltshire   SP2 0AW

Tel: 0722 743712

Hal Leonard Books
8112 West Bluemouth Road
Milwaukee
WI 53213   USA

Hammond
Potash House
Drayton Parslow
Bucks
MK17 0JE

Tel: 0296 72787

Harman
Mill Street
Slough
Berks
SL2 5DD

Tel: 0753 76911

Hayden Labs
Hayden House
Chiltern Hill
Chalfont St Peter
Bucks
S19 9UG

Tel: 0753 888447

HHB Communications
73-75 Scrubbs Lane
London NW10

Tel: 01 960 2144

Hohner
Bedwas House Industrial Estate
Bedwas
Newport
Gwent   NP1 8XQ

Tel: 0222 887333

Hollis Research
c/o First Rate
La Ramée
St Peters Port
Guernsey
Channel Islands

Tel: 0481 23169

Hugh Symons
223-227 Alder Road
Poole
Dorset
BH12 4AP

Tel: 0202 745744

HW International
3-5 Eden Grove
London N7

Tel: 071 607 2717

Hybrid Arts
24-26 Avenue Mews
London
N10 3NP

Tel: 081 883 1335

Hybrid Technology
273 The Science Park
Cambridge
CB4 4WE

Tel: 0223 420360

IBM
PO Box 41
Northern Road
Portsmouth
PO6 3AU

Tel: 0705 323088

Intelligent Music - see MCM

JBL - see Harman

Jim Miller - see Computer Music Systems

J.L. Cooper Electronics - see Sound
    Technology

John Hornby Skewes
Salem House Garforth Leeds
LS25 1PX

Tel: 0532 865381

Kawai
Sun Alliance House
8-10 Dean Park Crescent
Bournemouth
BH1 1HL

Tel: 0202 296629

Key Electronics
7515 Chapel Ave
Fort Worth
TX 76116
USA

Tel: (817) 560 1912

Korg
Units 8-9
The Crystal Centre
Elmgrove Rd
Harrow
Middx
HA1 2YP

Tel: 071 427 5377

Kurtzweil - see Hammond

Ladbroke Computing
33 Ormskirk Road
Preston
Lancs
PR1 2QP

Tel: 0772 203166

Lexicon- see Stirling Audio

Lyre - see Computer Music Systems

Magnetic Music - see Digital Music

Maranatha Systems - see Computer Music
    Systems

Maranz
15-16 Saxon Way Industrial Estate
Harmonsdworth
Middx
UB7 0LW

Tel: 081 897 6633

Mark of the Unicorn - see MCM

MCM (MCMXCIX)
9 Hatton Street
London
NW8 9PR

Tel: 071 724 7104

Mellotron Digital - see MidiMusic

Michael Stevens
Invicta Works
Elliot Road
Bromley
Kent   BR2 9NT

Tel: 081 460 7299

MicroIllusion - see SDL

Midi Master - see Digital Music

Midiers Land - see Digital Music

MidiMusic
25 Middlelease Drive
Middlelease
Swindon
SN5 9GL

Tel: 0793 882108

Midi Quest - see Computer Music Systems

Music Quest - see Digital Music

Neumann - see FWO Bauch and Aries
        Gotam Electronics

New England Digital
Unit 7
Elsinore House
77 Fulham Palace Road
London   W6 8JA

Tel: 081 741 8811

Newtronic
66 Beaulieu Avenue
London
SE26 6PW

Tel: 081 659 0744

NeXT Computers
1, Heathrow Boulevard
286 Bath Road
West Drayton
Middx
UB7 0DQ

Tel: 0573 831853

Nomad Audio
North Road Farm
Wendy
Nr. Royston
Herts

Tel: 0234 207979

Oberheim - see Sound Technology

Opcode Systems - see MCM

Panasonic
Willoughby Road
Southern Industrial Estate
Bracknell
Berks   RG12 4FP

Tel: 0344 853174

Pandora - see Hugh Symons

Passport Designs - see MCM

Peavey Electronics
Hatton House, Hunters Road
Corby
Northants
NN17 1JE

Tel: 0536 205520

PG Music - see Zone Distribution

Philip Rees
Unit 2, Clarendon Court
Park Street, Charlbury
Oxford

Tel: 0608 811215

Philips Consumer Electronics
City House
420-430 London Road
Croydon   CR9 3QR

Poke - see Computer Music Systems

Precision Software
6 Park Terrace
Worcester Park
Surrey   KT4 7JZ

Tel: 081 330 7166

Raper and Wayman
Unit 3
Crusader Estate
167 Hermitage Road
London   N4 1LZ

Tel: 081 800 8288

Realistic - see Tandy

ReVox - se FWO Bauch

Rogers - see Michael Stevens

Roland
West Cross Centre
Brentford
Middx TW8 9EZ

Tel: 081 568 1247

Sansui - see Fabulous Audio Technology

SDL
Unit 10, Ruxley Corner Industrial Estate
Sidcup Bypass
Sidcup
Kent   DA14 5SS

Tel: 081 300 3399

Sennheiser - see Hayden Labs

Showtune - see Digital Music

Shure - see HW International

Shuttlesound
Unit 15, Osiers Road
London SW18

Tel: 081 871 0966

Simmons Electronics
Alban Park
Hatfield Road
St Albans
Herts
AL4 0JH

Tel: 0727 36191

Sonic Solutions - see FWO Bauch

Sony Broadcast & Communications
Jays Close
Viables
Basingstoke
Hampshire
RG22 4SB

Tel: 0256 55011

Soundbits Software
48 Galton Tower
Civic Close
Birmingham
B1 2NW

Tel: 021 233 3440

Sound Quest - see Computer Music
        Systems

Sound Technology
Unit 15, Letchworth Point
Dunhams Lane
Letchworth
Herts
SG6 1ND

Tel: 0462 480000

SSE Marketing
Unit 2
10 William Street
London
NW1 3EN

Tel: 071 387 1262

Steinberg Research - see Evenlode
        Soundworks

Stick Enterprises
6011 Woodlake Avenue
Woodland Hills
CA 91367
USA

Tel: (818) 884 2001

Stirling Audio
Kimberly Road
London
NW6 7SF

Tel: 071 624 6000

Studer-Editech - see FWO Bauch

Studio Spares
61-63 Rochester Place
Camden Town
NW1 9JU

Tel: 071 482 1692

Studiomaster
Studiomaster House
Chaul End Lane
Luton
Beds
LU4 8EZ

Tel: 0582 570370

Symetrix- see Sound Technology

Systems Design Associates - see
        MidiMusic

Take Control
Jonic House
Speedwell Road
Hay Mills
Birmingham   B25 8EU

Tel: 021 706 6085

Tandy
Tameway Tower
Bridge Street
Walsall
W. Midlands WS1 1LA

Tel: 0922 710000

Tannoy
Coronation Road
Cressex Industrial Estate
High Wycombe
Bucks   HP12 3SB

Tel: 0494 4506060

Tascam (Teac)
5 Marlin House
The Croxley Centre
Watford
WD1 8YA

Tel: 0923 225235

Teach Services -see CMS

Technics - see Panasonic

Temporal Acuity Products - see Digital
     Music

T.F. Barrett
Box 130
Westminster Station
VT 05159
USA

Tel: (802) 722 9063

TOA Electronics
Tallon Road
Hutton Industrial Estate
Hutton
Essex
LM13 1TG

Tel: 0277 233882

Trilogic
Unit 1, 253 New Works Road
Bradford
BD12 0QP

Tel: 0274 69115

Turtle Beach - see Computer Music
          Systems and Digital Music

Twelve Tone Systems - see Digital Music

Umusic
17 Parkfields
London
SW15 6NH

Tel: 081 788 3729

Vestax - see Arbiter Group

Voyetra - see Computer Music Systems

Waveframe - see Stirling Audio

XRI
390-394 Birmingham Road
Wylde Green
Sutton Coldfield
W. Midlands
B72 1YJ

Tel: 021 382 6048

Yamaha (Yamaha-Kemble Music)
Mount Avenue
Bletchley
Milton Keynes
MK1 1JE

Tel: 0908 371771

Zone Distribution
15 Abeville Road
London SW4

Tel: 081 766 6564

Year books, periodicals and magazines

British Music Year Book and *British Music Education Yearbook* published by Rhinegold, 241 Shaftsbury Avenue, London WC2H 8EH

British Phonographic Industry Year Book published by the BPI (see above)

BASCA News published by the British Academy of Songwriters, Composers and Authors (see above)

Directory of Record Companies published by DML, Victoria House, Main Street, Stanton-Under-Barton, Leicester LE6 0TQ

Electronic Musician published by ACT III Publishing, Suite 12, 6,400 Hollis Street, Emeryville, CA 94608, USA

Home & Studio Recording published by HSR Publications, Alexander House, Forehill, Ely, Cambridgeshire CB7 4AF

International Music and Recording Industry Year Book published by Kemps, 12 Felix Avenue, Crouch End, London N8 9TL

International Songplugger published by More News, Dalling House, 132 Dalling Road, London W6 0EP

Keyboard published by Miller Freeman Publications, 500 Howard St, San Francisco, CA 94105, USA

Making Music and *The Making Music Handbook* published by Track Record Publishing, 20 Bowling Green Lane, London EC1R 0BD

Music Business Directory published by Sound Technology (see above)

Music Technology published by Music Technology Publications, Alexander House, Forehill, Ely, Cambridgeshire CB7 4AF

Music Week Directory published by Music Week, Ludgate House, 245 Blackfriars Road London SE1 9UZ

The Songwriter published by the International Songwriters Association (see above)

Sound on Sound published by SOS Publications, PO Box 30, St Ives, Cambridgeshire PE17 4XQ

Glossary

Italicised words are Glossary entries

acoustic instrument musical instrument which produces sound by physically vibrating

active sensing automatic scanning of a *MIDI* set-up to detect errors

A/D Analogue to Digital

ADSR Attack, Decay, Sustain, Release: the four stages of an *envelope*

AES Audio Engineering Society

aftertouch altering a sound by changing the pressure on a key after it has been struck

alias spurious additional *frequency*

algorithm series of steps to be followed in performing a task

algorithmic composer computer program used as an aid to composition

ambience background sounds

AMPLE Advanced Music Programming Language and Environment

amplitude the strength of a vibration; loudness

APC Association of Professional Composers

APRS Association of Professional Recording Studios

analogue continuous; real life; as opposed to *digital*

anechoic free from echo

arranger device or computer program for producing musical arrangements

ASIC Application Specific Integrated Circuit

asynchronous communication non-synchronised computer communication as used in *MIDI*

audio signal electrical signal of varying voltage

aural exciter device for adding *harmonics* to an audio signal

authoring creating exercises in a music-education program

auto-correction *quantisation*

AWM Advanced Wave Memory (method of sound synthesis)

bank set of stored sounds

BASCA	British Academy of Songwriters Composers and Authors
basic channel	*MIDI channel* used for main instructions
baud	equivalent of *bps*
BCC	British Copyright Council
binary	working arithmetically to base 2; 0s and 1s
bit	smallest unit of computer data; also subdivision of an *SMPTE* frame
block	section of music in a sequencer marked with a beginning and an end
BPI	British Phonographic Industry
bps	*bits* per second
BSEM	British Society for Electronic Music
bouncing	method of moving sounds recorded on the tracks of a multi-track tape recorder to another track
bridge board	slot-in *card* allowing one computer to emulate another
buffer	area of computer memory used to store data temporarily
byte	group of *bits*
capacitor microphone	*condenser microphone*
card	microchips and circuitry fixed on a board
CD-ROM	compact disc used to store digital data of all kinds
cent	subdivision of a semitone
CGA	Colour Graphics Adapter
channel	used in *MIDI*, and of mixers and other devices, to indicate a separate pathway or sound source; type of *aftertouch*
chase lock	method of audio synchronisation
chorus	effect which makes one instrument sound like many
clone	copy
close-miking	putting a number of microphones close to instruments in an orchestra
compressor/limiter	device for filtering a sound signal
condenser	type of microphone
console	mixer
controller	electronic instrument with no internal sound-producing capability; type of *MIDI message*

click	action of using a *mouse*
clock	division of a beat in *MIDI*
clock speed	speed at which a *processor* runs
CPU	Central Processing Unit; the *processor*, the heart of a computer
crosstalk	sound leakage between stereo channels or between *tracks*
cursor	moveable (usually flashing) small block on a computer screen
CV	Control Voltage
D/A	Digital to Analogue
daisy chain	*MIDI* devices connected in series
daisy-wheel printer	printer which uses a spoked wheel of pre-formed characters
DASH	Digital Audio Stationary Head
DAT	Digital Audio Tape
data byte	part of a *MIDI message* following the *status byte*
dB	decibel
dbx	noise reduction system
DC	Direct Current
DC	Dynamic Component: a method of synthesis which combines *analogue FM* and *PCM*, devised by Ensoniq
DCC	Digital Compact Cassette
dedicated	(of a piece of equipment) designed for one task
de-gauss	de-magnetise
de-esser	device for cutting out sibilant sounds
default	condition or setting which applies if no instructions are given to the contrary
delay	effect such as *echo* created by splitting a signal then introducing a time lag
desk	*mixer*
digital	handled as numeric values; as opposed to *analogue*
digital delay	effects unit for producing *echo*
digital encoder	device for recording sound on video tape
DIN socket/plug	standard fitting on *MIDI* cables
distortion	alteration of an audio signal producing a metallic sound

Dolby	noise reduction system
dot-matrix printer	printer which forms its characters out of dots
dot pitch	factor affecting the resolution of a computer screen
download	send data (from)
dpi	dots per inch
DPM	Digital Phase Modulation (method of sound synthesis)
Drop Frame	audio synchronisation standard
dry signal	signal untouched by an effects unit
DSP	Digital Sound Processor
dump	send data to a storage medium
dynamic	type of microphone; also, type of allocation of *polyphony*; not to be confused with the musical term meaning loudness or softness
EBU	European Broadcasting Union: audio synchronisation standard
echo	effect created with a *delay*
EGA	Enhanced Graphics Adapter
EIN	Equivalent Input Noise; measurement of *signal-to-noise ratio*
electret	type of microphone
envelope	graphic representation of the *frequency, amplitude* and *timbre* of a sound over time
enhancer	*aural exciter*
equaliser (graphic or parametric)	devices for shaping a sound signal by altering its tonal balance
expert system	type of artificial intelligence
event	any *MIDI* action
expander	*sound module*; also, opposite of *compressor/limiter*
fader	sliding knob
file	data stored as a defined entity on computer disk
Film	audio synchronisation standard
first generation	live recording
fixed disk	*hard disk*
flanging	adding a metallic quality to a sound
flat-bed	in a flat case rather than *rack-mounted*
floppy disk	computer storage medium

Fourier analysis	process used to separate the component parts of a waveform
FM	Frequency Modulation (method of sound synthesis)
frequency	rate of vibration, measured in *Hertz*
FSK	Frequency Shift Keying; used in audio synchronisation
fundamental	the lowest frequency of a sound
GEM	Graphics Environment Manager
graphic equaliser	see *equaliser*
handshake	equalised connection of two devices
hard copy	material printed on paper
hard disk	large-scale computer storage medium
hardware	tangible equipment; opposite of *software*
harmonic series	series of *overtones* each of which has a whole-number ratio to the *fundamental*
harmoniser	device which uses *pitch shift*
Hercules	mono computer screen adapter
Hertz (Hz)	cycles per second (repetitions of a sound wave)
hex(adecimal)	working arithmetically to base 16
HX Pro	type of *Dolby* noise reduction system
IAC	Inter Application Communication
icon	representation of an object or idea on a computer screen
identity code	part of a *System-exclusive MIDI message* indicating the manufacturer of a MIDI device
IMA	International MIDI Association
Implementation Chart	chart indicating the MIDI capabilities of a device
ink-jet printer	printer which forms its characters by spraying ink
interface	*hardware* connection, and the standards of that connection, between two devices
inversion	in a *sequencer*, transformation of notes to give a mirror image
iPD	Interactive Phase Distortion (method of sound synthesis)
ISA	International Songwriters Association
jack	type of audio connection
joystick	pointing device for controlling a computer program

jukebox	facility for automatically playing one performance *file* after another
Kilobyte (K)	1,024 *bytes*
KiloHertz (KHz)	1,000 *Hertz*
knowledge base	database accessed by an *expert system*
LA	Linear Arithmetic (method of sound synthesis)
LAN	Local Area Network
laser printer	high-quality printer which works with laser light
LCD	Liquid Crystal Display
LED	Light-Emitting Diode
LFO	Low Frequency Oscillator
line level	high-level audio signal
local control	turning on or off the internal sound-producing capability of a synthesising device
loop	repeat of *sampled* data
LSB	Least Significant Byte
lumpy recordings	recordings on tape, records and so on
mastering	making a final recording
master keyboard	*controller* keyboard; keyboard controlling *sound modules*
MCA	Micro Channel Architecture
MCPS	Mechanical Copyright Protection Society
MDA	Mono Display Adapter
Megabyte (Mb)	1,024 *kilobytes*
MegaHertz (MHz)	1,000,000 *Hertz*
menu	list of options in a computer program
microtonality	use of the pitches in between semitone steps
MIDI	Musical Instrument Digital Interface
MIDI message	series of *bytes* containing *MIDI* data
MIDI-exclusive	*system-exclusive*
mixer	sound mixer
mixdown	the master recording
MMA	MIDI Manufacturers Assocation
Mode message	type of *MIDI Controller message*

modem	device for sending data to and from a computer via a telephone line
mother keyboard	*master keyboard*
mouse	pointing device for controlling a computer program
moving-coil microphone	*dynamic microphone*
MPA	Music Publishers Association
MSB	Most Significant Byte
MS-DOS	PC *operating system*
MU	Musicians Union
multimedia	mixing of text, images and sound
multi-tasking	the ability (or apparent ability) of a computer to perform more than one task at a time
multi-timbral	capable of producing more than one *timbre* simultaneously
NAMM	National Association of Music Merchants (USA)
natural instrument	*acoustic instrument*
noise gate	device for filtering out *noise*
offset time	the point at which *SPP* messages are sent to a *sequencer* by a multi-track tape recorder after *SMPTE* code begins
operating system	set of instructions which tell a computer how to operate
optical disk	computer disk read and/or written to with a laser
opto-isolator	optical device for protecting delicate circuitry
oscillator	sound-producer within a synthesiser
overtone	a *frequency* higher than the *fundamental*
pan	moving an audio signal across, or position of a sound in, the stereo spectrum
parallel port	type of communications port on a computer
parametric equaliser	see *equaliser*
partial	*overtone*
patch	collection of parameters defining a sound
patch bay	unit for connecting sound devices
PCM	Pulse Code Modulation
performance memory	stored sounds
peripheral	piece of equipment connected to a computer

phantom power	power supply for condenser microphones
phasing	effect in which the sound appears to travel between source and listener
ping-pong	*bouncing*
pink noise	sound used to set an *equaliser*
pitch bend	moving a note away from its original pitch
pitch shift	split signal producing thickening of a sound or a harmony
pixels	dots on a computer screen which make up an image
phono	type of audio connection
polyphony	multi-part
pop	sound produced by plosive consonants with microphones
port	inlet/outlet on a piece of electronic equipment
Porta-Studio	cassette recorder and sound mixer in one
ppqn	pulses per quarter note
processor	*CPU*
program	computer software; also, group of sounds stored in a synthesising device
PRS	Performing Rights Society
pseudo many	*chorus*
psycho-acoustic enhancer	*aural exciter*
Punch In/Out	facilities for recording between specific points in a *score*
PZM	Pressure-Zone Microphone
quantisation	adjustment of *MIDI* data to fit within defined limits
rack-mounted	fitting in a 19-inch equipment rack
RAM	Random Access Memory
random composer	*algorithmic composer*
real time	playing or recording as a performance, as opposed to doing so in *step time*
retrofit	kitting out an analogue synthesiser for *MIDI*
reverb(eration)	sound reflections in a confined space
ribbon	thin strip of metal in a ribbon microphone
riff	musical phrase
RISC	Reduced Instruction Set Computer

ROM	Read-Only Memory
sampling	turning an analogue audio signal into a digitally stored waveform
SCART	type of connector
score	piece of music printed on paper; also, performance stored in a sequencer
score editor	computer program for printing out traditional musical notation
screen dump	screen image printed on paper
SCSI	Small Computer Systems Interface: a standard interface for connecting certain *peripherals* to a computer
sequencer	device or computer program for storing sequences of notes
serial port	communications port used for sending and receiving *MIDI* data
signal-to-noise ratio	level of an audio signal in relation to background noise (such as hiss) produced by the system
SISC	Society of International Songwriters and Composers
slave	device under the control of another
software	computer program or other digital instructions; opposite of *hardware*
song	sequences of stored notes ready for performance
song chain	*jukebox*
Song Select	type of *MIDI message*
SMPTE	Society of Motion Picture and Television Engineers: time-code synchronisation standard
S/N	*signal-to-noise ratio*
sound module	keyboard-less synthesiser (*expander*)
spectrum analyser	device for analysing *frequency* bands
SPP	Song Position Pointer, used in audio synchronisation
star network	method of connecting *MIDI* devices
Start bit/Stop bit	*bits* marking the beginning and end of a *byte*
status byte	the first *byte* of a *MIDI message*
step-time input	process of entering notes one by one into a computer, as opposed to playing in *real time*
stripe	to record *time code* on a track of a multi-track tape recorder

studio	range of electronic equipment for creating and handling music
sync	synchronisation
synthesiser (synth)	see Preliminaries at the beginning of this book
system message	*channel*-independent *MIDI message*
System-exclusive message	*MIDI message* used for a specific make of device
timbre	the colour or texture of a sound
time code	*SMPTE*
track	band running along a tape (or area of computer memory) which can be recorded independently of other tracks
Tune Request	type of *MIDI message*
UART	Universal Asynchronous Receiver and Transmitter
UKMA	UK MIDI Association
upload	send data (to)
velocity sensitivity	ability to sense the speed at which a key is pressed on a keyboard
VGA	Virtual Graphics Array
voice	a line of music; a part; also, a sound in a synthesiser
Voice message	type of *MIDI Channel message*
VS	Vector Synthesis (method of sound synthesis)
weighted keys	keys on a keyboard having the feel of those on an *acoustic* piano
wet signal	sound completely altered by an effects unit
white noise	random noise signal whose *amplitude* is the same at all *frequencies*
WORM	Write Once Read Many; type of *optical disk*
write-protect	disable the ability of a floppy disk to have its data changed
WYSIWYG	What You See Is What You Get
XLR	type of audio connection

INDEX

A

A & R personnel, 254-256
A/D & D/A conversion, 2, 3, 35, 123, 128, 135, 199-201
Accelerandos, 65
Acoustic booths, 192
Acoustic instruments - classification, 124
Acoustic sounds, *passim*; 188-214
Acoustic tiles, 192, 205
Acoustics, 178, 201-205
ADAM, 200
ADD synthesis, 134
Additive synthesis, 134
ADSR, 116, 125-126, 156-157, 161
AES/EBU standard, 208, 213
AFM synthesis, 134
Aftertouch, see *Keyboards (musical)*
Aids to composition, 12, 15, 215-222
Algorithmic composers, 216-218
Algorithms, 134-135, 158, 216-217
Aliases, 136
Ambience, 190
AMPLE, 34
Amplification/amplifiers, 3, 69, 123, 201-203
Amplitude, *passim*
Anechoic chamber, 205
Armstrong, Louis, 250
Arrangers (automatic), 119, 219-222
Artificial intelligence, 155, 215-216, 221
ASCII, 42, 139
Aural exciters, 182
Authoring tools, 247
Auto-accompaniment, 219, 222
AWM synthesis, 134

B

Bach, J.S., 133, 165
Baker, Janet, 188
Baud, *passim*; 39-43
Beaming, 240
Beatles, The, 254, 261
Beethoven, 249, 254, 261
Bell, Alexander Graham, 171
Berlioz, *v*
Bernstein, Leonard, 261

Bias control, 206, 214
Binary system, 40-42 *et passim*, 45, 66, 199-200
Bits, 19, 42-45, 49-57, 137
– Start/Stop, 44, 62
Block editing, 93, 101, 161, 208, 230
Bouncing, 194-195
Breath control, 52, 143, 160
Breath sensitivity, 116
Brymer, Jack, 188
Buffers, 63, 68, 86, 226
Bulk dump, 155
Bytes, 20, 41-42, 49-57, 62, 66
– LSB/MSB, 54-55
– Status/Data, 50-57, 66

C

Cage, John, 153
Carlos, Wendy (Walter), 133
Carriers, 134, 158
CD-ROM, 135
Chase lock, 63, 197
Chipboard sounds, 138
Chords and arpeggios, 100
Chorus, 16, 134, 143, 181-182
Close-miking, 191
Communications
– Serial/parallel, 43
– Synchronous/asynchronous, 43-44, 62
– Software, 25
Compact discs, 135-137, 198, 207-208, 256-257
Composer (definition), *xvii*
Composers (automatic), 12, 15, 215-218, 221
Compression/expansion, 183-184, 208
Computers, *passim*; 18-37
– Amstrad, 35, 74
– Apple, 227
   Apple II, 30, 71
   Lisa, 30
   Macintosh, 24, 28, 30-33, 71-72, 89, 217, 219, 225, 251
– Acorn
   Archimedes, 19, 28, 34-35, 74,
   BBC, 33-34, 74, 251

– Atari 28-29, 31-33, 35, 72-73, 75-76, 217, 219, 225, 251
– Choice of, 36-37
– Clock speed, 19, 30
– Commodore
  CBM64/CBM128, 32, 74
  Amiga, 28, 32-33, 73-75, 217, 251
  CDTV, 22, 32-33
– Emulation, 31
– Files, 20
– Floppy disks, 20-21, 31
– Hard disks, 21, 232
– IBM
  PS/2, 28-29, 68
  PC (& compatibles), 28-32, 34, 67-76, 217, 219, 225, 229, 251
– Keyboards, 13, 20-25, 36, 42, 86, 89, 106-108, 223-226, 230
– Mice, see *Mice*
– Monitors, 21-22, 233
– MSX, 35
– NeXT, 35
– Operating systems, 23
– Optical disks, 135, 208, 209
– Ports, 4, 25, 74-75
– Processors, 19, 29
– RAM, 19-20, 29-33, 37, 70, 83, 89-90, 101
– ROM, 19-20
– Spectrum, 74
– Yamaha
  C1, 30, 70
  CX5, 35
Copland, Aaron, 261
CPU, 19
Crosby, Bing, 261
Crosstalk, 185

D

D/A conversion, see *A/D conversion*
Daisy-chaining, 46
DASH, 208
DAT, 200, 207-208, 213
Data-entry pads, 120
dbx, 194, 211
DCC, 208
De-essing, 184, 189
Debussy, Claude, 261
Decibels (dB), 171-172, 177, 204, 213
Delay(s), 16, 95, 180-182, 201
  – Delay time, 180-182
  – Digital, 180
Digital encoder, 207
DIN connections, 46
Dolby, 194, 211-212, 214
Doppler effect, 182
Dot pitch, 21-22
DPM synthesis, 134
Drum machines, 48, 81, 85, 117, 129, 131-132, 139, 143, 146

DSP, 19, 35, 139
Dual mode, 163
Dubbing, 206
Dynamic allocation, 142

E

Ear training, 248
EBU, 64,
Echo, 16, 66, 85, 95, 134, 143, 162, 174, 178, 180, 182, 205-206
Educational software, 12, 14, 247-251
Effects units, 66, 85, 163, 169, 173, 178-179, 183, 185-187
EGA, 22
EIN, 177
Electronic organs, 112
Enhancers, 16, 182, 195
Envelopes, 124-125, 133, 138, 155-157, 159-161
Equal temperament, 164-165
Equalisation, 173-175, 177, 182-187, 202-206
  – Graphic, 182-184, 203-205
  – Parametric, 174, 183, 204
Evans, Geraint, 188
Expanders, see *Sound modules*
Expansion/compression, 183-4, 208
Expert systems, 215, 216, 219, 221

F

Faders, 66, 84, 120, 169, 175-176, 201
Film (synchronisation), 64
Films, 257, 258
Filtering, 16, 62, 68, 88, 102
  – in algorithmic composers, 217
First-generation recording, 211
Flanging, 181, 182
Flat-bed equipment, 169
Flatness (of response), 191, 203, 205-206
FM synthesis, 134-135, 139, 158-159, 216
Frequencies, 127-128, 134, 136-137, 164-165, 173, 174, 178, 182, 184, 191-194, 202-208, 238
FSK, 63 *et passim*, 195-198
Fundamental (frequency), 164

G

Gating, 183-184
Glissandos, 98, 100, 141
Goodman, Benny, 188
GUIs, 23, 31, 35, 89, 97, 102

H

Handshaking, 62
Harmonics, 114, 127, 164-165, 178, 182
Harmonisers, 182
Headphones, 202
Hercules display, 22
Hexadecimal system, 45
Hitchcock, Alfred, 258

I

Integrated packages, 12, 14, 224
Inversion, 95
IPD synthesis, 134, 158, 159

J

Jack sockets, 169
Jackson, Michael, 261
Jarre, Jean-Michel, 16, 81, 106, 143, 261
Jones, Quincy, *vi*
Jordan, Chris, 34
Jukebox, 89

K

Keyboards (musical), *passim*; 6, 13-14,
    108-113, 122, 129-132, 139-142,
    145-147, 149, 164-5, 222, 226
    – Aftertouch, 9, 55-57, 88, 110-111, 113,
    120, 122, 133, 143, 145, 218
    – Breath controllers, 112-113
    – Controller (Master, Mother), 108-109
    – Pedals, 112-113
    – Pitch bend, see *Pitch bend*
    – Keys, 6, 113, 122, 140-141, 145,
    – Local On/Off, 111-113
    – Modulation wheel, 52, 110
    – Note range, 113
    – Scaling, 160
    – Skills, 249-250, 251
    – Split, 111, 113
    – Velocity sensitivity, 6, 9, 50, 109, 113,
    115, 119, 143, 145, 160
Kilobaud, 39-40 *et passim*, 62
Knowledge bases, 215, 217, 219

L

LA synthesis, 134, 138-139, 158-159
LANs, 27
Legato effects, 217, 249
LFO, 160
Librarians, 13-14, 155, 163, 166
Library music, 256-257
Limiting, 183-184
Line level, 171, 172
Looping, 161
Loudspeakers, 3, 11, 116, 123, 128, 201-204,
    205, 210
LSB, 54-55

M

Machine code, 45
Madonna, 103
Manufacturer's Identity Code, 57
Mastering, 17, 80, 201, 206
Maths co-processor, 19
MCA, 29, 68
MDA, 22
Metronome, 63, 68
Mice (mouses), 13, 22-23, 35, 74-75, 86,
    155-156, 160, 217-226, 230, 232

Microphones, 16, 114, 119-120, 135, 169,
    174, 177, 183, 185, 189-193, 203-204,
    209-210, 248
Microprocessors, see *Computers - Processors*
Microtonality, 143, 161, 163-165
MIDI, *passim*
    – Baud rate, 43
    – Channels, 39, 66, 76, 84, 86-87, 113,
    115, 140-142, 162-163
    – Clocks, 91
    – Connections, 3, 46, 61-62
    – Implementation chart, 57, 107, 120,
    143
    – Instruments, 6, 87-88, 106-122, 188
    – Accordions, 119
    – Drums, 117-118
    – Guitars, 87-88, 106, 114-115
    – String, 106, 118
    – Wind 106, 112, 119, 115-116, 188
    – Interfaces, *passim*; 5, 8, 10, 48, 82,
    29-31, 35, 61-79, 86, 98, 168, 196-197,
    229
    – Lighting, 143, 145
    – Merge, 72, 76-78, 122
    – Messages, *passim*; 47-60, 262-267
    – Networking, 66
    – Patch bays, 72, 77-78
    – Pedals, 119
    – Ports, 5-6, 45-46, 61-62, 64, 66-76,
    129-130
    – Specification *passim*; 262-267
    – Split, 72, 77
    – Standard files, 7, 99, 102, 219, 226,
    229
    – Studio, *passim*; 1-17
    – Switches, 77-78
    – Sync, 65 *et passim*
    – Theory, 38-60
    – Through units, 47, 76, 78
MIDI-to-CV converters, 77, 79
MIDI-to-FSK devices, 65
Miller, Glenn, 153
Mixdown, 168, 175, 183
Mixers - see *Sound mixers*
Modems, 25, 74-75, 229
Modulation wheel, see *Keyboards (musical)*
Modulators, 134, 158
Monitoring, 201-204, 206
Moog, Robert, 133
Mozart, 153, 249, 261
MS-DOS, 32, 35
MSB, 54-55
MTC, 65 *et passim*
Multi-tasking, 26-27
Multi-timbrality, 140-142, 145, 148-152,
    161-162
Multi-track recorders, 7, 15-16, 81, 86, 169,
    177, 193-195, 198-200, 211-212
    – Analogue/digital, 198-200
Multimedia, 22, 33

Music
 – Companies (addresses) 269-277
 – Organisations and official bodies, 259-260, 268
 – Publications, 259, 277
 – Publishers 255-257, 259
 – Theory, 236-247, 250
 – History, 251
 – Symbols, 231
 – Terms, 236-247
   Glossary of, 244-247

N

Natural harmonic series, 164-165
Networking, 27
Notation software, 12-13, 223-235, 253

O

Octal system, 45
Offset time, 197
Online communications, 25-26
Operators (oscillators), 134, 158
Opto-isolator, 39
Oscillators, 132-134, 138, 157-160
Overtones, see *Harmonics*

P

Pad-to-MIDI converters, 117
Panning, 120, 175, 184
Parsons, Alan, *vi*, 188-189
Partials (harmonics), 164
Partials (oscillators), 158
Pascal, Blaise, 256
Patches/patch editors, 13, 161
Patch bays, 72, 77-78, 163
PCM, 137
Performance memory, 141, 161-163
Phantom power, 177, 185, 190, 209
Phasing, 16, 181-182
Phono sockets, 169
Phrase buffers, 86
Pianolas, 82, 139-40
Ping-pong, see *Bouncing*
Pink Floyd, 143
Pink noise, 203
Pitch bend, 7, 52-55, 88, 93, 109-110, 113, 115, 120, 133, 143, 160
Pitch shifting, 16, 182
Pitch-to-MIDI converters, 114, 119-120, 248
Pivot note, 95
Pixels, 21
Plotters, 227-228
Polyphony, 9, 11, 133, 137, 140-142, 145, 148-152, 158, 162, 231
Porta-Studios, 194-195, 211
Portamento, 160
Postscript files, 227
ppqn, 65, 87, 91, 95
Presley, Elvis, 261
Previn André, 258

Printers/printing, 24, 74, 223-235
 – Types of printer, 226-228
Products/price categories, *xvi-xvii*
Production music, see *Library music*
Pseudo-many, 16, 181
Psycho-acoustic enhancement, 182
Pure-tone generators, 204

Q

Q factor, 174
Quantisation, 96, 102, 200, 224, 230, 233

R

Rack mounting, 3, 142, 169, 185
RAM cards/cartridges, 145, 163
Random composers, see *Composers (automatic)*
Ravel, Maurice, 221, 261
Real-time input, 86, 108, 223, 226
Record companies, 252-253, 255-256, 259
Recording to disk, 70, 83, 208, 214
Retrofit, 77
Reverb, 16, 66, 85, 134, 143, 162, 174, 178-180, 182, 190, 201, 205-206
RISC, 19, 34
Ritardandos, 65
ROM cards/cartridges, 145, 163, 219

S

Sampling 10, 35, 119, 129, 131, 134-139, 149-152, 160-161, 167, 207-214
Sample editing, 161, 167
SCART connections, 22
Score editors, 12-13, 223-235, 253
Selling music, 252-260
 – Copyright & royalties, 259-260
Sequencers, *passim*; 6-8, 11-14, 80-89,
 – Change parameters in Play mode, 88-89
 – Clock resolution, 87, 102
 – Count-in, 87
 – Editing, 89-91
 – Graphs, 97
 – Grids, 90-91
 – Hardware, 80, 105
 – Humanising (random) quantisation, 96
 – Inversion, 95
 – Linear/pattern, 83, 101
 – Events lists, 91-92
 – Mute/Solo, 88
 – Notepads, 101
 – Pitch transformations, 94, 102
 – Play range/Loop play, 88
 – Punch In/Out, 87, 101
 – Quantisation, 102
 – Recording, 86
 – Reverse in time, 100
 – Save functions, 98
 – Time offset, 95, 102
 – Time Signature/tempo, 87

– Tracks, 84-86, 93, 97-98, 101
– Traditional notation, 90-91
– Transformations, 95
– Undo, 101
– Velocity changes, 96
Sight-reading, 248
Signal-to-noise ratio, 177, 185, 193-194, 213
Six, The, 261
Slaving (synchronisation), 63, 98
Smith, Dave, 1
SMPTE, 64 *et passim*, 78, 195, 197-198, 209, 257
Song chain, 89
Song Position Pointers (SPP), 59, 63 *et passim*, 98, 101, 197-198
Sound banks, 13, 51, 100, 155-156, 162-163
Sound editors, 12-14, 154-158, 160-162, 166
– Keyboard scaling, 160
– Performance settings, 160-162
– Samples, 160-161
Sound effects and effects units, 16, 171, 178-187
Sound layering, 163
Sound mixers, 3, 11, 66, 84-85, 168-177, 185, 196, 201-202
– Analogue/digital, 176, 186
– Channel Volume, 175
– Channels (tracks), 169-171, 174, 177
– Clip level, 172
– Effects Return/Send, 174-175, 177, 185
– Equalisation, 173-174
– Gain, 172
– Input Select, 171
– Insert point, 173
– Line, 172, 177
– MIDI control, 176, 186
– Mute, 175
– Overall Volume, 176
– Pan, 175
Sound modules, 3, 10-12, 66, 71, 77, 108, 117, 119, 130-131, 134-135, 140, 142, 146, 148, 150, 154, 156, 158, 161-163, 168, 171, 220, 229
Sound-level meters, 204
Sound waves, 124, 126-129, 131-135, 199
SPDIF, 208, 213
Spectrum analysers, 203
Spiegel, Laurie, 218
Staccato effects, 217, 230, 249
Star networks, 47, 76
Step-time input, 7, 86-87, 108, 223, 233
Stock, Aitken & Waterman, *vi*
Stokowski, Leopold, *vi*
Strauss, Johann, 82
Stravinsky, Igor, 261
Striping, 64, 197
Structures (algorithms), 158
Sustain pedal, 52, 141
Sweep equalisation, 173

Synchronisation, *passim*; 63-66, 98, 195-198, 257
Synthesis, *passim*
– Explanation, 123-134, 138, 157-158
– Carriers/modulators, 134-135
– Types of, 134, 145, 148
Synthesisers, *passim*; definition, *xvii*
– Analogue, 81, 133, 161
– Digital, 133-134
– Synthesiser voice editors, 12-13, 154-156, 158

T

Tangerine Dream, 81
Tape recorders (stereo), 202, 206-208, 214; see also *Multi-track tape recorders*
Tape recorders (video), 207
Tape-sync, 15, 63 *et passim*, 196-197
Tchaikovsky, 249
The Music Network (TMN), 26
Timbre, 6, 51, 100, 128, 134, 140, 142-143, 157, 164, 182
Time code, see *SMPTE*
Time offsets, 217
Tomita, 16
Traditional notation, 90-91, 223-235, 240-241, 243, 248
Transposition, 94, 162, 219, 239
Tremolo, 100, 120, 160
Trills, 98, 101

U

UART, 62
Universal editors, see *Librarians*
Universal Synthesiser Interface, 1

V

Vangelis, *iii-iv*, v, 16, 258, 261
VCRs, 207
Velocity curves, 109, 122
Velocity sensitivity, see *Keyboards (musical)*
VGA, 22
Vibrato, 7, 52, 39, 107, 133, 143, 160
Volts/voltage, 77, 81, 128, 132-133, 135, 171-172, 190
VS synthesis, 134

W

Wakeman, Rick, 1, 16, 133
Watts, 171
Waveforms, 131, 134, 155, 159-160, 208
White noise, 127
WIMP, see *GUIs*
Wonder, Stevie, 104
Workstations, 131-132, 139, 146-147
WORM, 208

X

XLR, 169, 185